# SPECIAL EDUCATORS

## *PERSONALITY AND TEACHING COMPETENCY*

# SPECIAL EDUCATORS

## *PERSONALITY AND TEACHING COMPETENCY*


*By*

**Dr. K.M. Mustafa**

*Honorary Director*
*Institute of Research in Learning Disabilities (IRLD)*
*Mahatma Gandhi University*
*Kottayam, Kerala*
*(INDIA)*



**DISCOVERY PUBLISHING HOUSE PVT. LTD.**
**INDIA**

*Published by:*
**Namit Wasan**
**DISCOVERY PUBLISHING HOUSE PVT. LTD.**
4383/4B, Ansari Road, Darya Ganj
New Delhi-110 002 (India)
*Phone* : +91-11-23279245, 43596064-65
*Fax* : +91-11-23253475
*E-mail*: discoverypublishinghouse@gmail.com
namitwasan9@gmail.com
sales@discoverypublishinggroup.com
*web* : www.discoverypublishinggroup.com

*First Edition:* **2019**

**ISBN: 978-93-86841-64-3**

**Special Educators:** ***Personality and Teaching Competency***



*Printed at:*
Infinity Imaging Systems
Delhi

# 1 Introduction

## CONTEXT OF THE STUDY

Education is very important in life. It can be conceptualized as learning and attainment of skills of utilizing knowledge for progress and development. In general it links the individual to the mainstream of development of society and nation as well. But, in our society, there are some people who cannot access such general education for progress because of some difficulties. Their problems of accessibility comprise special talents in sensory, cognitive and physical areas of functioning. It requires special care and training for survival of such people and their contribution in mainstream of headway. Education of such people is called special education. As a definition it can be said that the field of special education studies those pupil who are different form average normal pupil.

In fact, development is a plant of slow growth. Similarly, the plant of special education has been nourished since a long gradual change in interests, attitude and behavior of people, which made education essential, accessible and advantageous for pupil with different disabilities.

In the beginning the disabled was protected by the parental instinct and also made able to cope with disability. All these were through the informal education and unscientific methods they knew. However, in case of external difficulty or lack of parent's instinct of self-protection abandoned the disabled. Only those survived who were able to resist the unpredictable change in their environment. This period is known as 'instinctive Darwinism'. In course of time, there was significant change in people's attitude and they viewed disability as a punishment of God. It was based on the 'Sin theory'. There fore the result was expulsion of the disabled from society. It was the 'Social Darwinism' phase.

The modern period of special education emanated form the 'Education Darwinism', which meant for attitudinal change in 'Social Darwinism' in to education for disabled. But there was no as such provision of education for them. Rather the attitude was very simple and full of sympathy, i.e., come if the person can, try to cope is he/she can, attempt for learning if they can.

There is a broad light at the end of every tunnel. So this period laid the foundation of organized care and education with the emergence of humanity and charitable organizations of people in many corners of the world. The legislative provisions, development of asylums, training canters, hospitals and other special institutions were tremendously emphasized and thought up, initially more for manifest disabilities. This in turn led to bipolar classification of handicapped and non-handicapped persons. The handicapped were thought of a distinct category, which helped the enterprise of integrated special education.

In addition, it stimulated the thrust on normalization of such handicapped people, in the form of deep consideration of needs of special education and mainstreaming of disabled.

The earliest source of reference of disability was the Ramayana period around 5000 BC. It was the reference of mental retardation when Queen Kaikayi's maid named Manthara was found dull. The philosophy of 'Sankya' mentions the different kinds of intellectual disabilities. Around 1000 BC, the Garba Upnishad suggested that the distressed parents give birth to defective babies. In 500 BC, the 'childish mind' model was given in the Upnishad explaining mental retardation. During 185-71 BC Patanjali included disabled person for yoga therapy. In the 4$^{th}$ century BC, the Maurya period, Kautilya came ahead and banned both verbal and behavioral insult of persons with disabilities, recognized their rights of property and employed many of them as spies in his region. Later on, emperor Ashoka established hospitals and asylums for the disabled. A significant milestone was achieved by Vishnu Sharma around 1$^{st}$ century BC. He was the courtier of King Amarsakti and wrote the world's first test on Special Education, titled, 'Punchtantra'.

In same tradition of care and protection from the state continued in medieval Indian period also, with some noticeable progress. The blind would become minstrel and sing hymns in praise and worship of God. Surdas is the epitome. He was a blind poet who worshipped Krishna and Spread Krishna Bhakti cult.

Similarly, a blind Muslim could memories Quran to become a hafiz. The Maratha and the peshwa appointed deaf as spies and along with dumb employed as copiers or duplicators of secret documents. Although confined to certain people, however this was indicated significant change in attitude and behavior of the people toward special education devising some indigenous methods of education and training of the disabled.

In course of time in first 3 decades of 19$^{th}$ century, global change in society led to the development in modern education and special education to much extent also. Special education began in North India in 1826 with an opening of an asylum for the blind at Varanasi by Raja Kali Shankar Ghosal.

In 1841 a development took place in Chennai when an asylum was opened for idiots, separating them from the mental illness. There were many centers established for the disabled throughout the country in the 2$^{nd}$ half of the 19$^{th}$ century including training centers and integrated schools. But the noticeable development became conspicuous when the first institute for the deaf and mute come into existence in 1884 at Bombay (now Mumbai). In 1886 the Brail

# Preface

This book is prepared on the basis of my Ph.D. research work. The problem I have selected for my research study was personality as correlates of teaching competency among teacher trainees of special education. The selection of the problem was based on my experience as a student teacher in special education, special educator and administrator in the field of special education and rehabilitation. The difficulties and challenges I faced in understanding the needs of special learner as a teacher trainee and the problems faced in the classroom management, my discoveries about what was applicable and inapplicable in the field, development of the teaching ability to effectively deal the children with special needs have become the underlying factors of my research and preparation of this book.

The book has been written to be used as a research reference or as a referral text in an introduction to courses in teacher training in special education and for the research studies in special education and pre-service teacher preparation. It is appropriate for pre-service teacher trainees as well as the trainers in the field of special education. Since the book is based on the research work, it clarifies a number of idea closely related to special education. Professionals can understand techniques used in identifying research problems, forming hypotheses, using data gathering instruments and employing statistical procedures in special education.

It is hoped that the book will be helpful and will serve as a useful resource for teacher trainees, special educators, research scholars and policy makers.

**Dr. K Muhamad Mustaffa**

# Contents

System came to India with the opening of the first school for the blind of Ambala in Punjab. These events are deemed to be the outset of special education of children with disability in India. The North East India registered its name in history when a school was opened in 1918 at Kurseong in Bengal to train those children who were having physical and mental defects and unable to profit by normal school teaching. Similar work began in Travancore in 1913 and in chennai (the Madras) in 1936. Contemporarily, the psycho medical retardation center was established at Ranchi in 1934. the Government Mental Hospital, Madras started a school for children with mental retardation in the year 1939, while the first home for the mentally deficient come up in 1941 at Bombay. This was the direct out come of the Children's Act. Mrs Vakil in 1944 started another school of mentally deficient in Bombay and surprisingly the number of institutions for the deaf, blind and mentally retarded rose to 34, 32 and 3 respectively by 1947. In 1954 Mr. Srinivasan began the first special class in a regular school at Andheri in Bombay.

The outset of constitutional obligations regarding the special education of universalisation of education in the age group of 6-14 years under article 45, which included the disabled children along with the normal. In addition, although article-41 also envisages that the state shall within the limit of its economic capacity and development, but this is contradictory in itself. Subsequently the Education Commission Report (1965-66) recommended placement of the disabled child, "as far as possible" in ordinary schools. The recommendation was endorsed in the 1968 National Policy Resolution of the parliament. The practice of the recommendation was mostly in special schools however; the integrated education was remaining in the back seat. The major reason behind this was lack of preparation for implementing the scheme, especially the trained staff and inadequacy of special support. Then, the scheme was transferred to the Ministry of Education form the Ministry of social welfare.

Initially, the efforts of the Education Ministry were confined to limited categories of disability and the aim was a range of education provision in terms of curriculum, instructional material, instrumental aid, besides medical, psychological and social supports. Although it was a well recognized fact that the disabled people have the same right to education as any citizen, however, because of the preoccupation of the developing countries (Third world countries) with survival needs and lack of resource the target was not achieved. Therefore, it was emphasized to improve access of the disabled children to education as per their needs as closely as possible to that of ordinary children in their environment.

In 1986, education for handicapped was included in the 'National Policy on Education' (NPE) passed during the premiership of Mr. Rajiv Gandhi. This NPE specified that the possible education of children with handicaps will be common with that of other normal children and these children were proposed to be enrolled in special schools with hostels at distinct head quarters. For fulfilling the target it was implicated that there would be a system for identification, diagnosis and assessment of the handicapped for placement in different special schools. In this connection, the National Building code of India (1983) and the Bureau of India Standard Code (1987) on Building and Facilities for the Physically Handicapped had provided guidance and provision for requirement of physically handicapped in the public building processes. In 1987 the Behrul Islam committee was constituted to study the problems of disabled persons in a comprehensive manner. This committee dealt with both the preventive and promotional aspects of rehabilitation such as education, employment, vocational training and creation of a barrier-free environment. This committee became bedrock of the persons with disabilities (Equal opportunities, protection of Rights and full participation) Act, 1995. This is a landmark legislation as an attempt to change the disabled scenario. It is a comprehensive legislation, which will provide the much needed legal protection and status to every disabled person in this country.

The Act is to remove all discriminations against persons with disabilities in sharing of development benefits and also to integrate them in to the social mainstream. It consists at 14 chapters and the 5$^{th}$ chapter deals with education for disabled persons.

- Provide free education to disabled children till they attain the age of 18 years,
- Promote the integration of students with disabilities in the normal schools,
- Promote the setting up of Special schools in Government and private sectors, in remote areas, to impart special education with vocational training,
- Make schemes and programmes for non-formal education,
    - Conducting 'Special Part-time classes' for children who have been educated upto class V and then could not achieve due to disability,
    - Conducting 'Special part-time classes' for providing functional literacy for children in the age group of 16 and above,
    - Conducting class and discussions through interactive electronic media,
- Undertake research for designing and developing new assistive devices and teaching aids.
- Set up teacher's training institutions to develop trained manpower for schools for children with disabilities.
- Prepare a comprehensive education scheme, which would provide for transport facilities, special books, uniforms and equipments needed
- For education free of cost. Thus it has presented highly commendable provision to the education for the disabled.

After 2 years of this landmark Act, the National Handicapped Finance and Development Corporation (NHFCD) was set up in January, 1997 for providing financial assistance through education and self-employment of their economic growth and development. The Ministry of social Justice and Empowerment has attained recent milestone in this context establishing 6 composite Regional Centers (CRCs) in different parts of India in the year of 2000 and 2001. Out of these 6 CRCs 5 have started working, i.e., in Jammu, Lacknow, Bhopal and Guwahati. All these centers have common goal of prevention, educations and rehabilitation with different kinds of disabilities.

Research is in the areas of developing learning potential Assessment Device, which is common to all areas of disability. Conceptually, it should focus on psycho-educational characteristics of the handicapped, efficacy of delivery system's community based programmes, curriculum modification, developmental research on instructional system, management of educational environment. Framework with the disabled, assessment techniques based on cultural specifics are in dire need in our country, with cooperative and partnership Endeavour since the field of handicap is a complex area and therefore can rarely be handled at an individual level.

Research in the field of exceptional children especially in the field of teacher preparation programmes for disabled is taking off at a very slow and insignificant level in our country. Virtually it has low priority among professionals. The attempts to implant all Western ideas and principles will not pay divided unless indigenous techniques and procedures are developed through research and development of materials.

A proper teacher preparation programme should enable the trainees to acquire the basic skill and competencies to be a good teacher such as the capacity to manage a class with pupils of varying abilities to communicate ideas logically and with clarity, to use the technological devices to make teaching more effective, to organize educative experiences outside the class and to learn to work with community and help the pupils to do so. For this, personality of the prospective teachers has a greater influence. But at present, the academic credits of the candidates are considered the only criterions for admission to teacher training course in special education.

Academic excellence is not enough to become a good teacher. Certain studies have shown that academic qualifications at graduates and post graduate level do not help to improve the efficacy of teaching caliber.

Krishna Battacharjee (1984) in his study had throws light in this regard and pleaded that the prospective teacher should be given admission only after assessing their attitude towards teaching profession. This warrants one of the reasons for the present study.

A person without genuine interest in teaching special children may be failure. Various studies conducted by Pillai (1985) and Kumar (1986) have substantiated this view. Intelligence of the candidate is not at all considered as a criterion for admission to teacher training courses in special education. Various studies conducted by Mutha (1950) Wangoo (1982) and Malik (1984) have proved that intelligence of a prospective teachers has a positive influence on teaching.

The researcher is of the opinion that the personality of the teacher trainees has a greater influence in their competency in teaching the disabled children. Hence he feels that a detailed examination is worthwhile to find out whether any relationship exists between the above factors and the efficacy of teaching professions in special education.

## NEED AND SIGNIFICANCE

It is fact that no technical device in the field of education can replace the teacher. He remains an integral part in the educational process. Teacher is a friend, philosopher and guide so he should be ready to help the students at any time. As such his role is higher than that of any modern scientific equipment. In such a situation the teacher should be competent enough to discharge his duties satisfactorily. Hence those who are capable alone should be selected for teacher preparation programmes.

Development of facilities for education of exceptional students are increasing day 'by' day. The manpower development, particularly that of teachers and rehabilitation personnel should go hand in hand. Such institutions and programmes are very rare in our country. The facilities with a historical perspective emphasizing the present state of affairs with respect to, Major handicaps: mentally retarded, visually handicapped, hearing handicapped, orthopedically handicapped etc. in the country, Programmes of the national institutes, programmes of rehabilitation council of India, programmes located in selected NGO level, are some of the developmental milestones in the field of special education and rehabilitation in our country.

Special education movement in India is relatively of recent origin. However, the institutions have come up for education, care and rehabilitation during the last two decades in a significant number, if not proportion to the target clientele yet significant enough form near zero base.

Training of disability wise special teachers has to be taken up a serious and most priority task for the smooth functioning of special education system. The ministry of human resource development and the ministry of welfare through the university grant commission (UGC), NCERT and regional college of education, National Institutes of Handicaps and selected university departments of special education may under take this task.

Since the teacher has the responsibility for the development of the child and for preparing him as a citizen having faith in and professing democratic secular and scientific values, the teachers own education, personality and training should lead to the inculcation of similar values and skills based on appropriate learning experiences. Teacher being responsible for the total development of the child, can fulfill the responsibility, if he understands the children, known their interests and attitudes and can develop necessary skills in them.

Competency in teaching is a must for teacher of special education. How can we able to promote these competencies is the major problem. The teacher himself should be capable to meet the challenge of children with special needs in the classroom as well as in the community. Hence anybody can be selected for teaching is not a good practice. The right person should be selected for the teacher training programme in special education. The applicants academic achievement in the basic degree alone can not be consider for the admission to training programmes . He/She should have favorable attitude towards the profession in which he/She is going to engage. The following words of the education commission (1964-1966) are worth noting. 'Of all different factors which influence the quality of education and its contribution to national development the quality, the competence and competency of teacher and undoubtedly the mod significant'. More recently the International Commission on Education stated that the importance of the role of the teacher as an agent of change, promoting understanding and tolerance has never been more obvious than today.

Teaching is an art no doubt, a science and skill as well (Pillai 1985). It is an activity unique, professional social, rational and human activity effective teaching is one that produces maximum learning out comes. The ultimate goal of teaching is to attain all round development of the child. As Rabindranatha Tagore remarked " The main objective of teaching is not explain in meaning, but to knock at the door of the mind".

The purpose of teaching is to maximize learning. Teaching in often thought of us something that comes rather naturally to people who know their subject. As education is viewed as an instrument to develop the cognitive faculty, tolerance and understanding among learning and prepare citizen to understand and face the challenges of global section the role of the teacher in the emerging society will definitely change form what it is today. Here it is to be reminded the words of Dr. Ananthamoorthy in a talk " You can remove a bad prime minister after five years. But you cannot remove a bad teacher till he attains the age of 55".

Playing a significant role in the all round development of the children with disabilities teacher's mental condition and personality un questionably affect the child. The teachers' mental condition is important, because it affect teaching effectiveness and also his/her happiness. The teacher obviously is an important person in determining the ways his pupils are effected by and react to their work. To a considerable extend he can control the condition of work chose tasks and methods suitable for his pupils.

A proper teacher preparation programme should enable the trainees to acquire the basic skills and competencies to be a good teacher such as the capacity to manage a class with pupils of varying abilities, to communicate ideas logically and with clarity, to use the technological devices to make teaching more effective, to organize educative experiences out side the class and to learn to work with community and help the pupils to do so. For this, personality of the teacher have greater influence. But at present the academic credits of the candidates are considered the only criterion for admission to BEd/DEd course in special education.

Academic excellence is not enough to become a good teacher. Certain studies have shown that the academic qualifications of graduate and post gradate level cannot help to improve the efficiency of teaching competency instead studies have included that the attitude of teachers towards teaching profession had a significant relationship with efficiency in teaching profession. This indicates that those who are having higher academic standards may not necessarily be very effective in the teaching profession. Krishna Bhattacharya (1994) in his study has throws light in this regard and pleaded that the prospective teacher should be given admission only after assessing their attitude towards teaching profession. This wants one of the reasons for the present study to assess the personality and to find out its correlation with teaching competency among teacher trainees of special education.

Special education refers to instruction that is specifically designed to meet the needs of exceptional children. It involves designing the physical environment in the classroom, teaching procedures, teaching content and using of equipment for a particular type of disability.

The teacher should be capable enough to meet all the challenges in the field especially in learning and teaching process of the children with disabilities. So mere academic achievement should not be the only criterion for the selection to teacher training courses is special education. The investigator is of the opinion that certain other factors like personality factors have very much influence on teaching competency. Hence the investigator identified the problem to find out the relationship between the personality and teaching competency among the teacher trainees of special education.

The competent and devoted teachers can only work satisfactorily for the disabled generation and thus for the development of the nation. The admission to teacher preparation programs of special education should be based on some thing more than academic achievement. Hence the investigator feels a thorough study of the relationship of personality on the teaching competency of teacher trainees of special education is essential for the improvement of the efficiency of education and training.

In brief, the need and significance of the present study is summarized in the following points.

(*i*) Though numerous studies on teacher personality and teacher effectiveness have been conducted , no study has been conducted on the line of the present study and hardly any attempt seems to have been made to study the relationship between student teacher's personality and his teaching competency with regard to special education.

(*ii*) The study will help in finding the personality patterns of successful student teachers which ultimately help the selectors and employers at the time of recruitment of teaching personnel in education.

(*iii*) It will fill a gap in Indian setting where no search seem to have been done on the lines of the present study using personality scale and teaching competency scale.

(*iv*) The study will put the policy makers and the managers of special education on the right track by providing knowledge of how why and when the special educators to be admitted and trained in the teacher training institutions, Which essentially beneficial to children with special needs.

(*v*) The study will help to improve the teaching learning process in special education and also will be able to equip the special educators to manage students with special needs in the classroom.

(*vi*) The study will help to strengthen the organization and functioning of teacher training institutes of special education and schools for children with special needs.

## STATEMENT OF THE PROBLEM

"PERSONALITY AS CORRELATES OF TEACHING COMPETENCY AMONG TEACHER TRAINEES OF SPECIAL EDUCATION".

## DEFINITIONS OF THE KEY TERMS

### Personality

Personality is defined as the dynamic organization with in the individual of those psychophysical systems that determine his characteristics behavior and thought. (Allport, G.W. 1961)

### Correlates

The word correlates is defined as a variable, which is correlated with a specified variable (Wolman, Benjamine, Ed. 1975).

### Competency

Competency refers to the ability to apply the knowledge in to practical situation and the essential principles and techniques of subject matter field.

### Teacher Trainees of Special Education

The student teachers who are undergoing training in the field of education of children with special needs.

### Definitions in the Contexts of the Present Study

#### Personality

The total psychological and social reaction of an individual is known as personality. It comprises in various personality factors.

#### Correlates

In this study correlates indicates the relationships between certain psycho -social variables with teaching competency.

#### Competency

The term competency denotes the caliber of the teacher trainee in transferring theoretical knowledge into actual practical situation.

#### Special Education

Special education refers to the education of the pupils who deviate so far physically, mentally, emotionally or socially form the relatively homogeneous group of so called normal pupils. In this study it refers to the education of students with hearing impairments, students with visual impairments and students with mental retardation.

## OBJECTIVES OF THE STUDY

The present study was under taken with the following objectives.

1. To asses the personality of the teacher trainees of special education.
2. To evaluate general teaching competency and to categorize the teacher trainees in regard to their general teaching competency.
3. To find out whether the personality of the teacher trainees of special education has significant relationship with teaching competency.
4. To understand the gender differences in the teaching competency of teacher trainees of special education.
5. To examine whether there is any significant difference in the General Teaching Competency of Teacher Trainees of Special education, who belongs to the family of disabled and who do not belongs to the family disabled.
6. To examine whether there is any significant difference in the general teaching competency of teacher trainees of special education on the basis of locality (i.e. Urban and Rural).
7. To find out whether there is any significant difference in the general teaching competency of teacher trainees of special education, who have teaching experience and those who have not teaching experience.

8. To find out whether there is any significant difference in the general teaching competency of teacher trainees of special education with the parental history of teaching and without the parental history of teaching.
9. To find out whether there is any significant difference in the teaching competency of teacher trainees of special education specializing in visual impairment, hearing impairment and mental retardation.

## HYPOTHESES

The following hypotheses were formulated for testing in the study.

1. There exists significant correlation between the personality and general teaching competency of teacher trainees of special education.
2. There exists significant gender difference in the teaching competency of teacher trainees of special education.
3. There exists significant difference in the general teaching competency of teacher trainees of special education, who belong to the family of disabled and those who do not belong to the family of disabled.
4. There exists significant difference in the general teaching competency of teacher trainees of special education on the basis of their locality (i.e. Urban and Rural).
5. There exists significant difference in the general teaching competency of teacher trainees of education, who have teaching experience and those who have not teaching experience.
6. There exists significant difference in the general teaching competency of teacher trainees with parental history of teaching and without parental history of teaching.
7. There exists significant difference in the teaching competency of teacher trainees of special education on the basis of specialization in visual impairment, hearing impairment and mental retardation.

## SCOPE OF THE STUDY

The investigator hopes that the findings of the present study will be useful to the teacher trainees, teachers, administrators and educational planners in the field of special education (1) The result of study would help to improve the teaching-learning process in special education. (2) It is looked forward to reveal many informative findings, and there by increase the quality of teacher training programmes. (3) Various recommendations could be made to teacher training institutions, special schools, Government, NGOs and policy makers on different issues in special education. (4) The finding will help the candidates who wish to apply for admission to the teacher-training courses. (5) The study might endure as a starting for further investigation on this field. Conclusively, the investigator hopes that the study would be of great use to the concerned students with special needs, student teachers of special education, special educators and all other who have interest in the field of education and the welfare of the children with special needs.

## LIMITATIONS OF THE STUDY

The investigator is aware of certain limitations in the present study:

1. The major limitation envisaged for the present study is that the study was conducted on a sample of 143 Teacher Trainees selected form 3 categories of specialization in special education.
2. Only certain psychosocial variables are considered for the present study. Variables such as level of aspiration of the trainees, stress, socio-economic background etc have not been considered for the present study.
3. Even though random stratified sample was used, the actual sample included more females and more rural teachers which might have influenced to the findings of the study.

Owing to the above limitations, the investigator would like to note that such limitations are not unusual in a study of this kind.

## ORGANISATION OF THE REPORT

The format of the thesis is as follows. The thesis consists of five chapters. Chapter I is the introduction, which has been written with care to cover all the adequate information that needs to be conveyed, so as to introduce the present topic of research work. Chapter II highlights the review of the background literature and the abstract of the previous research findings, which had provided the baseline, to proceed with this research work. Chapter III describes the methodology, which is the backbone of the thesis, that depicts the method of study, description of the samples, sampling procedure, the tools used, the data collection procedure, the statistical techniques used and the analysis of the data. Chapter IV discusses the analysis and interpretation of the results, which stands as the brain baby of the research work that had been carried out. Chapter V concludes with the summary, implications and suggestions.

# 2 Theoretical Overview

## SPECIAL EDUCATION AND SPECIAL EDUCATORS

Special Education refers to instruction that is specifically designed to meet the individual needs of the exceptional student t. The teacher who is involved in the teaching of exceptional children after proper training in the concerned area is generally called as special educator. Special education actually involves many components , each of which must be considered by the special educator when working with exceptional student. These include the physical environment the teaching procedures, the teaching content and materials and the use of adaptive equipment. Even though the sample selected for the study (which was base of this book) comprised of teacher trainees of special education, they were also treated as special educators.

The Special Educator is supposed to educate children with special needs to the maximum extent possible. The perfection of special educator is a challenging, rewarding and sometimes frustrating endeavour. Through research and continued teaching, special educators discover more and more about the characteristics, capabilities and educational needs of exceptional students.

## MEANING OF SPECIAL EDUCATION

Special education means specially designed instruction which meets the special education and related needs of an exceptional child. It is distinguished from regular educational programme meant for non-exceptional children by some unusual quality, something uncommon, noteworthy. It is something special–special materials, special training techniques, special equipment and special help and/or special facilities may be required for special categories of children having special needs. For example:

1. *Visually impaired* children may require reading materials in large print or Braille.
2. *Hearing impaired* children my require hearing aid, auditory training , lip reading etc.
3. *Orthopedically handicapped* children may require wheel chairs and removal of architectural barriers.
4. *Mentally retarded* child may need skill training. Related service such as special transportation, medical and psychological assessment, physical and occupational therapy and counseling may be required if special education is to be effective.

## SPECIAL EDUCATION AS TEACHING

We may look at special education in terms of who, what, where and who? Special education meant for exceptional children whose special needs or abilities necessitate an individualized programme of education.

An inter-disciplinary team of professionals–special educators ,regular classroom teachers, psychologists, speech therapists, physiotherapists, specialist doctors bear the primary responsibility for helping exceptional children maximize their capabilities.

What? Special education is sometimes differentiated from regular education by its curriculum – that is by what is taught. For example teaching self- help skills or training in reading and writing Braille is an important part of curriculum for severely handicapped children (the blind) in special education institutions which is not found in regular education the school system dictates the curriculum, but in special education the child's individual needs dictate the curriculum.

What? Special education can sometimes by identified by where it takes place, Whereas regular education is provided in the regular classroom, special education may be provided in special class, resource room, special school or in residential school.

How? Special education can be differentiated from regular education by the method used by teachers. One special educator may use sign language to communicate with his students. Another special educator may use task analysis and skill training for mentally retarded children. Still another special educator may use multisensory approach and process training while teaching a learning disabled child.

1. *Preventive Efforts*: Keeping possible problems from becoming a serious handicap.
2. *Remedial Programme*: Overcoming disability through training or education.
3. *Compensatory Efforts*: Giving the child new ways to deal with the disability.

Special education is a profession, a service with tools and techniques to meet the special needs of exceptional children. It is individually planned, systematically implemented, and carefully evaluated instruction to help exceptional learners achieve the greatest possible personal self-sufficiency and success in present and future environments.

## OBJECTIVES OF SPECIAL EDUCATION

Special education has the same objectives as those of regular education – human resource development through providing appropriate education to children, national development, social reconstruction, civic development, vocational efficiency, etc. In addition to these objectives special education has certain special objectives such as the following:

1. Early identification and assessment of special needs to handicapped children.
2. Early intervention to prevent a handicapping condition from becoming a serious one for remediation of learning problems and compensation by teaching the child new ways of doing things.
3. Parent counseling about prevention and remediation of defects care, and training of handicapped children in daily living skills, self-help skills, pre-academic skills and communication skills.
4. Community mobilization and awareness of problems of handicapped children and their education.
5. Rehabilitation of the handicapped.

The National Policy of Education (1986/1992) clearly stipulates that :

6. By means of this, the realistic self-concept of that strategically determine for effective living.

## PRINCIPLES OF SPECIAL EDUCATION

Special education is based on the following principles:

1. **Individual differences:** There are inter-individual differences and intra-individual differences. In other words, some students are very different from most in ways that are specific regarding education, and special education is required to meet their educational needs.
2. **Zero rejection:** All children with disabilities must be provided a free and appropriate education. The school systems do not have the option to accept or reject a child for education in a regular school.
3. **Non-discrimiantory evaluation:** Students who need special education must be clearly identified to ensure that they receive appropriate services. Each student must receive a full individual examination before being placed in as special education programme with tests required at intervals to assess his progress and difficulties in learning.
4. **Individualised education programme:** Student with special needs require individualized education programme either in a resource room or a special class in the regular school for some part of the day. Such education must match with their current level of functioning and their special needs.
5. **Least restrictive environment:** As much as possible, children with handicaps must be educated with children who are not handicapped in the regular classroom. The regular classroom provides the least restrictive environment for handicapped children.

6. **Special process:** The provides implies that the parents of handicapped children have the right to evaluate the efforts of the school system to identify and assess the handicapped children, to modify the programme of the school to meet the special needs of these children and, if they are not satisfied with the programme of the school, they have the right to withdraw their children from that school for a better programme in any other educational institution.
7. **Parental participation:** Special education can be made effective if parents participate actively in the educational programme designed for handicapped children.

## NEEDS OF SPECIAL EDUCATION

It is true that the backward children and the talented children need specific facilities for their development. So educationists feel the importance of special education for them.

1. Special classes necessary for backward children because they require specific teaching methods and techniques.
2. Talented children face difficulties in adjusting themselves with average children because they belong to a higher IQ group. In general, it is found that the teaching expert moves at his speed, it is found that the teaching expert moves at this speed which suits average children. But a child with superior intelligence finishes the task much earlier. Here the problem is how a talented child will spend the rest of his time while the teacher continues the same take for the average children. Very often, the talented child is up to mischievous pranks. Also the curriculum meant for the average child id too simple and gets monotonous for the gifted one. Here the talented children do not get any kind of stimulation and lose interest in their studies.
3. Special teaching facilities are required to meet the personal and social needs of exceptional children. So additional facilities enable the children to realize their potentialities and to minimize the handicaps arising from their anomalies. Here superior chidlrne are provide with the opportunity to work according to their talent. In an average class, a bright child feels the handicap. With little endeavour he comes out exceptional. He can stand and keep a position in the class with minimum effort. Of course, accelerated promotion call for many drawbacks.
4. Experimental data reveal that social maladjustment is found to be rampant with bright children in regular schools. The talented children stay idle in the class due to the light load of work. So they engage themselves in mischievous pranks and unapproved behaivours.
5. In the special classes, the bright children get a chance for proper stimulation, but it becomes a problem for teaching experts to provide

proper stimulation to both the talented and average students in an average class. Generally gifted children are more sensitive in comparison with the average children. They are quick and alert in thinking. So they require special techniques for being handled.

6. In a special class of gifted children, every student feels that he is not superior alone, but there are some other bright ones. This thought helps a great deal in developing confidence. Again, special classes also provide opportunities for developing leadership in special branches. Among the group, there may be some children with special interest in poetry, drama, games and in other branches of knowledge. Proper encouragement and training under special programme of education may help them in the long run.
7. Selective placement is entitled through special education. It involves the complete assessment of children as well as their social environment by professionally qualified experts form different fields. Physical examinations and evaluations by specialists and experts like ophthalmologists, audiologists, ophthalmologists, psychiatrists, pediatricians, neurologists, psychologists and educational personnel are necessary for proper selective placement of many types of exceptional children.
8. Special education requires many auxiliary services. For example, the orthopedically handicapped require physical therapy, occupational therapy and periodic physical examination. Some exceptional children need to be kept under constant medical supervision. Periodic examination may be necessary for blind children and the children who are practically blind and hard of hearing. Occupational and physical therapy with psychiatric and psychological services are also necessary for some exceptional children.
9. The importance of special education can be associated with the problem faced by a teacher in the average class. An average class, generally, consists of children of many categories such as handicapped (both physically and normal) gifted (bright and superior) and some average or normal. The teacher has to devise a method of instruction which is suitable for all. But in putting this into practice, it is difficult for the teacher, for the students also face problems to understand. Here the need for a special class is seriously felt. In a way, special education is not only meant to help the exceptional children but is also conductive for the regular class teachers.
10. Very often, it is said that education begins where medicine ends. Providing a hearing aid to a hard-of-hearing child is of course, of medical concern. But teaching the child to use his vision of hearing capacities effectively is certainly the child to use his vision or hearing capacities effectively is certainly an educational function. If the hearing

anomaly is corrected, then it is also a medical concern. But if it is not corrected, then it becomes an educational concern. For totally blind children, instruction in Braille, provision of special Braille materials, travel training and counseling are advised by educationists through special education.

Unfortunately only 5 percent of the physically handicapped children (i.e. blind and deaf) are estimated to be in special schools and special care is being taken to educate them by experts in different disciplines., But most of these special schools are located in the metropolitan cities or in urban areas. But children by having rural background remain practically unserved by these educational schools. This accentuates the fact that a large number of special schools are needed to accommodate these children.

First, special education needs the identification exceptional children and some provision made for experts to take them into account. This special education may be imparted in the reualr classroom, special or in combination of both. Previously it was primarily confined to special classes. But now a special education programme development for exceptional children is a part of total general education.

However, exceptional children require special education which include three elements, and these are as follows:

(*i*) Trained professionals including teachers, educationists, psychologists, physiotherapists and others are required.

(*ii*) Special curriculum is made for the children which suit different areas of exceptionally such as mental retardation, giftedness, deafness, blindness, orthopaedic handicap, cerebral palsy and social and emotional problems and

(*iii*) Some facilities including special building features, study materials and equipment are also collected for this purpose.

## CONCEPT OF INTEGRATED EDUCATION

Integration is another expression used to mean mainstreaming. Integration cannot be reduced simply to an educational issue or employment issue. Its achievement will require the successful coordination of a whole series of transitions for the handicapped, ranging from early identification to early intervention to school programme to community, jobs and finally to community living.

An approach to integration that takes the individual needs of the special child into full consideration may result in one or more of the following:

(*a*) **Physical Integration:** Planning for the location of special programmes in school buildings with regular education programmes.

(*b*) **Social Integration:** Planning for regular personal interactions between students who have handicaps and those who do not.

(*c*) **Academic Integration:** Planning to ensure students with an without handicaps simultaneously use school resources.

(*d*) **Sacietal Integration:** Planning designed to enable students with moderate and severe handicaps to work, live and spend issuer time with their fellow non handicapped citizens.

## Meaning of Integration

The term 'Integration' means:

1. Providing special services within the regular schools.
2. Supporting regular teachers and administrators.
3. Taking parents concerns seriously.
4. Having students with disabilities follow the same schedule as non-disabled students.
5. Involving disabled students in as many academic classes and extracurricular activities as possible including music, art, field trips, assemblies and exercises.
6. Arranging for disabled students to use library, playground, and other facilities at the same item as non-disabled students.
7. Encouraging helper and buddy relationships between disabled and non-disable students.
8. Arranging for disabled students to receive their education in regular community environments when appropriate.
9. Teaching all children in the same schools they would attend if they did not have disabilities.
10. Providing an appropriate individualized programme.

## Concept of Integrated Education

The National Policy on Education, 1986, has given priority on an equity basis in the rield of education and recommends to provide opportunity to all not only for access but also for success. "Equalization of education opportunity" includes the opening of schools within walking distance, providing communities to schools, reducing the dropout rate and increasing the retention rate of children through various measures. Besides all the above facts, provisions should be made for non-formal education centers for non-attending children and various ancillary services to facilitate schooling of children.

The very term integration signifies the process of interaction of disabled children and normal children in the same educational setting. Of course, there are two separate terms which are, very often, synonymously used with integration. These terms are : (*i*) Mainstreaming and (*ii*) Normalization.

Basically integrated education is the result of Mainstreaming movement in America. This movement makes provision for mainstreaming the disabled children, in other words, mainstreaming refers to integrating handicapped or disabled children into regular classes and helping them thorough specialized techniques.

Again, sometimes integration is interchangeably used with normalization. The reason is that in integrated education, the disabled children are treated with normal children. There is every limitation to think that these two groups are different from any aspect.

Moreover, integrated education is an educational programme in which exceptional children attend classes with normal children on either part of full-time basis. Such a combination may be taken as social integration or academic integration or both. Some educationalist think that integrated education is the placement of the disabled children in ordinary schools with some specialized educational help and services.

The definition given by Stephnes and Blackhurt reveals "Mainstreaming is the education of mildly Handicapped children in the regular classroom. It is based on the philosophy of equal opportunity that implemented through individual planning to promote appropriate learning achievement and social normalization.

## Meaning of Integrated Education

Integrated education movement flows directly from the recognition of equal rights for all citizens and equal educational opportunity for all children with special needs, their education should be provided in the least restrictive and most effective environment. The least restrictive environment which disabled children need can only be provided in general schools. Thus, integrate education refers to education of disabled children in common with other in general schools with provision for extra help for the disabled. It refers to integrating the physically and mentally handicapped children with the non-disabled children in regular classroom and providing specialized services to meet the special needs.

Four key processes are important in integrated education .

1. Normalization 2. Deinstitutionalization 3. Mainstreaming and 4 Inclusion.

The details of these processes are given below:

1. **Normalization** is the process of creating a learning and social environment as normal as possible for the exceptional child and adult.
2. **Deinstitutionalization** is the process of releasing as many exceptional children and adult as possible from the confinement of residential institutions into their local community.

3. **Mainstreaming** is the process of bringing exceptional children into daily contact with non-exceptional children in an educational setting.
4. **Inclusion** is the process of bringing exceptional children of whatever condition into the general classroom for their education.

Integration is the opposite of segregation. Segregation is the process by which a special group in society is identified and gradually the social and physical distance between this group and the rest increases. A feeling of otherness develops in the group which alienated the former group.

Integration is the process of bringing the 'part' (the handicapped handicapped) to the 'whole' (the society). The indicators of integration are that (*i*) handicapped persons enjoy the same right as the rest; (*ii*) have equal opportunity for growth and development in environmental conditions available to the rest (*iii*) have access to the quality of life like any other citizen and (*iv*) are treated as equal partners in the community. The process begins by physical proximity i.e. reduction of physical distance. It continues with mutual sharing of the physical facilities and progresses towards reduction of social distance. The reduction of the physical and social distance results in social integration in which the group becomes equal partners in the community.

## Characteristics of Integrated Education

It has the following main features:

1. Integrated education is an education setting in which disabled children receive education along with non-disabled children in the regular classroom with provision for extra help for the disabled. Thus, integrated education is a practical solution to the problem of segregation of disabled children.
2. Integrated education is not alternative to special education. Rather it is complementary to special education. Only mildly and sometimes moderately handicapped children can be enrolled in integrated schools. Severely handicapped children who are enrolled in special schools can also be admitted in integrated schools after they acquire communication skills, daily living skills, study skills, and other pre-requisite skills.
3. It is designed to provide equal education opportunity to the disabled and to prepare them for independent living like other members of the society.
4. It provides the least restrictive and the most effective environment in disabled children so that they may grow and develop like other children.
5. It is an educational setting which promotes a healthy society relationship between the disabled and the non-disabled children at all levels and reduces the physical distance between them through equal participation in social activities.

6. It is an arrangement in which disabled children are considered as important as their non-disabled peers.
7. It accepts the disabled child as an individual in his own rights.
8. It ensures civic rights to the disabled in order to raise their standards of living.
9. It is an economic system for the education of disable children and solves the psychological problems which these children face in special educational settings.
10. It is based on cooperative efforts of regular classroom teacher, the specialist teacher, parents and community members.
11. It is a viable approach to attain the goals of universalisation of elementary education by providing equality of educational and development opportunities to the disabled who have been denied equality so far.

### Needs of Integrated Education

Many educationalists nullify the idea of special education on the ground that it never equalizes educational opportunities, rather it creates a feeling of differentiation among children. Special classes create a feeling of inferiority complex among disable children. Recently, psychologists think that integrated education should be introduced in our school system to provide equal opportunity for education of all children. Educationalists justify this type of education under following points.

1. **Normal mental growth is possible:** Psychological complexes are prominent under special educational settings. The disabled children think that they are inferior to others for which they are being treated separately. In integrated educational system, the disabled get the chance to enjoy along with normal children from developing psychological complexes. Every child feels that he is, in no way, inferior to anyone. Thus, the integrated educational system leads to normal mental growth of children.
2. **Social integration is ensured:** Certain social qualities are very much pertinent with the disabled children when they tend to get education with normal ones. Children get wider community integrated set up and this is conductive for the disabled ones to learn social virtues include love, affection, cooperation, sympathy and adjustment etc. The students in integrated setting not only get special attention but are also taught in a wider educational arena.
3. **Integrated education is less expensive:** Non doubt, special educational set ups are very costly and expensive. Besides that, Training programmes for special teachers and teaching experts are time–consuming. Considered from another angle, integrated education is

less expensive and advantages. To establish a special school, generally we seek the assistance from various corners, i.e., trained personal, experts physiotherapists, doctors etc., Again keeping a disabled child in a normal class is less expensive than placing him in a special set-up.

4. **Integration is possible through integrated education:** Social interaction is pronounced in integrated educational setups in comparison with special educational set-ups. A natural environment is created for interaction of the disabled with non disabled peers. Learning to adjust in this environment, to accept and to be accepted by their friends are possible through integrated education. The students in normal set ups also acquire a sense of competency and emotional adjustments.
5. **Academic integration is possible:** Academic integration is possible through integrated set ups educationalist believe that once a child is placed in a special school, below par academic abilities of the disabled ones under the teacher are developed. The teaching experts always have the idea that the students in the special schools or the disabled children are under achievers. Owing to the placement of the children in special schools, they fail to score well in academic studies. In a way we can say that, with a sophisticated environment and up-to date curriculum, integrated education brings academic integration.
6. **Principle of equality is maintained:** Particularly in India, constitutional provisions were made to universalize the elementary education and to provide educational facilities to the disabled children. They very objective of equality should be maintained through integrated set-ups, so that no student would think himself inferior to the other.

## Levels of Integrated Education

Various types of integrated education for disabled are found. Among them seven important types of models are worth noting here.

1. The first category of integration is the full time integration in normal schools. In regular classes, the teachers teach the disabled children throughout out the day. Student also support from teaching experts only when they are in need.
2. Another category of such children attend regular classes. But some classes are suspended due to the arrangements so special classes.
3. The third category includes education of the disabled in a special class. But the students are required to maintain their attendance at normal classes. Again they have to engage themselves in co-curricular activities of the normal school.
4. The fourth category of the integration includes the educational in residential schools with some lessons in neighbouring normal schools.

5. The fifth model integration. Here a large number of normal children are placed with the disabled children to ensure academic and non academic participation among themselves.
6. Education in normal classes with home–bound programme is included in the sixth category of integrated education.
7. The seventh category of integration is the short term education in hospitals or in other establishment.

## Scope of Integrated Education

Integrated education is proposed to provide educational facilities to the types of disabled children.

1. Children with locomotor handicap (orthopaedically handicapped).
2. Mildly and moderately hearing impaired.
3. Partially sighted children including one-eyed children.
4. Educable mentally retarded.
5. Children with multiple handicaps (blind and orthopaedic, hearing impaired and orthopaedic, EMR and orthopaiedic, visually impaired and hard of hearing).
6. Children with learning disability.
7. Blind children who have completed preparation in braille reading and writing, orientation and mobility training.
8. Deaf children who have acquired communication skills and learnt speech reading.

The scope of integrated education includes pre-schools training for the disabled, counseling for parents, primary education, secondary education, +2 levels of education and vocational courses.

## CONCEPTS OF MAINSTREAMING

The concept of mainstreaming owes its origin in the work and idea of Samuel Gridley Howe, and American Physician, who took keen interest in the education of blind and deaf children. As early as 1891, Howe has stressed that blind children should be educated in regular schools because of the social advantages of such a setting. He was advocating in favour of "exposing the disabled to an educational experience as close to that of non disabled as possible" In other words He has advocating in favour of mainstreaming the handicapped children in the general schools. It was in (1975) that the concept of mainstreaming was introduced in the education for all the handicapped act (USA).

Mainstreaming refers to educational placement procedure and process in which disabled children are educated in the least restrictive environment to satisfactory provide for their educational and related needs. The concept of mainstreaming is based on the following convictions.

1. Disabled children have wide range of special educational needs.
2. The special educational needs of disabled children very greatly in intensity and duration.
3. There is a continuum of educational settings which may be appropriate for an individual children needs.
4. Disable children should be educated with non-disabled children.
5. Special classes, special schools and other ways of segregating the disabled from the non disabled may be necessary only when the special needs of disabled children cannot be satisfied in general schools even with the provision of supplementary aids and services.

According to Kaufman et al., (1975) Mainstreaming refers to the temporal, instructional and social integration of eligible exceptional children with normal peers based on an ongoing, individually determined, educational planning and programming process and requires clarification of responsibility among regular and special education, administrative, instructional and supportive personnel.

## Components of Mainstreaming

According to this operational definition, there are three components of mainstreaming.

1. Integration in education
2. Educational Planning and programming
3. Clarification of responsibilities.

**1. Integration in education:** Integration is the opposite of segregations. Segregation is the process by which children with special needs or the disabled children are identified as a separate group and are educated in special schools in the company of the other disabled children of the same category being alienated from the parents, siblings, non-disabled peers and their own community. Gradually the social and physical distance between this group and the rest increases. A feeling of otherness develops in group. Integration is the process of bringing the parts (the handicapped children) to the whole (the society). The indicators of integration are that disabled children enjoy the same right as the rest, have equal opportunity for growth and development in the least restrictive and most effective environment, have access to the quality of life like any other children, and are treated as equal partners in the school and community. The process begins by reductions of physical distance. It continues with mutual sharing of the physical facilities and proceeds towards reduction of social distance. The education of the physical and social distance results in social integration in which the groups become equal partners in the community.

Integration is basic to mainstreaming integration should be temporal, instructional and social. The child with special needs should be placed in a regular class with other children for a period of time which may vary from two periods to six periods every day. Along with temporal integration there should be social and instructional integration. The special child should be accepted by his peers, regular teachers and should be participate in all social activities of the school. Instructional integration is the most difficulty component for mainstreaming. The special child's instruction should be so designed that the participates in class room activities which normal peers yet does not have difficulties. In learning the efficiency of mainstreaming depends in part up on the amount of time the special child spends in the regular classroom, the extent to which he is accepted by normal peers and participates in social activities, and the success of instruction in the classroom.

**2. Educational planning and programming:** Simply placing the special child in the regular class room with other children in not enough for mainstreaming to succeed. The educational programme of the mainstreamed child needs to be planned carefully. Special efforts must be made to plan the programme for the unique needs of such children so that they can achieve the maximum benefits participation in the regular classroom. For this to occur, supportive personal and services should be provided both to the child the regular class teacher.

**3. Clarification of responsibilities:** In some mainstreaming situations the regular teacher assume total responsibility for the special child. But usually resources teachers are appointed in mainstreaming situations when both regular teachers and the resources teacher are working with the child. There may be confusion regarding who is responsible for what. The child's total needs can be met when their respective rules are clearly and carefully delineated. The efficiency of mainstreaming depends up on both the regular teacher and the resource teacher discharging their respective responsibilities sincerely.

### Characteristics of Mainstreaming

In summarizing what has been discussed above it can be said that the effectiveness of mainstreaming depends on the following conditions.

1. There should be temporal, social and instructional integration of handicapped children.
2. Educational programmes for the mainstreamed handicapped children should be planned carefully to meet their special educational needs.
3. Supportive services and personal should be provided both to the children and the regular class teachers.
4. The responsibilities of the regular teacher resources teacher should be clearly delineated.
5. The regular class teacher should ultimately take the responsibility of educating the handicapped children in the general school.
6. Only mildly handicapped children should be exposed to mainstreaming situation. Severely handicapped children who have completed their

preparation and learnt the pre academic skills daily living skills, communication skills and other pre-requisite skills in special school settings may be later mainstreamed in the general schools.

7. The regular teacher must accept and agree to implement mainstreaming in their classroom and schools.
8. The regular teacher must prepare themselves for their new and difficult role. The authorities must arrange to provide in services and pre service training on characteristics and special education in needs of handicapped children to the children teachers.
9. In all case parent should be involved in the care, training and placement of their handicapped children.

Over the years, things have improved diagnosis has multidisciplinary, education has become the emphasis trained professional are available. Hence, the need for integration and mainstreaming is more felt. Mainstreaming is an approach that emphasis integration and as such it is the antithesis of the earlier institutionalization movement which emphasized segregation. But not until the 1970s was it though fit to integrate retarded children, even though it was known earlier that special classes were not superior to regular classes and that placement in special classes stigmatized those children, Hence efforts are directed towards a less restricted educational environment.

The Council for exceptional Children (CEC) has specified the essentials of mainstreaming the mildly disabled.

1. Providing the most appropriate education for each children in the least mainstreaming the mildly disabled.
2. Concentrating of specific educational needs than on labeling.

## DEINSTITUTIONALIZATION

'Deinstitutionalization' means that removing retard persons from institutions and placing them in other environments. 'Mainstreaming' means educating retard persons as much as possible in classes with non-retarded person. 'Integration' basically means mainstreaming. Normalization means that the individual's total environment should be as close as possible to that of non handicapped person's environment segregation is only desirable when the nature of the handicap is such that education in regular class with the use of supplementary aids and service cannot to be achieved satisfactory.

Deinstitutionalization includes three process (1) reversing institutionalization by finding alternative placement, (2) returning to that community all residents who have developed the skills necessary for successful transition. (3) establishing residential environments and protect right and leach reports on Deinstitutionalization, (*a*) placement in nursing homes where the quality of care is less than at institutions (*b*) primary medication was the treatment (*c*) readmission to institutions since community facilities are not available, (*d*) poor medical diagnosis, (*e*) regression in adaptive behaviour, and (*f*) in component staff to look after the inmates.

Deinstitutionalization is a trend which grew in reaction to institutionalization. In institutions, disabled children were considered physically or mentally ill and received treatment but no care and education. Around 1800 such institutions sprouted and as grew in size they become less cos effective and housed people with out much of treatment either. The trend continued 1950s and 1960s a number of social movements took place to help the retarded e.g. President Kennedy's approach to mental illness which led to the establishment of community centres which provided impatient and out patient care, treatment, consultation and education.

**Differences Between Special Education and Integrated Education**

| Special Education | Integrated Education |
|---|---|
| 1. Special education for exceptional or disabled children is and old notion. | 2. Integrated education is relatively a recent development of special education. |
| 2. This system isolated the disabled from the normal children. It segregates the disabled from the main stream and provide extra help. | 3. The provisions of integrated educational system call for socializing the disabled participants with normal children and academic and non-academic area. |
| 3. Special education is somehow clinical. | 4. But integrated education is based on the principles of Psychology. |
| 4. Special education is based on the laws of discrimination. | 5. Integrated education is based on principles of equality. |
| 5. Special education systems provide necessary arrangements for severely handicapped children. They also benefited by special education. | 6. But mildly disabled children get benefit through integrated education. An all around development is possible through it. |
| 6. Education for the disabled children is not considered as an integral part of the total education. Provisions for the establishment of special class are rather encouraged by it. | 7. Education for the disabled children is a part of total education. It provides extra help for the disabled children. It does not segregate the disabled children. |
| 7. Special education provides vocational training and prevocational guidance etc. | 8. Integrated education provides general education with some special provisions. |
| 8. Special education is truly special in every accept. It is established outside the ordinary school systems. | 9. Integrated education is an educational programme in which disabled receive education along with the normal child. |

## INNOVATIONS IN SPECIAL EDUCATION

Innovative steps have been taken and are in operation in recent years to make mainstreaming and/or integration effective. Teachers who know how to individualize instruction will have little difficulty integrating disabled pupils in the classroom. Individualize instruction in a classroom does not mean 30 students doing 30 different things at the same time. It means that after general discussion, the class can be divided in to three to five small groups for part of their instruction. It is in the small groups that the most pressing needs of the children can be met.

According to I.K. Devies, Teacher should be manager of learning, facilitates of the learning experience rather than disbursers of information. All teachers need time to work with individual pupils of groups of pupils. Experience teacher keep catch up time in the few minutes before recess during lunch, or after school to help those pupils who need extra instruction. During this time they also help children begin homework.

### Group Instruction for Teaching

Using small group instruction is another way to make mainstreaming more effective. Before using this technique the teachers should have sufficiently develop their class room grouping skills to enable small pupils to functions smoothly. They should be taught how to work in groups. The following instructions could be a starting point.

1. Choose your two most trustworthy pupils.
2. Assign them each a specific task to be completed outside class, such as preparing for science demonstration.
3. Excuse the pupils from regular class work. Make the assignment a choice one.
4. Have the pupils put on their demonstration.
5. Compliment pupils for a job well done.
6. Get ready for complaints from others for such choice assignments. Now the stage is set.
7. Select a reliable pupil and one of the less reliable ones.
8. Gradually extend this procedure over five or six weeks to more and more small groups.
9. Make sure that having a group assignment remain a privilege, this will encourage good behaviour.

### Mastery Learning Strategy

Mastery learning techniques offer a systematic way to give pupils longer periods of time master skills and concepts without penalty.

In order to use mastery learning the following steps may be used. Use Mastery Learning by:

1. Restricting mastery learning to the basic curriculum.
2. Beginning with the most essential basic skills.
3. Providing pupils with a short list of skills to learn.

4. Having each pupil study, practice, self-test, recycle, and rates, with final checking (testing) by the teacher until mastery is achieved.
5. Initially, allowing about 10 to 15 percent more time for handicapped children.
6. Drawing on assistance of tutors from other grades or the same grade, teacher aids, parent volunteers, programmed instructional units, micro computer drills.

Mastery learning is an optimistic theory about teaching and learning that any teacher can virtually get all students to learn excellently, swiftly and self-confidently. Both exceptional and non-exceptional children can benefit from the system of instruction if it is systematic, if the tasks are broken into small steps, it goals are clearly stated, if sufficient time is given to the learners, and there is some criteria of what constitutes mastery.

*Bloom asserts* that native intelligence matters in learning. But when instruction is matched to learner's present level of functioning, all students can learn fast. Mastery learning programmes are used successfully in special education programme under IEP. Some of the materials used in special education classes are based on mastery learning principles. In order to make it more effective a resource room with a resource teacher are required.

## TEACHER IN SPECIAL AND INTEGRATED EDUCATION

A teacher always tries to bring out the best in each child. When children stay away from their family, the teacher is the person who contributes a lot for them. Again teachers for deaf and disabled children have special roles in schools. Besides some additional qualities, they must have the primary aim of teaching and guidance. To make the children interested in the class is very important for a teacher. The teacher must try to satisfy the needs of the children as far as practicable, so that the relationship becomes strong. He should remain alert always in order to meet the needs of the students.

Again, the teacher should have pleasant personalities. They must try to develop a tendency to understand the child and the situation. Readiness to work hard is highly appreciated. Good teachers always have knowledge of up-to-date methods of teaching. Some teachers must develop skills in teaching and handling the problems of exceptional children.

No doubt, the education of exception of exceptional children either in special school or in an integrated set-up depends on the efficiency of the teacher. The following steps are noteworthy for effective teaching.

1. Problems of children should be intimated to the parents by the teacher within a minimum span of time.
2. Records of every child should be maintained properly by the teacher, so that a programme of action can be executed immediately.

3. A teacher must have a clear concept of special education and integrated education.
4. Remedial teaching programmes should be worked out by the teachers which may be conducive for children with specific educational needs.
5. A teacher should prepare instructional materials to teach in integrated set-ups.
6. Cooperation of other faculty members must be sought by the teacher to provide best possible education for disabled children.

Emphatically speaking, education of exceptional children special schools or in common schools, is a tough task. Their early identification, assessment of disability, enrolment in school, specialized help and successful placement in a vocation and life is not limited to primary schools or secondary schools only. Through joint effort and in collaboration with various departments, effective implementation of integrated education is possible.

## DEVELOPMENT OF SPECIAL EDUCATION

*(History, Policy and Legal Provision)*

The education of disabled children never received such amount of consideration and special efforts by government and non-government agencies in past as in present days. The attitude of the community in general and the attitude of parents in particular towards the education of the disabled have undergone change with the development of society and civilization.

In the *first phase,* disabled children were treated with hostility and were neglected. They were considered as 'Curve of God' and a burden for the parents. They were often killed by their parents.

In the *second phase* the disable children were kept in protection and wardship. Mankind was subjected to a Meath that "the disabled are useless, incapable of doing anything on their own, a species to be pitied and looked after as long as they are alive. "Thus, no attempt was made for their education, training, habilitation, and rehabilitation.

In the *next phase,* an attempt was made for their education. But disabled children were considered distinct from their peers. They were considered to be incapable of receiving education in general schools. Thus, for the first time, special schools and institutions were established in different countries for the education and training of such children. They were educated in special schools being separated from their parents and their non-disabled peers.

In the *second half of the twentieth century,* new thinking and new realization have opened new directions for education of disabled children. It is now realized that a disabled child is not a different kind of person. He is a child with special needs. Like all other members of the society, the disabled must have the same rights to education, work and full participation in the society.

It is also recognized that the disable, particularly those with mild to moderate degree of disability and the orthopedically handicapped, can be educated along with their non-disabled peers in general schools with provision for extra help. Moreover, education of disabled children in common with non-disabled children in general schools has been found to be an economical system in terms of expenses and coverage. These realizations, recognition and thinking on the part of educationists, planners and teachers have led to the conceptualization of integrated education for the disabled children.

## History of Special Education in other Countries

There have always been exceptional children , but there have not always been special educational services to meet their needs. The historical roots of special education are found in Europe and America primarily in the 19th century. In ancient civilization handicapped children were either killed or subject to abuse and neglect. Prior to the 19th century there were isolated instances of acceptance, kindly care, and education of disabled children.

Systematic efforts to provide special education to handicapped children started in the 19th century in Europe and America. Most of the originators of special education were European physicians. But the Americans who were initially concerned with the care and training of the handicapped kept themselves informed about the development that took place in Europe. Even some Americans used to visit Europe to get first-hand knowledge about the education of handicapped children. It is fact the European physicians were initially concerned about the education of mentally retarded children. Similarly much of the initial work in the field of special education in America entered around *deaf children and blind children.*

The history of special education does not indicate "Europe, good-America bad". But it is true that important ideas in special education found their way for Europe to America. Many European and American physician and educators contributed greatly to the development of special education, most prominent among them were:

1. J.M.G. Itard, Physician
2. Samuel Gridley Howe
3. E. Seguin, Teacher of MR
4. T.H. Gallaudet
5. Sigmund Freud
6. Philipe Pinel
7. Ann Sullivan

*J.M.G. Itard's contribution.* Itard, a French physician, is the person to whom most historians trace the beginning of special education. In the beginning years of 19th century. Itard set about to educate a wild boy of 11 or 12, named Victor.

The boy was apparently abandoned in a forest in Southern France at the age of 3 or 4. He managed to survive until his capture. At the time of capture he was animal like an appearance and behavior. He was naked, dirty, scarred, and unable to speak, and he selected food by smell. Itard could not make him normal, but he did dramatically improve his behaviour through patient and systematic educative procedure.

Itard was the originator of instructional devices, the inventor of behavior modification techniques, the first speech specialist, creator of oral education of the deaf, and father special education for the mentally retarded and the physically handicapped. His work with Victor firmly established that the retarded could learn and improve.

***Seguin's Contribution:*** Seguin is known as the greatest teacher of the mentally deficient. Being influenced by the achievements of Itard he established the first public school for the feeble-minded in Paris in 1837. I 1846 he published his classic textbook *Idiocy and Its Treatment by the Physiological Method.* His concept of education was the promotion of the harmonious physical, intellectual and moral developments of the child. His techniques and materials later become the basis for the so-called *Motessori Method Seguin* migrated to America and worked in collaboration with *Samuel Howe* for the education of mentally retarded.

The sensational discoveries and revolutionary ideas of Itard, Seguin and their successors during the 19$^{th}$ century which have formed the foundation for present day special education are as follows:

1. Individualized instruction for the mentally retarded children.
2. A carefully sequenced series of educational tasks for the MR.
3. Emphasis on stimulation.
4. Meticulous arrangement of the child's environment.
5. Immediate reward for correct performance.
6. Tutoring in functional skills.
7. A belief that everyone should be educated to the greatest extent possible.
8. An assumption that every child can improve to some degree.

## Development of Special Education in America

It is true that much of the initial work in the development of special education took place in Europe. But there were many Americans who contributed greatly during those early years.

***Louis Braille's Contributions*:** Louis Braille was the most important figure in the history of education of the blind. Braille, who became blind due to an accident during his early childhood, developed a revolutionary system of reading and writing for the blind. The Braille method is still recognized as the most appropriate method of reading and writing for the blind.

***Howe's Contribution***: Samuel Gridly Howe was one of the first physicians in the United States to develop keen interest in the education of blind and deaf children. His phenomenal success with one of his pupils. *Laura Bridagmen,* a deaf-blind-mute, earned him international fame.

***Anne Sullivan's Contribution***: Sullivan was a student of Howe. She was greatly influenced by her teacher's training methods. Although she was visually handicapped, she served as *Helen Keller's* tutor. Helen Keller was deaf-blind-mute. Sullivan's dedicated efforts could bring astonishing results. Helen quickly learned the names of objects and events in her environment. By the age of ten, she learned to say aloud "I…am….not….dumb….now". Later she became a graduate and wrote a number of books.

***Gallaudet's Contribution***: Thomas Hopkins Gallaudet had keen interest in the education of the deaf. He established the first American residential school for the deaf in 1817 in Hartford. The Gallaudet College in Washington D.C. which is the only college for the deaf was named in his honour.

## FALL AND RISE OF SPECIAL EDUCATION

There were many other European and American physicians and educators whose fascinating and brilliant careers helped to shape special education. In fact, the early years of special education were vibrant with the pulse of new ideas of great physicians and educators. The results they achieved with handicapped children were truly remarkable. But despite the energy, optimism, and achievements of these early leaders, special education lost its momentum during the last part of the $19^{th}$ century. Pessimism took hold humane and effective treatment turned to ineffective institutionalization and human warehousing, hope turned to despair. The special schools which were opened in the late 1800s became dumping grounds for all kinds of misfits. Many factors were responsible for the decline of special education such as:

1. Too much expectation of parents for their disabled children to achieve miraculous cure too soon.
2. Total failure of special education personnel in some cases.
3. Disagreement among professionals about the appropriate method of education.
4. Lack of financial support for providing special education service to a large number of disable children.
5. Social, political, and economic turmoil resulting from the civil war.
6. The idea that the handicapped were inherently inferior and no amenable to improvement thought education.
7. The influence of *Charles Darwin's theory of Evolution* the survival of the fittest.

After the World War II special education made a comeback with wealthy and powerful people like President *Kennedy* and President *Johnson* taking interest in the education of all handicapped. Education of the handicapped was initially considered as a privilege. With the development of democracy and socialism in different countries of the world education was considered to be a basic right of the child. This realization paved the way for mainstreaming disabled children.

## PROVISION IN LEGISLATION

Over the years, the objective of the struggle has changed from survival to equality. The concept of equality, includes the rights of the disabled as approved by the United. General Seembly in 1973.

Despite inclusion in the *U.N. Charter*, these rights have not become a practical reality for millions of handicapped persons throughout the developing world.

India is committed to the welfare and uplift of its less privileged citizens. Towards this goal, several provisions have been included in the Indian Constitution for care and protection of disadvantaged groups.

Explanatory efforts began in 1980 to suggest a comprehensive law for the disabled. These continued and intensified in this decade. The goals of 1981 which was declared as a *International year for Disabled persons (IYDP)* were equality and full participation.

The *Baharul Islam Committee* (1989) felt that the rights of the handicapped should be protected. The general purpose of the proposed legislation is to promote the welfare of physically and mentally handicapped persons so that they can a lead dignified, full and productive life by giving them equal opportunities enshrined in article 16 and 46 of the Constitution of India.

Through the proposed legislation, the state should be made responsible with regard to the fundamental policies for the physically and mentally handicapped through proper medical care, habitation, rehabilitation training, protection, education and vocational training, recreation, promotion of employment, social security etc. by providing various benefits and provisions. *Rehabilitation Council of India Act,* 1992 has been enacted which authorizes the Council to control quality of special education.

Different western countries have instituted statutory provisions in favour of integrated education of the disabled.

In India, however, there is no such law but policies of education from 1964 onwards have recommended placement of these children in regular schools with adequate support system.

The centrally sponsored scheme for *Integrated Education* for *Disabled Children* (IEDC) was initiated in early seventies by the Government of India in various states. The scheme has been revised and now covers the following types of the handicaps:

1. Mental Retardation
2. Learning Disability
3. Visual impairment
4. Hearing Impairment
5. Speech Impairment
6. Physical Disabilities

Education, Care, Training and Rehabilitation of exceptional children has a long past, but a short scientific history. An understanding of the origin and development of the special education movement would help to understand where we stand now in the field, particularly in India. Children with defects were not cared for in prehistoric societies. Defects like mental illness in the good old days were considered the result of some kind of sin. Children suffering from them were either killed or punished. The physicians and scholars in ancient Greek and Roman societies made some efforts to treat and preserve the lives of the handicapped and provided asylums for them. The renaissance brought a small change in the earlier attitudes. This was the state of affairs until the late $18^{th}$ and early $19^{th}$ centuries.

The early history of special education started with the hearing handicapped as early as 1555 when the *Spanish* monk *Pedro Ponce de Leon* (1520-1584) taught a small number of deaf children to read, write and speak and learn academic subjects. *Jnan Pablo Ronet* in 1620 wrote the first book on the education of the deaf and developed a one handed manual alphabet that is being used even today. In England *John Bufwer* published another book on the education of the deaf in 1644, followed by the Deaf and Dumb Man's Tutor by *George Dalgarno* in 1680 which set out instructional methods.

The first school for the deaf in Great Britain was established in 1767 in *Ediburgh by Thomas Braidwood. Braidwood's method* combined oral and manual method teaching alphabets and signs.

At about same time *Samuel Heinicke* (1729-1784) developed the oral method emphasizing lip reading and speaking skills in *Germany at Leipzing* in 1778 which was further developed by *F.M. Hill* (1805-1874).

In France, *Michel del' Epee* (1912-1789) who established the first school in Paris in 1755, and *Ambroise Sicard* (1742-1822) were developing sign language. The French system also emphasized training of the senses of sight and touch which became the forerunner to Montessorie's sensory training approach.

Education of deaf children was started with *Gallandel* (1787-1851) using the French method *Gollander* established the first school of the deaf in 1847 (which is today known as the American School for the deaf). The New York School for the deaf opened the next year. By 1863 there were 22 schools for the deaf in USA. The first oral school of the deaf in Massachussets Was established in 1867.

Day school classes for the deaf were started in 1869 at *Beston*. Adult education for the deaf began in New York City in 1874.

Subseuqently *Grahma Bell* (1847-1922) worked tirelessly for the deaf. *Helen Keller* (1880-1957) who was deaf and blind herself from early childhood, was a living example of the effectiveness of special education in overcoming the disability. The development so services for the deaf were hindered because the conflict over oral and manual method of instruction, but these have been reconciled over the years. In 1880, an international congress of education of the deaf was held in Milan, Italy. It made two recommendations.

1. Oral method must be preferred to the manual method
2. Oral method must be preferred to lip reading/sign language.

In Europe, oral method continued to prevail unchallenged during more than half the 20th century. After World War II the progress in electro acoustic technology gave new impetus to oralism. The increased belief that early education and intervention would allow most deaf children to attend ordinary schools for normal hearing or special unit to these schools. The mainstreaming movement progressively gathered more and more strength in great Britain, then in the United States, and continental Europe.

In France Education of the blind began with *Valentin Hany* (1745-1822) a French philanthropist who in 1784 founded the national Institution for the blind in Paris. It is an integrated school and its success led to the establishment of seven schools in Europe during the next 15 years. The first school for the blind in Watertown, Massachusetts was instituted in 1829 by *Samuel Graindley Howe* (1801-1876), This gave rise to residential schools for the partially sighted until the development of special classes in public schools in 1900 at Chicago Special Classes for the partially sighted was begun 13 years later in Boston. Hany developed embossed letters to be read with fingers and using this he printed the first book for the blind. *Louise Braille* (1809-1852) blind from childhood himself developed the system of Braille using raised dots to represent letters or alphabets, manually prepared for many years. The Braille typewriter was developed by Frank Hall (1943-1911), and a Braille printing system was standardized internationally in 1932.

Education of children with mental retardation began with the attempt by a French physician *Itard* (1775-1835) to educate an 11 year old boy who had been found living as a savage in the woods. This was documented in the book *"The Wild Boy of Aveyron" Edward Seguin* (1812-1880) followed the technique in France and United States and Maria Montessorie (1870-1952) in Italy. *Seguin* published his book "Idiocy and its treatment by the physiological method" in 1866. It contained ideas which are relevant even now-total education of the child, individualization of instruction, beginning instruction at the child's current level of functioning, and rapport between teacher and pupil. These were included in the famous method of Motessories for the education of the handicapped and non-handicapped.

*Decroly* (1871-1932) in Belgium developed a *curriculum* for mentally retarded children early in the 20th century and established schools throughout Europe *Binet* (1857-1911) made and immense contribution with the invention of intelligence testing.

In 1839 the first blind and mentally retarded (MR) child was enrolled in the Perkins Institute for the Blind in the USA. In 1848 the first residential school for the MR was opened in Massachusetts. By 1917 all states except four provided instructional care for the mentally retarded in the USA.

The first public school with special classes for children with mental retardation was formed in *Germany* in 1859 and thereafter in other European nation in the next decades. In the USA the first public school with special classes for the MR was opened in 1896 at Providence, Rhodes Island.

There were very few special treatment and provisions for the orthopaedically handicapped and the health impaired prior the 20th century. In the USA the first special class was established in Chicago in 1899, for children with low vitality in 1908 at Providence, Rhodes Island, and a class for children with epilepsy in Baltimore, Maryland in 1909.

*Esquirol* (1772-1840) published the first description of childhood psychosis in 1838 in a volume on scientific treatment of mental illness. For the first time in 1871 the New Haven Connecticut Public Schools provided a class for emotionally disturbed (ED) boys in New York City in 1874, These were first attempts made in USA. It was not until the 1930s that ED children were studied in a systematic way. The years since world War II have been characterized by the rapid development of services for handicapped children.

Special education services expanded rapidly after World War II both in numbers and types of children served. Legislative measures. Parental involvement, early education on pre-school education fro handicapped children all took off, including the education of those suffering from cerebral palsy, the learning disabled and the physically handicapped. By the 1970s facilities were available for all categories of the handicapped in the advanced countries of the world, and after 1981 in the developing nations.

Vocational Rehabilitation, occupational therapy, physical therapy were brought into the services for the handicapped. Expanded technology, use of computers, transportation devices, learning and visual aid technology, telecommunication systems, tele typewriters for the Deaf all came into use. Talking boons for the blind, which convert print into vibrating images that can be read with fingers were invented. The *Kurzwell* Reading Machine which converts print into spoken English, mobility aids etc. have further revolutionized the education of the disabled.

Besides, the 1970s have seen the emergence of mainstreaming and least restrictive environment as dominant concept in special education. The special class has doubtful efficacy and that is why there is a shift from placement in residential school and special day schools and increased enrolment in regular classes. Segregation is now discouraged unless the handicap is very, very severe.

## DEVELOPMENT OF SPECIAL EDUCATION IN INDIA

The *Kothari Commission* (1964-66) observes that the coveted goal of universalisation of elementary education depends upon the extent of success in bringing special groups of children within the education network. Unless educational services are extended to this group of children on mass scale, the universalisation of elementary enrolment of the handicapped children in relation to total children at the elementary state is 0.07 percent. This figure of enrolment has gone up to one percent as per review of NPE (1992). This low percentage of enrolment speaks volumes for the serious neglect and denial of educational opportunity for millions of disabled children in the country even thought the constitution of the country prescribes compulsory education for all children upto primary level. Most of the special groups of children are either not enrolled at all or drop out due to one reason or the other after stagnation. The slow progress towards bringing the disabled within the education network has been due to liner provision in special schools despite the fact that about 90 percent of the can be catered to in regular schools.

Integration of the handicapped into the regular school programme enunciated by the Kothari Commission leads to (*i*) reduction of costs of education and (*ii*) promotion of mutual understanding between the handicapped and non handicapped. However, many handicapped children find it difficult to cape with normal ones as they tend to be neglected. It is increasingly felt that every attempt should be made to bring in as many children into integrated programems as possible.

He had been reinforced in the *National Policy on Education* (NPE) 1986 stipulates that wherever possible education of children with locomotor handicaps and other mild handicaps will be common with that of others. The children with severe handicaps are proposed to be enrolled in special schools with hostels at district headquarters.

The ideal scenario for education of the handicapped is universalisation of primary education along with other children by 1995.

The *Programme of Action* (POA), 1986 and 1992 suggest pragmatic placement principles. It postulates that a child with disability who can be educated in a general school should be educated in general school only and not in a special school. Even those children who are initially admitted to special for training in plus-curriculum skills (that are required in addition to their regular school curriculum) should be transferred to general schools once they acquire daily living skills, communication skills and basic academic skills.

For achieving equalization of educational opportunities, POA (1992) also envisages that children with disability should have access to quality education comparable to other children. It postulates:

1. For children who can be educated in general primary schools:
   (*a*) Universal enrolment by the end of 9th five year plan.
   (*b*) Ensuring achievement of minimum level of learning (MLL) through adjustment and adaptation of curriculum and teaching to special needs.
2. For children who require to be educated in special schools or special classes in general schools:
   (*a*) Universal enrolment by the end of 9th five year plan.
   (*b*) Ensuring achievement of level of learning commensurate with their potential.
3. Reduction of dropout rates at par with other children.
4. Providing access to disabled children of secondary and senior secondary school with resource support and making special provision for vocational training of these children.
5. Reorienting pre-service and in-service teacher education programmes to meet special needs in the classroom.
6. Reorienting adult non-formal education programmes to meet educational and vocational training needs of persons with disability.

## Legal Provision for Special Education

The persons with disabilities (Equal opportunities, Protection of Rights and full Participation) Act, 1995.

The Gazette of India: Extra ordinary, Part-II, Section-1 No.1 of 1996, 1st January, 1996, Ministry of Law, Justice and Company Affairs, New Delhi: Chapter –V of Education p. 12-13.

1. The appropriate Governments and the local authorities shall:
   (*a*) Ensure that every child with a disability has access to free education in an appropriate environment till he attains the age of eighteen years;
   (*b*) Endeavour to promote the integration of students with disabilities in the normal schools;
   (*c*) Promote setting up of special schools in government and private sector for those in need of special education, in such a manner that children with disabilities living in any part of the country have access to such school.

(*d*) Endeavour to equip the special schools for children with disabilities with vocational training facilities.

2. The appropriate Governments and the local authorities shall be notification make schemes for:
   (*a*) Conducting part-time classes in respect of children with disabilities who having completed education upto class fifth and could not continue their studies on a whole time basis;
   (*b*) Conducting special part-time classes for providing functional literacy for children in the age=group of sixteen and above;
   (*c*) Imparting non-formal education by utilizing the available manpower in rural areas after giving them appropriate orientation;
   (*d*) Imparting education through open schools of open universities;
   (*e*) Conducting class and discussions through interactive electronic or other media;
   (*f*) Providing every child with disability free of cost special books and equipment needed for his education.
3. The appropriate Government shall initiate or cause to be initiated research be official and non-governmental agencies for the purpose of designing and developing new assistive devices, teaching aids, special teaching materials or such other items as are necessary to give a child with disability equal opportunities in education.
4. The appropriate Governments shall set up adequate number of teacher's training institutions and assist the national institutes and other voluntary organizations to develop teachers' training programmes specializing in disabilities so that requisite trained manpower is available for special schools and integrated schools for children with disabilities.
5. Without prejudice to the foregoing provisions, the appropriate Governments shall by notification prepare a comprehensive education scheme which shall make provisions for handicapped.
   (*a*) Transport facilities to the children with disabilities or in the alternative financial incentives to parents or guardians to enable their children with disabilities to attend schools;
   (*b*) The removal of architectural barriers from schools, colleges or other institutions imparting vocational and professional training;
   (*c*) The supply of books, uniforms and other materials to children with disabilities attending school;
   (*d*) The grant of scholarship to students with disabilities;
   (*e*) Setting up of appropriate fora for the redressal of grievances of parents regarding the placement their children with disabilities;

(*f*) Suitable modification in the examination system to eliminate purely mathematical questions for the benefit of blind students and students with low vision;

(*g*) Restricting of curriculum for the benefit of children with disabilities;

(*h*) Restructuring the curriculum for the benefit of students with hearing impairment to facilitate them to take only one language as part of their curriculum.

6. All educational institutions shall provide or cause to be provided amanuensis to blind students and students with low vision.

## EQUALIZATION OF EDUCATIONAL OPPORTUNITY

From 1950 onwards India has switched over to democracy. Its main tenets are equally, liberty, fraternity and justice. Equality implies equality of opportunity. In a democracy system all men are born equal and enjoy equal rights without any differentiation and discrimination of poor and rich and high and low. It is the prime duty of the government to minimize inequalities, disparities and imbalances as far as possible. To get education on equal footing is everybody's right in a democracy and hence should have full opportunity to develop his mental faculties. In this te interests of minorities, backward classes and deprived sections of the community need special consideration. People living in hills, rural areas and remote place need greater attention. Facilities of freeship, mid-day meals books assistance and scholarships etc. should exist for poor but meritorious children in schools and colleges. There is need to devise ways and means to identify the talent and help it grow to its full stature without economic impediments and hurdles. Rich person and philanthropists should also contribute generously towards their education and the help the government in all possible ways. Any discrimination between the education of boys and girls is improper. Both have equal rights to develop their individuality. This will go a long way in the evaluation of an egalitarian, democratic and socialistic pattern of society in the country and develop a healthy social and economic order.

### National Policy Education (1986, 1992)

The objective should be to integrated the physically and mentally handicapped with the general community as equal partners, to prepare them for normal growth and to enable them to face life with courage and confidence. The following measures were to be taken in this regard.

1. Wherever it was feasible, the education of children with motor handicaps and other mild handicaps would be common with that of other.
2. Special schools with hostels would be provided, as far as possible at adequate arrangements would be made to vocational training to the disabled.

3. Adequate arrangements would be made to give vocational training to the disabled.
4. Teacher's training programmes would be reoriented, in particular for teacher of primary classes, to deal with the special difficulties of handicapped children;

### Recommendations of Ramamurthy Committee, 1991

The Government of India set up the Ramamurthy committee to comment upon NPE/POA stipulations. Some of the specific observations made on the handicapped as stated in the NPH IW6 were as follows:

NPE advocated the policy of integrating the physically and mentally handicapped with the general community as equal partners.

The POA mentioned the detailed measures to be taken, important amongst them being massive in-service training for teachers, orientation programmes for the administrators, development of supervisory expertise in die resource institutions like the SCHRT and DIET, etc. It also called for provision of incentives like supply of aids, appliances, text books and free uniforms.

The causes for the low coverage of handicapped children in education are the following.

1. Education of the handicapped is viewed as a social welfare activity.
2. Child to child help leading to sensitization of the future generation, child to parent help for community sensitation and special and genera pedagogy reinforcement were missed.
3. Most of the special centres for the handicapped are located in metropolitan cities and urban centres. The non-government organisations barring a few exceptions have not significantly begun to operate at district or sub-district levels. Reportedly, 215 districts in the country do not have special schools for any disability though there an over 1000 documented special schools.
4. The scheme of Integrated Education for Disabled children which was conceptualised by the Department of Social Welfare in 1974 was implemented for several years in terms of running 'Mini Special Schools within general schools. The reason was that there was no provision of sensitisation and involvement of all the teachers.

The NPE, so far as it relates to education of the handicapped, is inadequate it the following respects:

1. It has not stressed the mobilisation of the total general education system for the education of the handicapped.
2. Special schools have been treated in isolation from other educational institutions from the point of view of providing the 3 educational

supervisory infrastructure, leaving it to the Ministries of social welfare and HRD to co-operatively develop the same.

The merit of the POA is in as call for establishment of special schools a district and sub-district levels; curriculum development apart from provision of infrastructural facilities; and specific target setting for universal primary education of the handicapped. While special schools for the education of those with sever handicaps are rightly emphasised by the POA, they have not lain emphasis on multiple delivery of services in special schools. While single disability mode is required I'm research, development and rehabilitation work, for delivery of education services, multi-service mode in special schools should be given importance. This is particularly so because doctors, dispensaries, public health centres and development functionaries are multi-purpose in nature. The POA has not called for redefinition of the role of special schools.

The department of Education has been implementing a scheme for the integrated education of the disabled under which 100% assistance is given to the stale. The scheme is at present being implemented in nineteen States and Union Territories. The annual provision under the scheme is of the order of Rs, 2 scores and as of now 20.00 children are being covered. Assistance provided to the states under the scheme is expected to be utilised to provide for salaries and incentives for teacher, setting up of resource rooms, carrying out assessment of handicapped children, training of teachers, provision of instructional material, etc.

## Recommendation of the Committee (1992)

Having comprehensively taken into account the problems faced in providing education to the handicapped with reference to their special and diversified needs, and having studied the history of implementation of the educational programmes for the handicapped, the Committee gave the following recommendations:

1. People should be made aware of the problems of the handicapped. The media should be effectively used for this purpose.
2. Every family with handicapped child should be provided support through incentives, dialogue and periodic training and evaluation. Parents groups and community education group should be formed.
3. The educational system of the handicapped should be flexible. It should offer a range of educated in general schools, special classes in general schools and integrated education for the disabled, vocational centres, etc.
4. Educational packages should be offered for hearing impaired children in a differentiated way purely oral oriented programmes for profoundly deaf children. Combined oral-manual programme for profoundly deaf children for the education of who pure oral programmes will not be

adequate. Segregated programmes for those children from whom such programmers are essential.

Integrated programmes for those whom this modality promise better emotive, cognitive, social and linguistic development.

5. For making boys and girls of impaired hearing economical!; independent, vocational training has to be specially organized Vocational training which is job-oriented and matched to the abilities and abilities of the hearing impaired, should be organised in a significantly diversified way.
6. Bharati Braille has been developed, at the National Institute in; the Visually Handicapped (NIVH). Dehradun This should In utilised maximally.
7. While work has been initiated for the development of Braille notations for mathematics and science, not much progress has been made.
8. For the moderately mentally retarded, special curricula should be developed and standardized - not merely for the purpose of base education in the three R's but also for training in self-care skills lib motor integration, perceptual and motor skills, language communication and conceptual skills.
9. Vocational schools for mentally retarded adults are not many. For their benefit jobs in sheltered workshops, farms and industries should be provided.
10. In the pre-service teacher training programme, education of the handicapped, should be made part of the pedagogy and methodology.
11. A programme of sensitisation should be implemented lm m services teachers as well. This should include various components, namely Non-formal Education, Vocationalisation of Education mid Distance Education.
12. Teacher training colleges should have special courses for teaching handicapped children; a special component on the education of the handicapped should be included in the B.Ed onuses as well.
13. At last one resource faculty should be provided in each DIET to provide teacher training inputs in the context education for the handicapped.
14. The role of the special schools should be clearly redefined as spell below:
    (*a*) Early identification of children with handicaps and formulation of stimulation programme for them.
    (*b*) Education of the handicapped children who cannot be educated in general schools up to the point when they can be integrated-thus breaking the insulation between the general and special schools.
    (*c*) Providing service as resource agencies for implementing the integrated education programmes in general schools.

15. A lot of development is taking place in the application of technology for the benefit of the handicapped. Several technological aids all already available, e.g., Brailleix produced in Germany which facilitates recording of whole encyclopaedia on cassettes, printing conversion devices like tectacon' which facilitates presentation of printed material in vibro-tactile form so as to enable blind persons to read, devices facilitating mobility of blind persons, etc. The technologies and techno-aids available for meeting the special needs of handicapped children should be reviewed, and measures for dissemination of information should be formulated.
16. Sustained researches should be undertaken to determine the needs of the physically handicapped and produce technological aids capable of helping in overcoming handicaps.

These recommendations were very comprehensive to shape the programme planning effectively, Subsequently another Committee was set up by the, government the *Janardan Reddy* Committee, which submitted its report in 1992.

The NPERC 1992 fell that the NPE was inadequate in the following respects:

(*i*) NPE had not stressed the mobilisation of the total general education system for the education of the handicapped.

(*ii*) Special schools had been treated in isolation from other educational Institutions from the point of view of providing the educational supervisory infrastructure, leaving it to the Ministries of Welfare and HRD to co-operatively develop the same.

The NPERC made very useful recommendations relating to the modelities of implementing programmes the education of the handicapped. Inter alia, it had advocated the line of media in creating awareness about the problems of the handicapped, providing support to every family with a handicapped child through incentives, dialogue and training and adopting a flexible approach to the education of the physically handicapped the NPERC examined at length the needs of different categories of the disabled such as the deaf, the blind and the mentally retarded, and made specific recommendations. The NPERC had also made important recommendations on the role of training, and of technological development in the education of the physics all handicapped.

The Programme of Action which was formulated in 1992 by MHRD. Government of India took all these historical antecedents into account and focused on an operational framework for implementing the plan of education handicapped.

### Programme of Action (POA) 1992 Salient Features

The POA made a stale of the art analysis of the situation. At the end of 1991-92 about 20000 children with disability were availing special benefits under the scheme of Integrated Education for Disabled Children (IEDC). In addition, about 60.000 children with mild disabilities received resources support without special benefits. A large number of children with disability were also receiving education in special schools which numbered about 1035 The Project Integrated Education for Disabled (PIED) is being implemented, as a Held demonstration. In one block each in ten Stales and Union Territories. In the blocks about 90 percent of children with disability arc receiving education in general schools. The cost per pupil in these blocks is now around Rs.2000 but is likely to come down as the number of beneficiaries increases. General teachers feel confident and motivated as their status in the community has improved due to the services they provide. The innovative multi-category-training of resource teachers has been found to be effective and has been institutionalised in the Regional Colleges and the training programmes organized by Non-governmental Organisations. Each DIET has been provided a resource centre for orienting elementary teachers and establishing field demonstrations in lab areas. Faculty from 102 DIETs have so far received induction training at die NCERT.

The ministry of social welfare had taken steps to ensure supply of trained manpower to special schools and improve standards in these school thought the National Institute for the handicapped and Increased support in NGOs.

The Ministry of labour manages 17 Vocational Rehabilitation Centres (VRC's) for the handicapped and helps in their placement. About 60.000 persons with disabilities had been rehabilitated under this schemes by September. 1991 Three percent of seats for admission to TTIs and under the Apprenticeship Training Scheme arc available for handicapped persons. These seats are being fillip Utilised.

The evaluation of special schools and I he scheme of lEDC has revealed some grey areas. The general education system has not yet been mobilised, to a noticeable extent, for education of the handicapped either at the Central or State Level. Inputs from different schemes like CUR, DRC, ECCE, non-formal education adult education, vocational and technical education, etc. are not being in ought together for the education of the physically handicapped. Sonic slates are still reluctant to implementing it rather indifferently. Few NGOs are active in rural areas. The standard of education in special schools needs improvement. Facilities for the education of children with multiple handicaps are yet in be developed. The early detection and intervention programmes so essential for education of these children have yet to be started. The goal of an unachievable dream unless concerted and urgent measures are taken.

## FINANCIAL RESOURCES FOR SPECIAL EDUCATION

For achieving equalisation of education opportunities, children with disability should have access to quality education comparable to other children. However, considering the financial resources likely to be available the targets for education of disabled children should be as follows:

1. Children who can be educated in general primary schools:
   (*a*) Universal enrolment by the cud of ninth Five Year Plan.
   (*b*) Ensuring achievement of minimum level of learning through adjustment and adaptation of curriculum and teaching to special needs.
2. Children who requite to be educated in special schools or special classes in general schools:
   (*a*) Universal enrolment by the end of the ninth Five year Plan.
   (*b*) Ensuring achievement of level of learning commensurate with their potential.
3. Reduction of drop rates to level on par with other children:
4. Providing disabled children access to secondary and senior secondary schools with resource support and making special provision for vocational training of these children, particular those with intellectual disabilities.
5. Reorienting pre-service and in-service teacher education programmes including pre-school teachers training programmes to meet special needs.
6. Reorienting adult and non-formal education programmes in meet educational and vocational training needs of persons with disability.

The strategy of area-specific and population specific micro-planning for UEE is equally relevant for this disadvantaged group. Planning for UEE and adult iteracy at the levels-centre, state, district, stale, district, block and project-should provide for the educational needs of this category of children.

Education of children with disability will be a component in the training of educational planners and administrators as well as pre-service and In-service teachers. District Institutes of Education and Training (DIETs), colleges of Teacher Education (CTEs) and the Institute of Advanced Study in Education (IASE) which have been provided with facilities for this component will have today particular attention to (his aspect of teacher training. While drawing up schemes for strengthening SCERTs, cells for education of the handicapped may be considered as envisaged in IEDC.

The material supplied under Operation Blackboard will have to take into consideration special needs of these children. School buildings will have to take note of architectural adjustments needed to ensure access to children with disabilities, at the construction stage itself so as to avoid expenditure line on modifications later on. Special schools need to be opened in the districts which have no special school facilities. The education of the handicapped should form essential component in all externally assisted basic education project being implemented or proposed to be implemented.

The following actions are needed for achieving the tai gels laid down; I

1. Adequate allocation of resources.
2. Provision for education of persons with disabilities should be made an integral component in externally assisted basic education projects.
3. Provision for education of the disabled should be made in the Centrally Sponsored Schemes of Operation Black Board Vocationalisalion of Education and Non-formal Education.
4. The NGOs have to be encouraged to implement IEDC, particularly in rural areas The NGOs involved in other educational activities should be encouraged to work in this area also and should be assisted in developing their expertise.

The Ministry of Labour bum is providing vocational training for the handicapped through the Craftsman training Scheme (CTS), the Apprenticeship Training Scheme and separate Vocational Rehabilitation Centres (VRCs). Three percent of the scats for admission to ITIs under the Craftsman Training Scheme and Apprenticeship Training Scheme are reserved for candidates who are handicapped but have the aptitude and are otherwise fit to undergo the required training. The slate/UTs have been advised from time to time to implement this reservation for the handicapped which will be continued during the eight plan also. Seventeen VRCs will continue to provide training to a large number of handicapped persons during the eighth plan. The instructors in ITIs will receive orientation to meet special needs of handicapped persons. This components will be added in ITI instructor's training programme. Adjustment and adaptation of equipment provide full access to disabled persons will be ensured.

## School Education for Handicapped

The first attempts at educating handicapped children were made in the last two decades lit tin-nineteenth century with the establishment of the first school for the hearing impaired in Bombay in 1885, Followed by the first school for the visual impaired in Amritsar in 1887. Growth of schools for the handicapped in the sixty sears until the advent of independence was extremely slow and sporadic. By 1947 India had just 32 school for (he blind. The number rose to 170 in 1980 Now there are 243 schools for (he visually impaired in the, country. Prior to independence I here were only eight codes available in the country but Bharati Braille has replaced all other codes now. Thirteen Braille presses are available in the country.

The number of schools for the hearing impaired was only 35 in 1947 but had risen to 180 by 1980. The present figure of schools for the hearing impaired is about 478 as per the Rehabilitation Council of India (RCI) directory of which

97 are secondary schools. The largest number is in the state of Maharashtra (139 schools).

Schools for the mentally retarded were three in 1947, but rose to 200 by 1980 and at present there are 600 schools for mentally retarded children. The first school for the cerebral palsied was started in 197.3. There are 12 schools run for the cerebral palsied at present, but no facility is yet available for autistic children. As regards the orthopedically handicapped most of them go to ordinary schools.

### Teacher Training for Special Education

Since 1981, systematic attempts have been made in the field of teacher training for handling special needs children. The leadership in this direction has been taken up by NCERT in designing courses of short term duration, mainly to implement the integrated education (IED) Scheme floated by the Government of India under centrally sponsored schemes (which has been now named as (PIED) project integrated education of the Disabled). NCERT has designed three level courses which are:

Level I. One week training of all primary teacher in the project area.

Level II. In-services training for six weeks for selected teacher.

Level III. One seal multi-category training of teachers since 1987 in its Regional Colleges of Education.

Besides, a six month's training course has been given to key persons at (lie NCERT headquarter. Several courses have been designed by 1 lie Rehabilitation Council of India Degree course have been started in some universities leading to B.Ed in special education.

## REHABILITATION FOR HANDICAPPED CHILDREN

Vocational Rehabilitation Centres (VRC) have been established. National Institutes have started functioning. A three percent job reservations for the handicapped and been brought in and special employment exchanges set up. National Awards, Tax concessions, self employment schemes, shellered workshops are also available for the handicapped. District Rehabilitation Centres (DRC) have been set up.

Community Based Rehabilitation (CBR) is in operation, where it is the responsibility of the community lo rehabilitate the disabled of all categories. Each level is equipped with Trained Personnel. Regional Research Training Centres (RRTC) have been set up in the four regions of the country. A rehabilitation technology centre and the National Information Centre on Disabled and Rehabilitation (NICDR) have been set up at Delhi. The NGOs have done commendable work in the area of disability over the years.

## Documentation of Disabled

The National Inhumation Centre on Disability and Rehabilitation (NICDR) undertakes collection, classification and storage of data on 12 different aspects of disability.

1. Concessions and facilities provided to the disabled by the central and state government.
2. Organisations and institutions working for the disabled.
3. Professionals working for the disabled.
4. Statistics about beneficiaries of various rehabilitation schemes and programmes.
5. Demographic statistics about the disabled.
6. Aids and appliance available for the disabled.
7. Statistics about national awards and awardees.
8. Schemes of scholarship-beneficiaries.
9. Scheme of assistance for purchase/fitting of aids/ appliances.
10. Scheme of organisations working for the disabled.
11. Employment statistics.
12. Research and Development Projects.

It is proposed to have Regional Centres of N1CDR too.

Non-government Organisations (NGOs) have contributed substantially to (he care, training and rehabilitation of the disabled in India. There are 315 voluntary organisations working for the disabled in the country at present. Among them, prominent are the Mahavir Viklang Kendra, Jaipur, Nevedic Prosthetic Centre. Chandigarh. Thakur Hariprasad Institute of Mental Retardation, Hyderabad, Amar Jyoti School, New Delhi. Pandy and Advani (1995) having given an exhaustive list of the voluntary organisations in this sector.

An All India Federation of (lie Deaf has also come up.

The Rehabilitation Council of India is now regulating the training, recognition and derecognition of the special education centres, institutes.

Training programmes for physiotherapists, occupational therapists. prosthetic and orthotic professionals, speech therapists, audiologists, mobility instructors of the blind. Vocational instructioners and counsellors, placement officers clinical psychologists, rehabilitation workers and other are being held in various National Institutes and Universities as per the norms of the Rehabilitation Council of India.

The major changes as regards exceptional children have been change from medical diagnosis to multi-professional assessment and treatment, treatment to education, meeting categorical needs to individual needs and to from category specific curricula and methods to appropriate variations in curriculum for all. There is a growing recognition of special education needs training services development of much close relationships between the staff and pupils with special needs.

## PRESENT FACILITIES IN OUR COUNTY FOR DISABLED

Administrative set up-The responsibility for implementing welfare schemes is being shared between the Central and State Governments. I he responsibility of Centre rests with the Ministry of governments. The responsibility of Centre rests with the Ministry of Welfare, and its activities are carried out through five bureau, viz. Handicapped Welfare, Social Defence Administration and Minorities. Tribal Development, and Scheduled Castes and Backward classes. According to estimates of national survey Organisation. The number of disabled persons is about 120 lakhs.

### Institutions of Special Education

The Government of India has established several special institutes Cot the handicapped. There are four national institutes, each for one special field:

1. National Institutes for Visually Handicapped at Dehradun.
2. National Institute for the Hearing Handicapped at Bombay,
3. National Institute for the Orthopaedically Handicapped at Calcutta
4. National Institute for Mentally Handicapped at Hyderbad

Besides, the National Institute for Rehabilitation, Training and Research at Olatpur (Cuttack), the Institute for the Physically Handicapped at New Delhi, the School for the Mentally Retarded Children at New Delhi and the Training Centre for the Adult Deaf at Hyderbad also assist in implementing the various programmes. The Artificial Limbs Manufacturing Corporal urn at Kanpur manufactures aids and appliances for the handicapped. These institutes have the main responsibility for training research workers, development of designs for finding and incentive. They should conduct research also.

There are 800-1,000 Special Schools for blind and deaf children, and for the mentally retarded. The majority of them are run by voluntary organisation. It is estimated that there are two million disabled children who will need special care, viz., improvement of health service, nutrition standards, mother care, and effective measures to prevent disability. The NPE plans to establish 10,000 schools for these children with 150 to 200 children in each.

There cannot be one model for special education programme. One can however, suggest a few alternatives. These models are: (1) Hospital Model, (2) Full-time residential or Day school, (3) Home bound model with peripatetic teaching, (4) Part-time special schools resource room help, and the like.

Influence of Other Disciplines: Special education did not suddenly spring up as a new discipline, nor did it develop in isolation from other disciplines. In the 20th century, members of the medical profession has continued to play important roles in the field of special education. The emergence of the disciplines of psychology and sociology and the widespread use of mental tests in the early years of the 20th century has enormous implication for the growth of the special education profession. Psychologists' study of learning and their prediction success or failure in school learning helped focus attention on children with special educational needs. Sociologists and social workers drew attention to the ways in which the family and the community affect exceptional child's learning and development.

Contemporary special education draws heavily on all disciplines concerned with child development – medicine, psychology, sociology and social work. Special education, which was initially the concern of physicians and later of psychologists, is growing very fast to become an independent discipline. Opening up of M.A. (special education) in different University Departments and colleges is an indication of this trend.

## EXCEPTIONAL CHILDREN

### Need

In a democratic country like ours every child has the right to education the right to receive help in learning to the limits of his capacity. Whether that capacity be small or great. It is consistent with a democratic philosophy that all children be given opportunity to learn whether they are average. Bright, dull. Retarded, blind, deaf, crippled, delinquent. Emotionally disturbed or otherwise limited or deviant in their capacities to learn. Equality of opportunity denotes two deviant in their capacitates to learn. Equality of opportunity denotes two things- equality of access to school education and equality of success in school.

In every classroom there are some children who have some learning problems. They need a little extra help from teachers to learn. Sometimes teachers understand their problems while at other time they are not able to understand their problems. The help they provide may not be sufficient. Their learning problems may persist and even accumulate despite special help by teachers. It teachers cannot understand the special needs of such children they will experience failure and frustration and later drop out from the school. In fact our failure to understand the special needs of such children have been major factors for our failure to reach the target of universilisation of elementary education within the stipulated period. These children with special needs are called exceptional.

### Definition of Exceptional Children

The term 'exceptional' means different things to different things to different people. Some use it when referring to the particularly bright children or the child with unusual talent. Others use it when they refer to any typical or deviant child. Telford and Sawrey (1972) said. "To be exceptional is to be rare or unusual."

"The term 'exceptional' is applied to a traitor to a person possessing trait upto the extent of deviation from normal possession of the trait is so great that because of if the individual warrant or receive special attentions from has fellows and his behavior responses and activities are thereby affected."

### W.E Cruickshank (1974)

'An exceptional child is he who deviates physically, intellectually and socially so marked by from normal growth and development that he cannot be benefited from regular classroom programme and needs special treatment in school."

### Samuel Kirk (1962)

"An exceptional child is he who deviates from the normal or average children in metal. Physical and social characteristics to such an extent that he requires a modification of school practices or special educational services or supplementary instruction in other to develop to his maximum capacity."

### Hewett and Forness (1984)

"An exceptional learner is an individual who, because of uniqueness inn sensory: Physical, neurological, temperamental or intellectual capacity and/ or in the nature and range of previous order of maximize this or here functioning level. " All children traditionally labeled as exceptional fall under this definition.

### Characteristics of Exceptional Children

1. It is applied to a trait of a person possessing upto the extent of deviation from normal.
2. It is commonly applied to children who differ notable from the average children.
3. An exceptional child deviates physically, mentally, emotionally and socially form normal growth and development.
4. An exceptional child is he who cannot be benefited from regular classroom teaching programmes.
5. An exceptional child requires a modification of school practices and needs special treatment in school to develop his maximum capacity.
6. An exceptional child belongs to both the extremes of physical mentally, social, emotional and educational achievement.

### Types of Exceptional Children

Exceptional children are of various types such as the following:

1. Children with Hearing Handicap
2. Children with Visual Handicap

3. Children with Mental Retardation
4. Children with learning Disability
5. Children with Orthopaedic Handicap
6. Children with Emotional Disturbance
7. Children with Speech Handicap
8. Children with Special Health Problems
9. Children with Multiple Handicaps
10. Gifted Children
11. Children with Creative Talents
12. Socially Disadvantaged Children

**1. Children with Hearing handicap:** The hearing handicapped are those children who have a damaged hearing mechanism face difficult in speech and language development. There is loss of hearing. The degree of hearing loss is less in some children while it is more severe in others. The hearing handicapped children may be hard – of- hearing or deaf.

The hard-hearing children are those children who have hearing loos but who can hear if spoken too loudly without a hearing aid. A hearing aid will enable them to hear better. For such children education in general school in common with other children is not difficult. Most of them are already studying in the general classroom.

The deaf are those who cannot hear even if spoken to very loudly. They require preparation in basic skills through special techniques before they are admitted in general schools. Hearing aids help them to become more functional.

Children with hearing impairment need hearing Aid auditory training, more of visual cues in the teaching- learning situation, services of audiologist, ENT specialists, special needs of such children differ depending upon the type and nature of hearing loos. The quality of previous training received in the home and pre-school centers etc.

**2. Children with Visual handicap:** The visually handicapped children are those who have problems with vision. Some visually handicapped children can read large print and are functional in their environment whereas some have sever vision loss and cannot be taught through visual methods. The degree of loss they may be partially sighted or blind.

The partially sighted are those who require large print or magnified print materials. Their visual acquity (sharpness of visual image) is very low (20/70 in the better eye). This means that the child can see at 20 ft. distance what a normal child see at 70 ft. Their eye-sight may be weak due to short sightedness, long sightedness, astigmatism, glaucoma or muscle detachment.

The blind are those who need to be taught through Braille or through aural method. Their visual acquity (sharpness of visual image) may fall at 2/20.9.

Such children must be prepared in pre- academic before they are admitted in general schools. They need orientation training, mobility training and more of oral instruction depending upon the degree of loss of vision.

**3. Children with mental retardation:** mentally retarded children are those who have a lower level of intellectual functioning and have problems in social adaptability. There are various degree of mental handicap. Consequently there are various categories of mentally handicapped children the educable mentally retarded (EMR), the trainable mentally retarded (TMR) and the custodial mentally retarded (CMR).

The educable mentally retarded are those who have minimum educational retardation in school subjects. Such children have problems of social adjustment, but are usually not recognized as mentally retarded at the pre- school level. The need repetition of instruction. The adaptive so that they can be identified in the early stages.

The custodial mentally retarded need help in developing daily living skills. They can be educated in special institution special classes. They are very poor in adaptive behavior. They need constant care and attention.

**4. Children with learning disability:** These children are like other children in intellectual functioning. They are not mentally retarded, nor spelling reading, writing, arithmetic, listening and comprehension. Their problems may be due to mental retardation, sensory handicap children may be categorized into mild learning disabled and sever learning disabled.

Such children and severe discrepancy between their achievement and intellectual ability. Such children may have the following specific problems.

Reading disability

Writing disability

Problems in comprehension and communication

Problems in numerical ability

Such children need repetition and drill, cognitive modeling process training,. Multisensory experiences and remedial instruction.

**5. Children with Speech Handicap:** Speech handicap refers to minor and major speech and language problems. There are children with mild languages and speech disorders in our classroom, and they often go unnoticed. While speak and writing they tend to omit, distort, add or substitute words, phrases, letters of the alphabet etc. They stammer and are quiet or have long gaps in speaking full sentences. Their problems should be corrected before they start school. The major types of speech disorders are:

(*i*) vice disorders

(*ii*) articulation or pronunciation disorders, and

(*iii*) fluency disorders

**Children with special health problems:** under this category we have children whose poor physical condition makes them inactive and who require special health precautions in school and adequate medical check – ups and support. Such children can be categorized into two groups.

(1) Children with mild health problems, and

(2) Children with severe health problems

Epilcpsy , diabetic problems, asthma, pain in the joints and anemia are some of the special health handicaps.

**7. Children with multiple handicaps:** Multiple handicap refers to more than one handicap in the child. A child may be blind and deaf, blind and orthopedically handicapped. Deaf and orthopedically handicapped, mentally retarded and orthopedically handicapped and so on. In case of multiple handicap one handicap may be primary handicap and the other secondary or one handicap may be severe than the other handicaps. It is therefore; important to identify the primary medical care, superior instruction form the teacher and a little love and affection from the parents and teachers.

**8. Children with orthopedic handicaps:** Some children have orthopedic handicap or locomotors handicap. Locomotors handicap refers to the problems with the functioning of bones. Joints and muscles. In some cases their crippling are so severe that they require artificial limbs to compensate for their crippling conditions. In other cases they need wheel chair or crutches. They need removal of architectural barriers and some environmental modifications in the schools, Usually mildly orthopedically handicapped children do not have learning problems. They can be integrated in the regular school without much difficulty.

**9. Children with emotional disturbance:** Children with emotional disturbances are very often considered as problem children in the school. An emotionally disturbed child has certain inner tensions which create anxiety. Frustration. Fears and impulsive behavior. Such a child may find excuses for this inner tension in some physical difficulty. An emotionally disturbed child may attempt to solve the anxiety by behaving in a premature or childish way. Becoming aggressive towards other people. Or withdrawing himself to the world of fantasy. Such children need love and protection. Security and recognition. Pleasant and success experiences in the home and the school.

**10. Gifted children:** Gifted children are in some way superior in intellectual ability to otter children of the some age. Gifted children are those who have demonstrated high ability (including high intelligence) . High creativity and high task commitment – a high level of motivation and the ability to see a project through to its conclusion. A variety of terms have been used to describe individuals who are superior in some way such as 'talented' 'creative', 'genius' and precocious (remarkably early development in particular areas like language, music mathematical ability). Most of these children remain unidentified in the class. Specific children who do not profit much from the regular school programme need early admission in schools and colleges and enrichment activities and materials.

**11. Children with creative talents:** In a school teachers may come across few students who have, the ability to produce something new- a composition, a system of ideas or a materials or a process which is essentially new or novel, and previously unknown to them. Such children behave differently. They are courage in their convictions. They have independent thinking and adjustment. They become absorbed and preoccupied in what they are doing. They are curious. They take risks. They are flexible in their opinions. They are intellectually self- confident. The prevailing school practices and situations create hindrance for their creative expressions. Teachers need to modify their attitudes towards such children and employ suitable strategies for promotion of their creativity.

**12. Socially disadvantaged children:** Most teachers encounter a group of children in their classrooms who appear lifeless, incurious, and deceptively unintelligent. They show lack of interest, involvement, and motivation for academic success. They underachievement the cumulative deficiencies in learning ultimately lead to their wastage and stagnation. These children and socially, economically, and educationally disadvantages. School readiness programmes in preschool centers, enriched experiences, and remedial instructions are very useful for them.

### School Provision of Exceptional Children

General school admitting disabled children should arrange to provide the following aids and appliances for

1. **Orthopedically handicapped children:** Adjustable furniture. Special writing materials (thich pen). Artificial limbs Wheel chairs and Crutches.
2. **Blind children:** Braille slate and stylus. Braille sheets Abacus. Taylor frame. Mobility canes. Cassette and taking books. Braille text books. Bulletin board. Flat desk. Embossed graph sheets with rubber band push pin tactile maps. Concrete objects to teach shape size, thickness, weight. Ascending and descending etc. number, texture and motor coordination.
3. **Partially- sighted and low vision children:** Magnifying glass, Spectacles. Portable reading lamps. White board in place of black board and Large print materials.
4. **Hearing impaired children:** Hearing aid (group hearing aid and individuals hearing aid). Speech trainer or voice trainer. Mirror (big and small). Special learning materials like flash cards, educational games and toy materials, hand-outs of classroom instruction.

5. **Mentally retarded and learning disabled children:** Educational games and play materials. Concrete objects for teaching different concepts. Pictures cards and pictures. Day, Date and Month Calendar.

   Tool bom. Aids for sensory – motor coordination and Alternation learning materials (simplified)

## CONCEPT OF HANDICAP, DISABILITY AND IMPAIRMENT

In the field of special education the three terms impairment, Disability and Handicap are very often used interchangeably. Thus, we come across expressions like hearing- impairment, hearing0 disability, and hearing – handicap to refer to hearing loss. These three terms actually mean different things.

An impairments is a permanent or transitory psychological, or anatomical loss and/or abnormality. This may be so from birth, or acquired later. Example on a hole in the ear drum, a missing or defective part of the body, paralysis after polio, myopia, low level of int5elleiegence etc.

Impairment may cause functional limitations. Functional limitations means partial; or total inability to perform those activities necessary for motor, sensory or mental functions within the range and manner of which a human being is normally capable such as walking , lifting loads, seeing , speaking hearing, reading, writing, taking interest in and making contact with surroundings. A functional limitations may last for a short time, be permanent or reversible limitations may be progressive or regressive.

Impairment leads to disability. Disability is defined as an existing difficulty in performing one or more activities which are generally accepted as essential components of daily living. Due to the impairment there is a reduction in functional ability. For example, due to the hole in the car drum, the child is unable to hear normally. A visually impaired child cannot see properly because of faulty image formation. An orthopedically handicapped child cannot use the arms and fingers for gippings. A learning disabled child cannot calculator or understand number relationship like a normal child, Depending in part on the duration of the functional limitations disability may be short term, long term, or permanent.

Medically, disability is physical impairment and inability to perform physical functions normally. Legally, disability is a permanent injury to body for which the person should or should not be compensated. Disability can be divided into three periods.

1. Temporary total disability
2. Temporary partial disability and
3. Permanent disability

Temporary total disability is that period in which the affected person is totally unable to work. During this time he may received orthopedic ophthalmological, auditory or speech or may other medical treatment. Temporary partial disability is that periods when recovery has reached the stage of improvement so that the person may begin some in of gainful occupation. Permanent disability refers to permanent damage to or loss of some part of the body even after any medical treatment.

Just as impairment leads to disability, disability handicaps the individual. Handicap means a restriction imposed/ acquired by the child's disability which affects the efficiency of his/her day – to day life activitites. The term handicap refers to the problems a person with a disability or impairment encounters in interacting with the environment. A disability may pose a problem in one environment. A disability may pose a problem in one environment but on in another. The child with an artificial limb may be handicapped when competing against non- disabled peers in a football match but experience no handicap in the classroom. Thus, a disabled person is not handicapped, however, unless the physical disability lad to educational, personal, social vocational or other problems The handicapping effects of a disability can be reduced by corrective service like hearing aids, artificial limbs, medical interventions etc.

The difference between these three terms can be summaries as follows. Impairment as structural, disability is functional and handicap is social psychological.

## Definitions of Handicapped Children

Impairment is defined as a loss of or damage to sensory organs. This may be so from birth, or acquired later. The impairment disturbs the normal functioning of the organ in its respective area. For example a child with a hole in the are dum cannot her properly because of the disturbance in the sound transmissions. Similarly, due to visual problems, there is improper formation of images and the child has difficulty in reading. An orthopedic impairment also refers to the loss of an organ. Or abnormality in any part of the organ or body which interferes with its normal functioning. For example, missing fingers or a polio infected arm. Such a child loses the grip of the fingers or the use of arm. For manipulation of objects in his/ her learning environment. A child with a mental impairment is unable to learn things as quickly as others.

**Difference Between Impairment, Disability and Handicap**

| | Type of Disability | Impairment | Disability | Handicap |
|---|---|---|---|---|
| 1. | Hearing Impairment | Damage in the ear mechanism (e.g. hole in eardrum) | Difficulty in transmission of sound | Unable to hear normally |
| 2. | Visual Impairment | Detachment of cay muscles(e.g. squint/ cross eyed) | Difficulty in focusing the eyes on a particular image | Unable to form single image |

| 3. | Orthopedic Impairment | Paralysis in arem | Difficulty in suing arm for grasping and manipulating | Unable to use the arem like others |
|---|---|---|---|---|
| 4. | Mental Impairment | Deficiency in mental ability | Difficulty in doing things like mothers | Unable to behave like others./ Difficulty in understating abstract concepts Unable to read and write like others |
| 5. | Learning Disability | Dysfuctioning of specific brain faculty ( for example motor area) | Difficulty in writing only Can speak and read normally | Unable to read and write like others |

can, Even the psychological process can be impaired. Impairment in the perceptual process can lead to learning disability. This implies that impairment leads to disability. Due to the impairment there is reduction in functional ability. For example, due to the hole in the eardrum the child is unable to hear normally. A visually impaired child cannot see properly because of faculty image formation. An orthopedically handicapped child cannot use arms and fingers for gripping and a learning disabled cannot calculate or understand number relationships like a normal child. Thus, a handicap is a restrictions imposed acquired by the child' disability which affects the efficiency of his/ her day to day life activities. Summarizes the differences between these terms.

Thus, impairment is loss or damage in an organ with result that the person is handicapped. The handicapping of a disability can be reduced by corrective services like hearing aids, artificial limbs, medical intervention, etc.

Now let us define the disability areas specifically. This will provide guidelines for identification, as manifestation of behaviours an characteristics will become clear.

1. The hearing impaired are those children who have a damaged hearing mechanism and face difficulty in speech and language development. There is loss of hearing. The degree of hearing loss is less in some children while it is ore in others. Four more details of. Appendix on definition of impairments on page 47 & 48.
2. Children with speech disorders are those who have difficulty in articulation, voice, and rhythm. In other words, we can say that they omit, substitute, distort and add sound while speaking a particular word or sentence. These problems can be due to organic defects or due to defective environmental feedback. Misarticulating lads to poor quality

of speech. Such children have law and high pitch problems and do not conform to the normal speech patterns. They may break the rhythm of sound white speaking which may lead to stuttering. It is also known as fluency disorder. For more information see page 30 of this chapter.

3. The visually impaired are those who have problem with vision. Some children can read large print and are functional in their environment whereas some have severe vision loss an cannot be taught thought visual methods. The visual loss is measured with the help of Snellen Chart given on page 26 and 27.
4. The orthopedically impaired are those who have problems with the functioning of bones, joints and muscles, to such an extent theta they require artificial limbs to compensate for crippling conditions, and some environmental modifications to be able to adjust in the classroom. Some children suffer from brain dysfunction and because of this, they have problems in performing motor activities.
5. Children with special health problems are those, whose weakened physical condition makes them inactive. They require special health precautions in school.
6. Mentally impaired children are those who have a level or intellectual functioning and have problems in learning, social and emotional behaviours. The degree for delayed development differs from one group to another. For identifying these children their adaptive behaviours should be assessed along with intellectual assessment.
7. The learning disabled are defined as those having disorder in one or more of the basic psychological process involved in understanding, or using spoken or written language. They show imperfect ability to listen, think, write, read, spell or do mathematical calculation. These children however are average in intelligence and do not have hearing or visual impairment.

   The definitions, given in brief, will help us in understanding the classifications of disabled children. Let us learn about the classification of disabled children which will facilitate the placement and education of these children in IED settings.

## Need and Problems of Exceptional Children

All children have certain basic needs. The need of children are often exceptional children or result in certain problems. The needs and problems of exceptional children are similar to and at the same time different from those for non-exceptional children. The needs and problems of mildy and moderately handicapped children are different from those of severely handicapped children. Similarly the needs and problems of handicapped children are different from those of children with superior ability. Even though the needs and problems of exceptional children are related to that characteristics they have certain common needs and problems such as need for appreciate education, need and problems such as, need for appropriate education, need for independent functioning, need for respect for their individuality, etc.

Disabled children are like non-disabled children except their specific disabilities. For example, a blind child is like any other sighted child except his loss of vision. Disabled children have a fundamental right to live and participate fully in all settings and programmes that are as normalized as possible. But consciously or out of ignorance we tend to treat them differently in school, at home, in the work place and in the community. Our differential treatment creates in them and among their peers a feeling of otherness.

Disabled children have a strong desire for independent functioning instead of assisting them to maximize their independent functioning normal environments we make them dependent on others. It is perhaps for this reason that many blind and orthopedically handicapped children resort to begging. One of the objectives of special education is to teach the disabled children self-help skills, daily living skills vocational skills and to assist them to manage their own affairs independently during adulthood.

An exceptional child, whether he is handicapped or gifted, has an individually of his own. He thinks, learn act and adapts in his own way . He has the capabilitites to live a better life and to improve his functioning level in the community. Teachers need to have confidence on his capabilitites and respect for his individuality. In schools exceptional children do not have the opportunity to express themselves fully. Their individuality is suppressed and at times punished by teachers.

Exceptional children need free appropriate education to maximize their capabilitites. Such education should not be provided to them out of sympathy or as a privilege granted to them. Education is a basic himan right and this must be granted to them just as we provide free and compulsory education to non-exceptional children. India is under pressure from international agencies to make education a basic right of the child. But it is surprising that the bill making education a basic right of the child is in the cold storage of the MHRD.

Many exceptional children and their parents experience difficulties relating to appropriate education. Appropriate education for exceptional children can only be provided in regular in the regular schools on the false impression that educating handicapped children in regular schools will adversely affect the education of non-handicapped children. In most cases the blind, deaf and MR children in regular schools. The principles of 'zero reject' stipulates that on in a school of his choice. Moreover there is no provision of appropriate education for gifted and creative children in our school excepting proving the same type of education that are provided to average students. There are also no special schools for gifted, creative emotionally disturbed and even the learning disabled children.

The handicapped children need equality of educational opportunity. The indicators of equal education opportunity for the handicapped have been spelt out by NCERT (1987) as follows:

1. Equal access to educational institutions in common with others.
2. Access to special education institutions where needed.
3. Resources facilities to support educational programmes
4. Equal access to curriculum
5. Curriculum adjustment to the needs arising out of a disability wherever needed.
6. Adaptive aids and equipment to ensure optimal access to curricula
7. Adjustment of instructional methods and materials to ensure optimal access to curriculum
8. Adjustment of evaluation of examination procedures to offset handicapping effect of the disability
9. Trained manpower for equal educational opportunity in general and special institutions.
10. Educational administrators response to the needs of the disabled children.
11. Commitment administrators responses to the needs of the disabled children.

The Programme of Action (NPE, 1986) also stipulates above mentioned measures for appropriate education of handicapped children. But handicapped children experience problems of access to and success in educational institutions. There are limited number of general schools enrolling handicapped children along with normal children. Even these schools are not properly children along with normal children. Even these schools are not properly equipped with materials, and special education provided in such schools in not appropriate to the needs of handicapped children. Special needs of such children.

1. Exceptional children need special education and related services. This requires proper assessment and classification of exceptional children. The problem is that in most cases the assessment procedure is not objective any systematic. This is why many children with temporary learning problems are classified mentally retarded or learning disabled. Moreover, what is cut off points between a mildy understanding about these children we tend to classify them

and label them as retarded, deaf, handicapped, cripples, disabled etc. Labeling itself is not a healthy practices for a number of reasons:

(*a*) Labels usually focus on a child's negative aspects. Once a child is labeled we tend to think about the child only terms of this inadequacies or defects.

(*b*) Labels lead to low expectations from teachers, parents and others about what a child can do.

(*c*) One a child is labeled teachers tend to explain the child's poor performance only in terms of his disability and not in terms of instructional failure.

(*d*) A labeled child may develop a poor self-concept.

(*e*) Labels create a sense of helplessness, inferiority and stigmatization.

2. Exceptional children need special aids, equipment and learning materials to profit from regular and special education programmes and to meet their special needs. The blind children need Braille materials and other aids; the low vision children need large print materials and magnifying glasses, the deaf children need learning aids, speech trainer visual materials etc. The MR children need games and play materials and other concrete objects, the LD children need alternate learning materials, encyclopedia etc. In most school's aids, equipment and learning materials are not able to maximize their capabilities. Discrepancy between what they are capable of doing and what they do gradually widens. This also causes a hug wastage of human resources.

Exceptional children, particularly the disabled ones, need incentives and financial assistance – conveyance allowances, allowance for purchase of learning materials, uniform dress, etc. The state Governments are not in position to provide such assistance to disabled children. They simply depend on the assistance provided by the MHRD. Governments of India. In most states the education of disabled children has been neglected due to withdrawal of assistance by the MHRD. Government of India. This is a recurring problem for most disabled children.

## Procedure of Educating Exceptional Children

There are various types of exceptional children. Educational programmes should vary from one category o to other categories of exceptional children. Education of each category of exceptional children will be discussed separately in later chapters of this book. In this section a general discussion on their identification, assessment, placement and education has been made.

**1. Identification and Assessment:** many exceptional children remain unidentified whether they are in the school or out of school. Consequently they are not able to maximize their potentialities. This calls for early identification of such children. Regular teachers should observe the behavioural characteristics of children suspected to be exceptional and refer them to specialists for medical and psychological assessments. In our country particularly in rural areas, school authorities have been facing difficulties for medical and psychological assessment of exceptional children due to non availability of specialists. In such cases teachers can conduct functional assessment which indicates what a child can do and he cannot do (Refer to Functional Assessment Guide developed by the Department of Teacher Education, special Education and Extension Service. NCERT, New Delhi). Functional assessment is to substitute for medical and psychological assessment. In every case exceptional children should be subjected to medical and psychological assessment if intervention programme is to be effective.

**2. Placement Service:** After medical and psychological assessment exceptional children should be placed in a suitable grade in a suitable educational institution. The degree of deviation of an exceptional child and the nature and range of his previous experiences usually determine his placement in an educational institution. So far as handicapped children are concerned the following placement programmes are followed in our country:

1. Full time placement in regular class
2. Part time placement in regular class with part time placement in special class.
3. Full time placement in special class.
4. Full time placement in special schools
5. Full time placement in residential schools.

Since we do not have special class and special school provision for gifted, creative, emotionally disturbed and socially disadvantages children. They are usually educated in regular schools. However, various type of scholarships such as NRTS, NTS, Merit scholarships etc, are available for bright students.

**3. Emphasis on Individuality:** Exceptional children constitute a heterogeneous group. There are various categories of exceptional children. Each category of exceptional children has unique characteristics. Again in each category there are various classes of children depending upon their degree of uniqueness. Education of exceptional children should match with their individuals characteristics. In fact the individuality of each exceptional child should be the basis of all that we doing and all that we want to for this education.

**4. Emphasis on Learning:** IT is worth noting that children are required to learn in the way the teachers. Since emphasis is being shifted at present from teaching to learning, teachers should teach in the way the child learns best. This emphasis on learning rather than teaching is rightly justified while planning any educational programme for exceptional children, whether they are disabled, disturbed, disadvantage or gifted.

**5. Special School Setting:** In our country a large number of special schools have been established for education for severely handicapped children, particularly the blind, the deaf and the mentally retarded children. In special schools severely handicapped children are educated by specially trained teachers with the help of special aids and equipment and curriculum adapted to their needs. Excepting a few Government Institutions, education in special schools is very expensive. Thus, many handicapped children are forced to out of school as their parents are not in a position to meet the expenses of their children's education in special schools.

**6. Integrated Settings:** The recent trend in the education of disabled children is to educate them in common with non-disabled children in general schools. The National Policy of education (1986) envisages that 'wherever it is possible, education of children with locomotor handicap and other mild handicaps will be common with that of others. Special schools with hostels will be provided, as far as possible at district headquarters, for severely handicapped children. Voluntary efforts for education of the disabled will be encouraged in every possible way.

**7. Provision of Incentives:** Government of India have made certain provisions of incentives for the education of disabled children. These include transport allowances, uniform allowances, purchase of books, escort allowances, attendances scholarships etc. Disabled children should be guided to take advantage of such incentives. In addition to these, gifted and talented children should be also guided to take advantages of NRTS, NTS and other scholarships.

**8. Preparatory Classes:** Disabled children should have some preparation before they receive formal education in as school. Such preparation can be made either in a special school or in ECEC centre, anganwadi, balwadi, or preparatory classes in a primary school. For this purposes the teachers should conduct a screening test first, and then administer individual teats, interviews parents and their disabled children to assess what the child knows and can do and what he does know or what he cannot do. A blind child knows must received mobility training, orientation training and training in daily living skills and Braille writing. A learning disabled child must be trained to sit and be attentive. Many disabled children need preparation in pre-academic skills. Such preparation is very essential for successful progress in primary grades. But once a child has completed preparation in pre-academic skills. Such preparation is very essential for successful progress in primary grades. But once a child had completed preparation in pre-academic skills, communication skills, daily living skills, mobility training and orientation training he should b encouraged to receive education in a general school in common with others.

**9. Resources Teacher Support:** Every school admitting exceptional children should have a resource teacher for every 8 to 10 exceptional children. The resources teacher may be a full time resource teacher or an it inerrant resource teacher. He is the person to provide support services to exceptional children in the resource room. Since he is an expert in the methodology of educating exceptional children he can also cat as a consultant to other regular teachers.

**10. Aids and Equipment:** Exceptional children who do not profit from the conventional instructional materials, teaching aids and equipment should be provided with aids and equipment in the resources room keeping in view their special needs. Braille materials, large print materials and magnifying glasses for the visually impaired, hearing aids, speech trainer, and visual materials for the hearing impaired, play and toy materials for the mentally retarded, alternate learning materials for the less abled ones etc. should be made available in school for proper education of exceptional children.

### Special Health Problems

Are those whose poor physical condition, make them inactive and who require special health precautions in School. Such children can be categorized in to the following groups.

1. Children with mild health problems: Come under the educable IED group. Their health problems do not interfere with educational learning. But precautions need to be taken in terms of getting adequate medical checkups and support.
2. There are children with severe health problems who cannot be integrated in regular schools. The severity of their health problems interferes with educational planning. They will need constant medical care and are therefore not able to participate in the academic and non- academic activities of general classrooms. Children with severe problems, like heart problem, diabetic, epilepsy, need to rest after 10-15 minutes of studying. It is difficult to accommodate them in general classroom since they require constant medical care and the full attention of the teacher. Such children need to be educated either at home/hospital or in special classes in general schools. Some health problems are discussed below.

The problem may occur in disabled children hence, the knowledge of the symptoms and their implications can help the teachers in minimizing these problems and helping the disabled to develop their talents like others.

**Epilepsy:** This is one of the special heath problems which a generally faced by children. The symptoms of this problems are : (*i*) the child shakes violently as if in the grip of hysteria, (*ii*) there is constant recurrence of fits, (*iii*) the child loses consciousness, (*iv*) he falls and moves arms and legs violently, (*v*) the child may become pale. (*vi*) he falls and moves arms and legs violently, (*vii*) purposeless activities such as rubbing of arms and body parts. (*viii*) the child starts taking off his clothes. The problem is due to brain injury or an extra growth in the brain. Some drugs are available to control the fits and the extra growth can be removed by surgery. Epilepsy is treated as a special health problems.

Since the fits are painless to the victim, it is important that the teacher should remain calm and not attempt to restrain the child's movements. All sharp objects that may injure the child should be removed from around him, but the movements must not be interrupted. If the mouth is open some soft objects such as handkerchief should be placed to prevent the tongue from being bitten. The child should be allowed to rest after the fit and the parents and doctor should boycott among peers and to protect the child form such treatment, the teacher should also explain to the other staff members and the community that the cause of epilepsy is not evil spirits but injury of the brain. The Child is normal in his/her intellectual functioning. This will help in better social, emotional and academic integration of such children.

## Children with Diabetic Problem

Children with the problems show the following symptoms: Frequent urination, abnormal thirst, extreme hunger, frequent change in weight, generally rapid loss, sleepiness, weakness, usual disturbances are felt more acutely and frequent skin infections such as boils and itching.

This problem can occur in both normal and disabled children studying in your school. As a teacher you are expected to identify these symptoms at an early stage. The problem is because the body not producing sufficient amount of the hormone called insulin and can be controlled by given insulin in the proper dose at the proper time. The teachers role is to help the child to get medical examination and to take medicine and diet according to the doctor's prescription.

1. **Asthma (Bronchical Problem):** Generally, the problem of asthma is overlooked in our classrooms but since it creates some social and emotional problems for the breathing trouble due to allergy. The commonly seen symptoms are: difficulty in breathing (The child takes large gulps of air) becomes pale, breathes noisily and perspires too much. Asthma is caused by allergens such as dust and the pollen of some plants. It may also occur due to excessive physical activity or emotional reaction. Drugs can be given orally or by injection, which help to control the problem. but it is not completely curable. Teachers who have such children in their class should help not be asked to do strenuous exercises. The teacher is also required to help the affected child to adjust to the problem and to involve in social activities that are not too rigorous.

3. **Juvenile Rheumatoid:** pain in the joint which occurs in younger children is known as Juvenile rheumatoid. Such children have a skin rash and swelling and redness of the eyes. There could be some retardation in growth since it is a disease that attacks the joints. It may cause stunted growth. Swelling and pain occur in the fingers, wrists, elbows, knees, hips and feet. In severe cases, it left untreated the joints become stiff,

making movements difficult and painful. Juvenile rheumatoid is a chronic infection of the connective tissue of the body. Drugs and special exercises can prevent the disease from becoming too severe. In the case of such children the role of teachers is very important. The teacher must be understanding and at the same time, not overprotective. Such children require more time to time to finish assignments. Various adjustments such children require more time to finish their assignments. Various adjustments such as writing aids and special paper and pencils can be provided to the children who have stiffened upper limbs. Since such children are physically weak, the teacher should not insist on their participating in all the activities.

3. **Anaemia health problem** is a condition in which the child suffers from severe loss of blood. Children who suffers from anaemia have periodic attacks of acute pain, may be weak and prone to jaundice an leg ulcers. They have pain in the abdomen, Knees. Elbows and other joints in the body. They suffer from consists headaches and may occasionally faint, feel ringing in the ears and see spots before the eyes. The major cause of this loss of blood is the loss of the red pigment of blood cells known as hemoglobin. The shape of the red blood cells change to sickle-shaped. A complete cure is not possible in server cases of the disease. Children affected with the disease need to rest frequently and be protected from further infection. The teacher should allow them more time to finish their assignments. Since it also leads to lack of oxygen, frequent hospital treatment is required. Teacher should get the children medically examined if the suspects any such problems in them. The children with mild type of anaemia need only periodic medical checks ups and medicines according the doctor's prescription. They can be integrated without any problems.

# 3 Review of Related Literature

## INTRODUCTION

A review of related literature is of vital importance to any investigation. It must be conversant with relevant theories in the field reports and records and also all other relevant literature. Knowledge of prior studies gives a good footing and direction for a research worker in the field of his investigation. According to Best (1990) knowing what data are available often serves to narrow the problem itself as well as the teaching that might be used. Only those studies that are playing relevant, competently executed and clearly reported should be included.

The problem under study is "personality as correlates of teaching competency among teacher trainees of special education". It is attempted to have a brief survey of similar studies conducted on teachers and student teachers to find out the relation between teaching competency and other variable such as socio economic status and sex difference. This is done in the hope that it will throw light on the problem under investigation and help to interpret the result with greater confidence and objectivity.

This Chapter covers the background literature that was drawn upon for the better understanding of the scenario. The bulk of literature that was compiled for this purpose is arranged in three sections. The first one examines the literature related to teaching competency variable. Section two reviews the studies on personality and section three examines the other studies related to the scenario.

## STUDIES RELATED TO TEACHING COMPETENCY

Teaching competence is defined by various authors. It refers to the set of knowledge, abilities and beliefs a teacher possesses and brings to the teaching situation (Mitzel, 1969). Some others perceive teacher competence as teacher behavior that produces intended effect (Medley and Mitzel, 1963). Rama (1979) define teaching competency "as the ability of a teacher manifested through a set of overt classroom behavior which is the resultant of the interaction between presage and product variables of teaching with in a social setting".

Ranganathan (2008) in a study of self esteem and teaching aptitude of DTEd students, found that there is a significant positive relationship between high self esteem and teaching aptitude and there is no significant difference between male and female and the level of self esteem and teaching aptitude.

Dash S. (2006) opines that the curriculum and the contents of teacher education programme should be rewritten and methods of teaching learning process should be reinvented, if we are to meet the challenges of the new millennium.

Nair, P.K. (2003) reported that the student teachers of the primary teacher education programmes face numerous problems regarding teaching practices, curriculum, availability of time, library and laboratory facilities and curricular activities.

Sivarajan K . (2002) opined that the sift of education from 'Gurukula system' to the learner-centered approach has necessitated the acquisition of several competencies for successfully meeting the functions of instructions.

Vijayakumariamma (2002) conducted a study on history and problems of teacher preparation programmes in Kerala. The study throws light to the historical developments of teacher preparation programmes and current issues in the teacher education system in Kerala.

Yearning and Walking (2000) investigated twenty seven student teachers personal self of teaching efficacy in Hong Kong. The result pointed out the teaching efficacy is viewed in terms of the dimension of concern for instructional participation and learning needs of pupils, communications and relationship with pupils academic knowledge and teaching skills, lesson preparations, managements of class discipline, teaching success, commitment and a sense of self confidence.

Cornelius(2000) investigated the factors effecting teacher competent of teacher trainees at the secondary leave revealed that intelligence, attitude towards teaching profession, and academic achievements of teacher trainees are the discriminating factor of the different groups of subjects.

Van Heyningen and Julie (1997) studied academic achievement in college students: what factors predict success?

This study evaluates first semester grade point average (GPA) in 96 first year college students to determine the ability of non- intellective variables to significantly predict GPA, and whether the predictive ability of these variables exceeds that of SAT scores. College students enrolled in Introduction to Psychology courses at Indiana University of Pennsylvania completed the Test of Reactions and Adjustment to College – Revised (TRAC – R), a self-report questionnaire that measures beliefs, behaviors, and emotions related to college, at the beginning and the end of their first semester in college. In addition, they completed the NEO Personality Inventory – Revised and a brief stress questionnaire the end of the semester. The student's SAT and first semester GPA were accessed after the completion of the first semester.

Analysis of data demonstrated that SAT scores were not predictive of GPA. The TRAC- R, however, was able to significantly account 21-32% of the variance in grades, dependent upon the time of semester the data was collected. A number of the scales on the TRAC – R were significantly correlated to grades.

The NEO PI – R did not demonstrate predictive ability for grades, except for the trait of Conscientiousness which demonstrated moderate predictive ability. Self- report of stress related to the amount of college course work demonstrated a significant correlation of the NEO PI – R. It did not moderate the relationships between these measures.

This study indicates that beliefs, behaviors, and emotions are able to predict GPA beyond that of SAT scores. They may be of benefit in future admission decisions. In addition, future research in the use of these variables to assist students who are not meeting grade requirements in college could point to future remedial uses of the TRAC – R.

Wills and Cora Deanne (1996) studied an investigation and non-succeeding disadvantaged college students.

Although over the past decade increased attention has been given in the literature to the task of identifying reliable predictors of academic success for college students, the majority of the research in this area has examined the use of traditional cognitive or intellectual variables such as high school GPA and scholastic aptitude tests such as the American College Testing Program (ACT) to predict college success. However, these variables alone have been found to account for less than 25 percent of the variability in college performance among disadvantaged college students (Miller & O'Connor, 1969).

A review of the literature reveals the personality variables of self- concept, locus of control, introversion- extraversion, and achievement motivation have all been examined and found to be repeated predictors of academic success among college students (Trachtman, 1975; Coopersmith, 1968; Rotter, 1963; Findley & Cooper, 1983; McClelland, 1961; Epps, 1969; & Eysenck, 1969). However, there are few studies which have examined the use of these personality variables as predictors of academic success among disadvantaged college students. Therefore, the purpose of this study was to determine if significant personality variables that effectively discriminate between disadvantaged college students who are succeeding and those who are not succeeding could be identified. This study investigated the differences between disadvantaged college students who were succeeding and those who were not succeeding with respect to the following personality variables: self-concept, locus of control, introversion – extraversion, and achievement motivation.

The participants were 26 Sophomores, 17 Juniors, and one Senior, from Berea College, who were required to enroll in, and had completed remedial English 015 – 016, Math 010 – 011, or all, thus defining these students as academically disadvantaged. Participants were classified as succeeding (G.P.A of 2.65 and above on a 4.0 scale) or not succeeding (G.P.A. of 2.60 and below on a 4.0 scale) based on their cumulative G.P.A at the end of the last academic semester completed. Personality instruments utilized in this study included the

Coopersmith Self- Esteem Inventory (Adult Form), Rotter Internal – External Locus of Control Scale, The Eysenck Personality Inventory (extraversion – introversion scale), and the Edwards Personal Preference Schedule (EPPS) (achievement motivation scale).

Results of the multiple analyses indicated that none of the four personality variables: self- concept, locus of control, introversion – extraversion, or achievement motivation significantly discriminated between those disadvantaged college students who were succeeding and those who were not succeeding. These results are not consistent with previous research findings that have repeatedly found a positive correlation between these personality variables and academic achievement. The implications of these results are discussed and recommendations for future research are given.

Bose (1993) studied the teacher effectiveness of 160 student teachers and found that positive significant relationship exists between teacher effectiveness and each of the predictor variable like intelligence, teaching attitude, self confidence and previous academic achievements .

Singh (1987) found that there is significant correlation between teaching aptitude and teaching effectiveness. He conducted his study on creative and non-creative B.Ed pupil teacher in relation to teaching effectiveness, self concept and some personal values.

Darga (1987) found that teacher aptitude is not a factor to control the adjustment behavior of the student teachers. The study also suggests that female teacher trainees are more adjusted than made trainees .

Sharma (1984) in his study 'Teaching aptitude, Intellectual lead and morality of prospective teacher' studied that the effect of sex and teaching aptitude. The result regarding this says that there is no significant effect of sex on teaching aptitude .

Girija (1980) studied the Intelligence and on –intellectual factors in Academic Achievement of advantaged and disadvantaged students from Professional colleges.

The purposes of this investigation were (i) to determine to what extent the intellectual (Verbal and non- verbal intelligence) and non- intellectual factors (study habits and skills, personality, values, motivation, anxiety, non-academic accomplishments and biographical factors) contributed to the improvement in the prediction of academic performance in addition to the admission criteria, and (ii) to explore whether the variables that were valid for academic prediction remained so for agricultural and animal science curriculum groups and advantageous an disadvantages groups.

The sample consisted of 788 students who were admitted to the University of Agricultural Sciences for the first degree in agricultural sciences. Of these, 588 were admitted to various courses in agricultural sciences and 200 were admitted to animal science courses. The instruments used in the study were the EPPS, Wrenn's Study Habit Inventory, Tyler and Kimber's Study Skills Test, Gordon's Personal and Interpersonal Values, Myer's Academic Progressive Matrics Scale, Raven's General Mental Ability test and a biographical questionnaire developed by the researcher Data were collected by administering the instruments and the criterion, the cumulative grade point average (CGPA) – the first – year college achievement scores were obtained from the records. Stepwise regression analysis and canonical correlation techniques were used to analyze the data.

The major findings were: 1. Pre-university marks (PUM) were the only common ad effective predictor of the CGPA for the total sample, for agricultural and animal science curriculum groups and for advantages and disadvantages groups. 2. The prediction of CGPA was significantly improved by the addition of intellectual and non-intellectual variables to the admission measure for all the groups. 3. The overall results of the various groups revealed that out of 62 predictor variables, 32 were potential contributions to CGPA. They were PUM, progressive matrices test scores, general mental ability, number of previous academic failures, study habits, skill in recognizing abbreviations, leadership qualities performance anxiety, desire for recognition, planning work efficiently, competitive, dependence, practical mindedness, achievement, need for support, conformity, benevolence, personal and biographical factors like casts, permanent residence, place of education, medium of instruction during primary education, source of income, guidance to choose vocation, parental aspiration, occupational aspiration, age, scholarship awarded, self estimated ability, accomplishment in areas of literature, social service, dramatic art and music.

Singh (1978) investigated into the relationship between teaching successes and behavioral changes in students. He used Critical Incidents Blank (C.I.B) and behavior Change Questionnaire (B.C.Q) to study the behavior change among the students. He revealed that teaching success is, to a great extent, dependent on adjustment. A positive attitude towards family – parents, wife and children, a sense of identification with people, place and profession and a growing concern for school, students and studies go a long way to make a teacher successful. He also investigated that a successful teacher was able to induce learning, develop interests and foster desirable attitudes in his students both by his teaching in the classroom and by his exemplary conduct in different social situations. An unsuccessful teacher, on the other hand, contributed significantly to produce little subject learning, developing aversion to the subject, creating misunderstandings and fostering undesirable attitudes.

Singh (1976) studied some personality variables related to teaching effectiveness. He found that most prominent needs of superior teachers were nurturance, achievement counter-action and aggression. The organizations pattern of superior teachers was generally logical and that of inferior teachers was emotional. The interpersonal relation as regards social behavior and adjustment were of very high degree in superior teachers but they were very low inferior teachers. The superior teachers had more strength of imagination while inferior teachers were weak in their imagination. The superior teachers were less entangled in family problems or were able to solve them quickly. But inferior teachers were sensitive to such problems. The superior teachers used more literary languages than average and inferior teachers.

Sharma (1975-76) in his study found that some selected organizational characteristics such as sex of teachers and type of management of the schools were related to teacher morale. Later Shrama (1977) studied morale of teachers at upper primary level of education and found exactly the similar results as those found in earlier study of Sharma (1975-76).

Raja Gopalan (1975) investigated the relationship of certain environment factors to teaching success in English achieved at the school stage. The sample included 225 teachers. Twenty headmasters and twenty-first assistants belonging to twenty schools. Tools used for the study were: (*i*) a teachers situation inventory; (*ii*) a rating scale; (*iii*) a peer rating and (*iv*) an over all rating scale administrated to the headmasters. Major findings of the study were: (*i*) the teachers were satisfied with the headmasters and the school organization; (*ii*) the teachers were most dissatisfied with the local community and the students; (*iii*) married teachers were more satisfied with their environment than unmarried teachers; and (*iv*) teacher's experience in teaching English determined his success, i.e., the more a teacher was experienced the more successful he was.

Buch (1975) and Sharma & Malhotra (1979) Opined about the general teaching competency in the following words." There were the times when it was believed that teachers are inborn and nothing can be done to improve teaching abilities of any person of any teaching ability level. Considering the possibilities.

Singh (1974) conducted a study to find out the relationship of teacher values with teacher attitude and job satisfaction. The sample consisted of 521 teachers from Higher Secondary Schools and University of Delhi. She found no difference in attitude due to age, education and training of teachers, but reports that female teachers expressed a more favorable attitude of teachers towards teaching as profession than the male teacher. Similarly Quraishi (1973) found that attitude of teachers towards teaching profession as independent variable did not show any significant result in predicting dependent variables.

Chhaya (1974) studied certain psychological characteristics of effective school teachers. He found that effective teachers had significant better personality adjustment and more favorable attitude towards teaching than ineffective teachers; effective teachers were significantly more emotionally stable than ineffective teachers were more authoritarian than effective teachers. Age and sex of teacher had a significant relationship with effectiveness of teaching

Mehrotra (1973) studied the effect of teacher education programmes on the attitude of teachers towards the teaching profession. He found that:

1. attitude of those who completed the course was more favorable than that of those who did not,
2. attitude of women students was more favorable than that of men.
3. the attitude of some age groups towards the profession at the end of the course was less than at the beginning,
4. the attitude was more favorable with higher age group and it increased except a decrease in between the age group 32-36 years and
5. the attitude became more positive with more teaching experience except for the group with 13-17 years of experience.

Khan and Weiss (1973) have reported, 'the actual availability and documentation of psychometrically sound attitude scales is, however, far from satisfactory". They have listed the available instruments to measure attitude of teachers and students towards education, school, teacher, teaching and school courses and have classified them according to their categories like Thurston, Likert etc.

Khan and Weiss (1973) have observed that. "it would appear that the relationship between teachers and student's attitudes has been regarded as axiomatic with no need for empirical research. It is likely that this premises has served as basis for the large number of studies conducted on students perceptions of teachers attitude, teacher's value and beliefs, and the effects of demographic characteristics and teacher education on teachers attitudes". Brown (1975) has remarked about the association between teachers and student attitude that "from an appraisal of other studies on student attitude and achievement, it is evident that teachers have an important influence on student's attitude". Ryans (1960) concluded that increase in age and experience of teachers influence the teacher characteristics in the negative direction.

Koul (1972) conducted a factorial study of certain personality variables of popular teachers in secondary schools. He found that the popular teachers had a favorable attitude towards teaching in schools and so they may be expected to maintain a state of harmonious relationship with their pupils characterized by mutual affection and sympathetic understanding. He also found that popular teachers were effective in their work as teaching.

Sharma (1971) studied the relationship of predictor of teacher effectiveness at elementary level and follow up after one year of training. Teacher effectiveness was evaluated on the basis of (*i*) U.P. Department Examinations marks in theory and practice teaching during the training course, (*ii*) the personality training scores of trainees and (*iii*) supervisors' rating of classroom teaching during training period. To estimate the relationship between teacher characteristics and teacher effectiveness after one year of training, a follow up study was conducted which included (*i*) personality rating scores by the headmaster, (*ii*) class rating scores by collogues and the investigator, (*iii*) pass percentage of the student taught by the teacher, (*iv*) evaluation through self perception, (*v*) the Minnesota Teacher Attitude Inventory scores and (*vi*) observation data of classroom verbal interaction by Flanders category system. A representative sample consists of 700 teachers (269 female and 431 male) obtained from normal Government Schools of U.P. was used in the study. He found that the combination of five predictors, i.e., teaching aptitude, academic grades, socio-economic status, teaching experience and age, in order of their arrangement appeared to be sound predictor of teacher effectiveness.

Samantroy (1971) studied teacher attitude and its relationship with teaching efficiency. The results showed that the teachers with favorable attitude had superior efficiency. The study also showed that there was a positive relationship between teacher adjustment and teaching efficiency.

Roy (1971) studied the nature of relationship among teacher attitude, teacher adjustment and teaching efficiency on a sample of 320 graduate teachers and came to the conclusion that there existed some degree of positive relationship between the variable teaching efficiency and teacher attitude and teaching efficiency and teacher adjustment.

Loree (1971) has done a review of research on attitude under four areas. These include the attitude measurement and attitudes related to teacher effectiveness. He has classified the tools for assessing teachers attitude into four categories and has described the tools available in each category. Use of these tools by various researchers has also been discussed. Among self-reporting inventories the Minnesota Teacher Attitude Inventory (MTAI) by Cook, Leeds and Callis (1951) has been reported as the most widely used tool for measuring attitudes. Studies on relationship of teacher attitudes with effectiveness have also been reported by Loree. He reports that Sprinthall, Whiteley and Mosher (1966) found a relationship between the cognitive flexibility (an attitude) and effective teaching. Rosenshine (1969) found in a review of research that teacher's enthusiastic and animated behaviors and pupil achievement are related.

Debnath (1971) studied the determinants of teaching efficiency. The study reveled that the important correlations of teaching efficiency were knowledge of the subject matter, sincerely in teaching, mastery over the method of teaching, academic qualifications, mode of exposition, sympathetic attitude towards students discipline, student participation, proper use of aids and appliances in teaching and the art of questioning.

Vicente (1970), who found that these factors do influence the morale of the adults. In more comprehensive study made by Heally (1970), teachers general status, feelings of financial security, administrative participation and certification were found to be positively related to their morale. Albert (1977) in his study found that emphasis on selflessness, a quality of human personality was highly related to human to morale. Age and social interaction factor were found to be related to morale by Samuel (1976) who found that both these factors had the capacity of affecting human morale. In Tellman's (1979) study principals reinforcing behavior, sex material status and educational preparation were found to be significant correlates of teachers morale. Spears (1974) found that morale is a function of incidents experienced by a person in his life. His study revealed that administrative support, institutional support and student outcome characteristics were significantly correlated with the morale of the faculty members. Dekhtawala (1977) found no relationship between teachers morale and their length of experience, size of the school, type of the school and locality of the school. She found significant correlation between teachers morale and their students achievement, their sex, age and marital status. Pillai (1974) in a recent study found that organizational climate was significantly correlated with teachers morale.

Prasad (1970) evaluated the professional efficiency of primary school teachers from three angles, namely, (*i*) efficiency in classroom teaching, (*ii*) efficiency in organising curricular activities and (*iii*) efficiency in organizing activities related to the school community relationship aspect of school life with the help of various devices. The study resulted in the development of Teacher Efficacy Observation Schedule.

NCERT (1969-70). The major hypothesis for this study was whether attitudes of teachers towards the profession are affected by the management of the school, location of the school, tenure of services, sex, marital status, age, experience, academic and professional qualifications. The findings include that sex, age and experience do not affect significantly the attitude of teachers.

Clarke (1970) teaching constitutes activities that are designed and performed to produce change in pupil behavior. Komisar (1966) has pointed out that teaching included so many activities as, introducing, demonstrating, citing, hypothesizing, reporting, conjecturing, confirming. Contrasting explaining, questioning, elaborating etc., which may be considered as constituent skills of teaching (Stones & Morris, 1972). Brown (1975) has considered teaching as a many sided activity which includes a number of activities like questioning, giving information, listening and such others.

Ryans (1969) extensive in nature was concerned with the identification of characteristics of teachers in general and able teachers in particular. Observations were made in classrooms, responses to personality inventories were recorded, interviews were conducted and life history information was gathered. Emphasis was placed upon both the intellectual and personality assessment of the teachers, Detailed assessment of superior teachers indicated that they seemed to be exceptional with regard to intellectual ability, personality adjustment and social interest and effectiveness. They have a strong liking for children and a personal admiration for such human characteristics as friendliness, permissiveness and fairness. The study of teachers attitude (Arora, 1976 and Goyal, 1980) rated low in effectiveness, suggested that they possessed a critical attitude towards others, less interest in social relationship and less favorable attitude towards pupils.

Aaron (1969) however, found that there was significant correlation between the attitude and achievement motives of teachers and pupils. Naidu (1975) in a study based on a sample on 360 teachers from Andhra Pradesh found that all teachers had favorable attitude. Bhogle (1970) conducted a study on psychological and organizational correlates of acceptance of innovations by secondary schools. She found that head teachers with favorable attitude towards teaching and older in age were more ready to adopt innovations.

Start (1968) analyzed 268 references relating to the ratings of teachers by their head teachers. He identified nine different criteria for teacher evaluation, viz., teaching ability, relation with colleagues, class control, relation with parents, administrative ability, relation with children, extramural contributions and relation with the head teachers.

Gage's views (1968) about teaching are "Teaching skills are specific instructional techniques and procedures that a teacher may use in the class-room. They represent an analysis of the teaching process into relatively discrete components that can be used in different combination in the continuous flow of the teacher's performance".

Beck (1967) devised and tested items for an instrument "About My Teacher" to measure pupil's perceptions of the merits of their teacher along the five dimensions of affective merit, cognitive merit, disciplinary merit, innovative merit and motivational merit. His conclusions are that sixth grade pupils perceive the teacher as warm, friendly and supportive person who communicates and disciplines pupils effectively flexible in methodology.

Deva (1966) used five predictor variables, viz., intelligence, social adjustment, personality adjustment, socio economic status and academic achievement to predict student teaching success. He found all the correlations between predictor variables and criterion measure to be significant. Personality secured to be most important and intelligence least important in predicting successes in student teaching.

Aggarwal (1966) conducted a study of the teacher educator's attitude towards their profession and found that they had a attitude towards the profession and that the factors like age, sex and experience did not influence their attitudes.

Sherry (1964), Deva (1966), Debnath (1971), and Singh (1978) have attempted to take into account a few correlates of teaching success. Other Indian researchers have touched only a few correlates of teaching efficiency. Recently, Kundu (1981) has reviewed 120 researches, category wise, conducted in India and abroad.

But no agreed upon criteria seems to have been evolved to measure teaching success. This shows that a further probing into the field is necessary taking into account the strong and weak points of the researches in the area already done.

Sherry (1964) constructed a predictive battery for success in teaching. The battery included the following tests: intelligence tests, interest inventory, personality and attitude scale intelligence was found to be the most important factor for success in teaching.

Parashar (1963) in a study of teacher attitude towards teaching found that age and teaching experience had no effect on attitude of teachers towards their profession. A study has been conducted by Sammantroy (1970) on teacher attitude and its relationship with adjustment and efficiency of teachers. He found that a large majority of teachers (78%) have a favorable attitude towards teaching, no significant difference was found between the attitude of men and women teachers, and the teacher attitude is related with adjustment efficiency to some degree.

Taylor (1962) studied the characteristics of a good teacher on a composite scale combining the three hypothesized areas of a good teacher's class room behavior, i.e., discipline, teaching and personal qualities. He administered the scale to 897 primary and secondary school children, 131 teachers and 43 training college students. The analysis of the responses showed that children in general evaluated most highly the 'good' teacher's personal qualities, particularly his patience, kindness, sympathy and understanding as did training college students. The minority of graduate teachers emphasized the good teacher's teaching. Teachers gave equal weight age to good teacher's teaching and discipline.

Jayamma (1962) constructed and standardized an inventory for predicting teaching efficiency on a sample of 500 school teachers drawn from sixty institutions of Mysore state. The variable studied were (*i*) professional knowledge and skill; (*ii*) acquaintance with the principles of psychology; (*iii*) class management, school organization and educational administration; (*iv*) relation with other and (*v*) individual qualities of humor, patience and sympathy. Factor analysis of the test showed that the order of sub- tests, in order of saturation, was professional skill and interest was the best measure of efficiency.

Evans (1962) summed up previous researches in this area. He arrived at the similar conclusion that children like teachers who are kind, friendly, cheerful, patient, helpful, fair, have sense of humor, show an understanding of children's problem, allow plenty of pupil activity and at the same time maintain order. They dislike teachers who use sarcasm, are domineering and have favorites, who punish to secure discipline, fail to provide for the needs of individual pupils and have disagreeable personality qualities.

Peronto (1961) found that good teachers differed from poor teachers in (1) Knowledge, (2) interest and proficiency in teacher-pupil relationships, (3) physical and emotional stability, (4) flexibility, (5) dominance and (6) professional motivation.

Barr et al. (1961) studied the validity of activity analysis in studying teaching. In an extensive study of 47 poor teachers and 47 good teachers in junior and senior high school levels they attempted to collect data of the activity method. In general the result of the study seemed to indicate that while there were doubtless factors contributing to success and failure in teaching, no critical factors which always distinguished the activities of good teachers from those of poor teachers were discovered.

Ryans (1960) compared the characteristics of teachers assessed as generally high and generally low. There was a general tendency for high teachers to be extremely generous in their appraisal of the behavior and motives of other persons; possess strong interest in reading and literary affairs, be interested in music, painting and the arts in general; participate in social groups; enjoy pupil relationships; prefer non-directive (permissive) classroom procedures; manifest superior verbal intelligence and be superior with respect to emotional adjustment. On the other hand, low teachers tended generally to be restrictive and critical in their appraisals of other persons; prefer activities which did not involve close personal contacts; express less favorable opinions of pupils; manifest less high verbal intelligence; show less satisfactory emotional adjustment and represent older groups.

Harris (1960) says "—the relation of student and teacher is a crucial factor in the teaching process and must be considered an important aspect of methodology". Haggerty (1932) in one of his earliest formal statements has indicated that "attempt to predict teaching success had generally failed to show any significant reliability because it had ignored one of the most important aspects of the teaching process-the relationship between students and teachers". A study by Bush (1942) shows that no single factor can be the cause of successful teaching, but he, on the basis of his findings, maintained that the students-teacher relationship is among the most important. Brookever's (1940) found that teachers who showed a high degree of person- to-person interaction with many students tended to be rated high respect to general teaching competence. The teachers who showed a high degree of person-to-person interaction with many pupils had intimate knowledge of their students and were likely to be popular among them. Ojemann and Wilkinson (1939) in their investigation found that the students, about whom teachers had intimate and superior knowledge, made greater gains in achievement, had better attitudes towards school, enjoyed school more, showed more mutual acceptance, exhibited fewer feelings of personal interiority, revealed a decrease in personal maladjustments and possessed a more logical motivation towards school work. The investigators also concluded that the intimate knowledge of students was helpful in establishing proper report and it was this which probably led the students to better educational achievement.

Harris (1960) said about the correlates of teacher effectiveness that "Measured intellectual abilities, achievement in college course, general culture and special subject matter. Knowledge, professional information, student teaching marks, emotional adjustment, attitudes favorable to students generously in appraisal of the behavior and motives of other persons, strong interest in reading literary matters, interest in music and painting, participation in social and community affairs, early experience in earning for children and teaching (Such as reading to children, taking a class for the teacher), history of teaching in he family, size of school and size of community in which teaching, cultural level of the community and participation in vocational activities, all appear to be characteristics of the teacher which are likely to be positively correlated or associated with teacher effectiveness in the abstract."

Edwards (1957) had reviewed the techniques of scale construction for attitude measurement and discussed in detail the merits and demerits of these techniques on the basis of research done on them. Among other major publications on attitude theory and its other aspects are by Fishbein (1967), Himmelfarb and Eagly (1974), Wilson (1972), Green (1954), Allport (1954). Green has observed that, "the method of equal appearing intervals is the most widely used of the judgment methods".

Anderson (1954) and Boyce (1912) in separate studies found no significant difference between men and women teachers in regard to teaching success.

Ryans (1951) found a tendency for teachers with five to nine years experience to be significantly higher with respect to success criterion scores than those with less or greater amounts. Moriam concluded that after a year or two experiences contributed little towards teaching efficiency.

Schwartz (1950) used assessment of the teacher in training and in his second year in profession to identify good from poor teachers. But he did not find a significant correlation between 16 P.F. scores and assessed teaching marks.

Von Haden (1949) and Webb & Nolan (1955) made studies in which various methods of judging success were compared. Measures of pupil gain as a means of evaluating teacher success did not correlate highly with other criteria of success.

Witty (1948) secured letters from some 14,000 pupils in the first and second contest respectively to choose the teachers who had helped the pupils most. The letters were analyzed to determine the predominant characteristics most often mentioned by the pupils. Being cooperative, having a democratic attitude, showing kindness and consideration, being patient, having wide interests, being fair and impartial and having a sense of humor were the characteristics the pupils mentioned most often in association with the helpful teacher. In addition, a random sample of letters were selected and analyzed for negative characteristics. The most frequently mentioned were intolerance, a bad temper, being unreasonable in demands made upon the pupils, being sarcastic and unfriendly and having an unattractive appearance.

Seagoe (1945) used University of California rating scale for practice teaching as the criterion of success. He concluded that tests of achievement had little predicative value. In 1946, again he used the same measure of success and found grade point ratio not significantly related to success in teaching practice.

Knight, Morris, Boardman and Lancelot (1940) throw light upon the qualities of teachers that need to be considered in studying the teacher at work. Though the data are of a highly diverse character, the main points of emphasis in these studies seem to be the following:

1. The teacher's personal fitness: such as poise refinement etc.
2. The teacher's professional equipment: such as knowledge of the needs of the child etc.
3. The teacher's mental capacity: such as intelligence, alertness etc.
4. The teacher's academic preparation: such as knowledge of the subject etc.
5. The teacher's emotional stability: such as self-control, balance etc.
6. The teacher's social adjustment and ability to work with others.

Simon's (1936) study pointed out teacher's unsatisfactory adjustment as the reason for the unpopularity of teachers among students. The teaching of such teachers was not found to be effective. Simon (1936) after studying the records of action taken in the dismissal of 769 teachers and administrators concludes: "They were unable to make satisfactory adjustment. The teacher's inability to adjust himself to the community or to the school environment will cause him to be unpopular with the pupils and parents and may cause boys and girls to dislike the subject he teaches".

Hart (1934) secured the reactions of some 10,000 seniors in 66 high schools in widely distributed sections of the U.S.A. to the qualities of merit in the teachers with whom they had studied. He found a total of forty three different reasons for "Liking Teacher A Best" and thirty different reasons for "Liking Teacher Z least". Not surprisingly, over fifty one percent of the students said that they liked best those who were "helpful in school work, who explained lessons and assignment clearly, and who used examples in teaching''. Also more than forty percent of the students responded favorably to teachers with a "sense of humor''. The teacher assessed most negatively were "unable to explain clearly, were partial to brighter students, and had superior, aloof, over-bearing attitudes". In addition, over 50 percent of the respondents mentioned behaviors such as "too cross, crabby, grouchy, and sarcastic" as reasons for disliking many teachers.

Hart (1934) in his study found that 80% of the pupils indicated that the teacher whom they liked the most, also was the most effective teacher, i.e. the best teacher.

Cattel (1931) surveyed professional opinion on the qualities of a good teacher through a questionnaire given to inspectors, training college staff, heads, teachers and students asking him them, among other things, to write down ten most important traits of a good-mature and ten of a good-young teacher. From replies he selected 22 qualities and claimed that various groups showed a fair agreement in their order of importance. The numbers in brackets show their overall order of importance.

(*i*) Natural gifts: Intelligence (2), Physical health (18), Presence of mind (19).

(*ii*) Character and Temperament: Self Control (13), personality and will, sense of humor (5), Kindness (8), Open-mindedness (4), Sympathy and Tact (3), Enthusiasm for the job (9), Perseverance (12).

(*iii*) General Direction of Sentiments: Enterprise (14), Conservatism (22), Alertness of mind (20), Orderliness and Precision (15), Idealism (6), outside interests (17).

(*iv*) Matters of Education and Acquired skill: Knowledge of Subjects (16), General culture (7), Social fitness (21), Knowledge of Psychology and Pedagogy (10), Classroom Technique (11).

Barr (1929) studied the characteristic differences in the teaching performance of good and poor teachers, selected on the basis of supervisory ratings. The teaching techniques and classroom behavior pattern of good and poor teachers were observed. He concluded that good teachers, as compared with poor teachers were more vigorous, more enthusiastic and happier, less attractive, more emotionally stable, possessed a better voice and displayed a keener sense of humor.

## STUDIES RELATED TO PERSONALITY

Studies related to personality with regard to teacher trainees of special education were quite unavailable. But there are many studies focused on personality factors of teachers, college students and other sections of the society in relations to other variables. The researcher reviewed such literature widely hoping that it may be helpful in his study. A brief description of such studies is reviewed below.

Sivarajan K (2002), stated that personality by conduct, behavior activities, movements and everything else are concerning the individual. In short personality is the way in which an individual adjust with environment. Personality is not a fixed stage. But a dynamic totality which is continuously changing due to interaction with the environment.

Paunonen and Ashton (2001) in a large-sample study of 717 subjects, 190 male and 527 female undergraduate students, described two broad Big Five factor measures, and were compared with two narrow personality trait measures in the prediction of final grades in an undergraduate psychology course. The two factors evaluated as predictors were Conscientiousness and Openness to Experience (or intellect). The traits evaluated, which were constituents of the respective factors, were need for achievement and need for understanding. In each comparison, the lower level trait measure did better than its higher-level factor measure in the prediction of course grades. It is concluded that the aggregation of narrow trait measure into broad factor measures can be counterproductive form the points of view of both behavior prediction and behavior explanation.

Polleys (2001) carried out a study with the purpose to investigate the relationships between self-regulated learning (SRL), personality, and achievement. Specifically, the study investigated whether a relationship exists between personality and self-regulated learning, whether a relationship exists between achievement based on assignment to a remedial group and sled-regulated learning, and whether achievement moderates the relationship between personality and self-regulated learning. Subjects were 126 college students, approximately half of whom were remedial students. All subjects completed both the Myser-Briggs Type indicator and the Motivated Strategies for Learning Questionnaire. Statistical measure, including multiple regression correlations, a series of moderated regressions, and a MANOVA procedure were performed in analyzing the data. Significant relationships between SRL and personality were found in 17 instances out of a possible 60 for the whole group of subjects. The multivariate test found no significant influence of achievement on SRL. When subjects were separated into the remedial and non-remedial groups, differing patterns emerged. The non remedial group showed relationships in only seven of the 60 possibilities. The remedial group, however, showed relationships in 15 of the 60 possibilities. The JP personality preference was the most powerful predictor of self-regulated learning for both remedial and non-remedial groups. Although the personality-SRL relationships were different in many factors between the non-remedial and remedial groups, the overall multivariate test showed no significance; hence, achievement was not found to be a moderator of the personality- SRL relationships.

Rindermann and Neubauer (2001) investigated the influence of personality on three aspects of cognitive performance, processing speed, intelligence and school performance. Stepwise regressions between personality scales and different processing speed measures (Zahlen-Verbindungs-Test, Coding Test), psychometric intelligence test (Kognitiver Faehigkeits-Test, Advance Progressive Matrices) and school performance (grades) were calculated in a sample of 280 students form German gymnasiums (aged 14-16 yrs). Results show a weak multiple correlation of personality with processing speed (R=0.32), a medium correlation with intelligence (R=0.51) and a high correlation with grades (R=0.69).

Processing speed tests allow one to measure cognitive abilities in a less biased form than intelligence tests, whereas school performance could be influenced in a positive or negative way by personality factors like self-concept, anxiety or motivation.

Busato et al (1999) investigated the relation between J.D. Vermunt's (1992) 4 postulated learning styles (meaning directed [MD], reproduction directed [RD], application directed [AD], or undirected [UD] learning styles), the Big Five personality traits, and achievement motivation among 900 university students. Extraversion correlated positively with the MD, RD, and AD learning styles. Conscientiousness was associated positively with the MD, RD, and AD learning styles, and negatively with the UD learning style. Openness to experience correlated positively with the MD and AD learning styles, and negatively with the UD style. Neuroticism correlated positively with UD learning style and negatively with MD and RD learning styles. Agreeableness was associated positively with RD and AD learning styles. Positive correlations were found for achievement motivation with the MD, RD, and AD learning styles, and a negative one with the UD learning style. Regression analyses confirmed these patterns. Although there was some systematic overlap for the 4 learning styles with personality variables and achievement motivation, the authors conclude that it makes sense to measure these 3 groups of variables separately in education settings.

Ngati and Jerry (1996) studied the relationship between personality characteristics and academic and demographic variables of adult learners.

The purpose of the study was to explore adult learners' personality and demographic characteristics and the way these variables relate to their academic performance.

**Method**

One-hundred-ninety-four adult learners from National University participated in the study by filling out a questionnaire. A correlation design, correlating personality, demographic, and academic achievement variables with GPA was used. The independent variables in the study were the adult learner's personality characteristics tested with the odd continuing learning inventory (OCLI), and four demographic characteristics: age, sex, marital status, and income. The dependent variable was the academic achievement measured by GPA.

**Results**

The results are as follows: (1) commitment to learning was positively and significantly associated with GPA; (2) cognitive openness was significantly associated with GPA; (2) cognitive openness was significantly and negatively associated with GPA; (3) age was significantly and positively associated with GPA; (4) married students had significantly higher GPA scores than single students; (5) students with higher family incomes had significantly higher GPA scores, than did students with lower family incomes; and, (6) the best combination of predictors of GPA was income and commitment to learning.

Johnson and Carol Bradley (1996) studied personality traits and learning styles: factors affecting the academic achievement of underachieving gifted students.

The purpose of this study was to examine the relationship between specific personality traits and learning styles and academic achievement in gifted students, resulting in their becoming underachievers and being considered at – risk in the educational system. Additionally, an attempt was made to determine when the rate of sharpest decline in academic performance occurs over a five – year period of time which would have essential implications in intervention strategies to prevent this occurrence. The population consisted of 46 gifted students in a South Carolina school district. Based on a median split of average cumulative end – of – year grades over a five – year period, the students were categorized into two groups: achievers and underachievers. The two groups afforded an opportunity to examine differences in personality traits, learning styles, and academic performance between the two groups within the population. Two tests, the sixteen Personality Factor Questionnaire and the Basic Assessment of Cognitive Organization, were administered to the participants to determine personality traits and analytic/global learning styles. The cumulative end – of – year academic grades were used to investigate whether or not there was an identifiable point in time over a five – year time span when the sharpest rate of decline in academic performance occurred.

Results of the Spearman Rank – Order Correlation Coefficients showed that there were significant correlations between ten personality traits and academic achievement, and mean differences between the gifted achievers and gifted underachievers confirmed that these personality traits contributed to the academic achievement of these students. There did not appear to be a significant correlation between analytic and global perceptual tendency and academic achievement although the majority of gifted students were either highly flexible or more global than analytic. In addition, no particular point of decline in academic achievement was readily identified. Findings of this study were consistent with the review of literature which suggested that personality factors may be related to academic achievement, and gifted achievers and gifted underachievers are generally global in perceptual tendency.

Giancarlo and Carol Facione (1996) studied critical thinking, culture and personality: predicting later academic success.

Observed differences in the high school graduation and college attendance rates of Latino students as compared to other ethnic groups have signaled the necessity for an understanding of the factors impacting academic achievement within this student population. The present study examines four sets of predictor variables attempting to cover four domains relevant to an individual's educational experience: critical thinking dispositions representing the meta-cognitive domain, cultural values representing the socio cultural context, personality trait representing the personal domain, and familial characteristics representing the home environment. The present study was not a cross – cultural comparison, rather it was an intra-cultural study of academic achievement among Latino students. The two study critical thinking and Latino high school student's academic achievement; and (2) investigate how gender, culture, personality, and familial characteristics influence Latino's disposition toward CT and academic achievement. Subjects were 205 female high school sophomores and 188 male sophomores from Southern California. Subjects completed a survey booklet in either English or Spanish. Academic achievement information regarding GPA, proficiency exams, math and science achievement was gathered from the student's school transcripts. Findings suggest that the strongest predictors of academic achievement were CT dispositions, modernity, respect for elders, sex role socialization, parent's education, parent's career attainment, subjects career aspirations, exposure to the American school system and regional economic circumstances. Subjects' career aspiration were significant for male students but not female students. No relationship between collective orientation and academic achievement was found. Respect for elders and traditional sex role orientation were negatively correlated with academic achievement among male subjects. This study establishes the disposition toward critical thinking as a significant meta-cognitive personality contrast within the psychological literature. This within – cultural group study demonstrates the importance of CT dispositions, biculturalism, modernity, and family educational background for predicting academic achievement among Latino students.

Sayles and Juliet Pamela (1995) studied the relationship among selected personality, identity status, and academic achievement factors among black adolescents.

## PROBLEMS

The academic performance of Blacks has been documented as being much below that of other racial and ethnic groups (Casenell, 1984; Jordan, 1981; Lee, 1994; White, 1984). This study attempted to determine the relationships among personality, the development of identity status, and academic achievement among black adolescents. Method. A total of 136 black adolescent students (64 males and 72 females) were used in this study. They were in the age range of 13 to 18 years and were members of classes from integrated middle, junior high, and high schools. The black identity scale (BIS) and the High School Personality Questionnaire (HSPQ) were group administered in one sitting and the California Achievement Test (CAT) was group administered separately in another sitting.

The data were analyzed using multiple linear regression analysis and canonical correlation analysis.

## RESULTS

(1) The overall academic achievement of black adolescents was related significantly to abstract thinking, affirmation of the values and worth of their blackness and origins, and being self-oriented as opposed to group-oriented, warm, sensitive, emotionally stable, and vigorous. Those who are more group-oriented rather than self-oriented tend to do well in comprehension and language expression and less well in language mechanics. (2) There was no relationship found between affinity and achievement. This is in contrast to Muhammad's (1991) finding of a negative relationship between affinity and achievement. From my findings, it appeared that the degree to which adolescents accept themselves as Black persons and accept black people in general is not related to achievement. This is in contrast to Muhammad's (1991) finding of a negative relationship between affinity and achievement. (3) Higher identity scores tend to be related to greater boldness, sensitivity, and vigor. The lower depreciation scores were related to greater boldness. The depreciation factor on the black identity scale was found to have very little relationship with any of the other variables in the study.

## CONCLUSIONS

The major significant relationships found in the study were those involving personality. Personality variables were significantly related to both achievement and identity. There were, however, few significant relationships between identity and achievement.

Barkley and Denyse Olivia (1995) studied role perception, personality type, and academic achievement in a practical nursing school.

A descriptive embedded single case study was conducted to develop a profile of practical nursing students enrolled in one class. In addition, this study examined the impact of information acquired during the fundamentals of nursing course on students' role perception. The dependent variable was role perception and the independent variables included (*a*) academic achievement, (*b*) health care experience, (*c*) gender, (*d*) educational level, and (e) age. Forty seven (47) students volunteered to participate in this study. Forty-three (43) participants completed all data instruments and were included in the sample. All participants were enrolled in Fundamentals of nursing, the introductory course for the licensed practical nursing program. Additionally, the group was international and of diverse educational backgrounds. All participants attended the sixteen week nursing course. Lecture discussion and self directed instructional methods were implemented to facilitate learning in the class room. The data were collected by using pretest and post test instruments: practical nursing students' role perception scale (PNSRPS), the Myers-Briggs Type Indicator (MBTI), the Demographic Data Questionnaire, and six fundamentals of Nursing examinations.

The PNSRPS, MBI, and the Demographic data questionnaire were administered at the beginning of the semester. After the introductory nursing content had been covered, the PNSRPS was administered again. Kendall Tau Coefficients were computed to examine the relationship between role perception and academic achievement. The difference between pretest and posttest role perception scores was analyzed using the Wilcoxon Matched-Pairs signed ranks test. A t-test for paired scores by instructional preferences. Independent sample Chi-square tests computed to analyze the differences between students' role perception scores as classified by healthcare experience, gender, educational levels, and age groups.

Findings indicated that there was a statistically significant difference between student nurses' mean test scores for the lecture discussion method versus the self directed method (t = $-$6.36, p = .0001). Although, no other satisfactory significant relationships or differences were found, the variables provided meaningful insight into developing a profile of the practical nursing student group.

Chitra, Thiagarajan and Krishnan (1994) studied 6 psycho-social factors that could augment the educational achievement,. Prestige and socio-economic status (SES) among scheduled caste (SC) communities. The factors studied were: personality, intelligence, occupational aspiration, SES, social distance, and awareness of facilities. The personality traits of 104 SC girl students and 100 non-scheduled caste girl students pursuing a higher secondary course were assessed. SC subjects differed form the NSC group only in their SES, and all 6 psychosocial factors were equally responsible for the academic achievement in both the groups. It was concluded that education causes a positive change in personality, intelligence, and occupational aspiration by narrowing down the gap between the 2 groups.

Leonoff and Deborah (1993) studied parental, peer, and personality factors in adolescent academic underachievement (underachievers)

The purpose of this study was to assess the relationship among parental, peer, and personality factors for the task of academic achievement during adolescence. One thousand one hundred and forty-two students from 3 suburban metropolitan Toronto high schools were screened to identity underachievers. The students, primarily middle class Caucasian, ranged in age from 15 to 18, with a mean age of 16. Students completed the Matrix Analogies Test (MAT) – short form (Naglieri – 1985) and the motivation and achievement inventory – form E (Friendland, Marcus & Mandel, in press) in class group sessions. Grade point averages (GPA) of the students were obtained from their school records. The final sample which excluded learning disabled students, contained 1069 students, 562 males and 507 females. Underachievement was defined as a statistical discrepancy between intellectual ability, as measured by the MAT and academic performance, as measured by GPA. A linear regression equation was used to identify underachievers. Using this method, 206 students were identified as underachievers. Forty-one underachieving students participated in semi-structured diagnostic interviews to assess their personality styles. Thirty eight students were reliably classified as one of the following personality types: overanxious, conduct disordered, academic problem, and identity. Forty-nine underachieving students and 67 achieving students, completed the Network of relationships inventory (NRI) (Furman, 1989) and the important people in my Life questionnaire (IPML) developed for the purposes of this study) in group sessions. The students rated their relationships with their mothers, fathers, two closet friends, and boy/girl friends. The student started their popularity with same and opposite gender peers, and indicated the size of their peer and adult networks. Underachievers reported significantly less power with both parents and close friends. Male underachievers reported decreased popularity with same gender peers with increased age. Male and female underachievers reported decreased popularity with opposite-gender peers with increased age. No significant differences were obtained as a function of the personality styles of the underachievers. Implications of these findings, limitations of the study, and future research directions were discussed.

Green, Peters and Webster (1991) examined whether personality profiles, using personality factor, or clusters of personality factors, are associated with academic success. 129 medical students completed the Sixteen Personality Factor Questionnaire (16PF) and were divided into 4 groups dependent on their academic performance. Most (62%) had no academic problems, but 16 subjects had serious difficulties, which entailed delaying qualification by at least 6 months. There was no relationship between the scores obtained for the subjects 1st attempt at A- level and their subsequent medical school academic performance. Academic success was not associated with any of the personality factors.

Abrami, Perry and Leventhal (1987), in Study 1, on 388 undergraduates (*a*) rated themselves on the Adjective Check List (ACL), (*b*) viewed a videotape that varied in instructor expressiveness and lecture content, (*c*) evaluated the videotaped instructor and a test on the lecture, and (*d*) completed the ACL for the instructor. In study 2, 87 subjects were also exposed to 2 videotaped lectures given 1 week apart. In Study 3, 108 subjects completed the ACL for themselves and their instructors, evaluated their instructor's teaching, and completed a test on common course material. No meaningful or consistent relationship between ratings and student personality characteristics appeared to exist. Personality characteristics of instructors were related to teacher effectiveness rating. Ratings predicted teacher-produced achievement equally well for classes that differed in the personality characteristics of the students enrolled. Teacher effects on rating appeared significantly greater than teacher effects on achievement.

Kazmi (1986) studied the personality profiles and cognitive factors of Academic failures amongst Science and Arts students at various levels.

The objective of the investigation to study the relationship between personality characteristics, cognitive factors , sex difference and academic failure among science and arts students at the high school, intermediate and undergraduate levels. Bernreuter's Personality Inventory, Raven's Progressive Matrices, Conformity – C – Scale, AAPAS Motive Test ( a measure of achievement motivation), Brown – Holtzman Survey of study Habits and Attitudes and Multi –dimension Inventory of Self Awareness , and a measure of memory span were administered to a random sample of 1000 failures (500 girls and 500 boys) of arts and science streams at high school, intermediate and undergraduate levels.

The major findings of the study were : 1. The relationship between different personality factors of Bernreuter's Personality Inventory, intelligence, conformity, achievement motivation, study habits and memory span, and academic failure was not significant. 2. Failure differed in their personality characteristics and cognitive make – up. 3. Sex differences did not interact with any personality characteristics for academic failure. 4. Failures did not have any significant interactional effects of sex difference and cognitive factors on their academic achievement. 5. The personality characteristics and cognitive factors interacted on the failure's academic achievement.

Singh (1984) studied the impact of social attitude on the personality characteristics of students of the Undergraduate level.

The objectives of the investigation were (*i*) to study the social attitude of undergraduate level students, (*ii*) to study the personality characteristics of the students. (*iii*) to compare the boys and girls with high and low social attitudes, and (*iv*) to study social-economic status of boys and girls with high and low social attitude.

The tools used for data collection were a Social Attitude Scale, a Personal Questionnaire, a Socio-economic status Scale (Kulshrestha), and a 16 P.F. Questionnaire. For the purpose of the study, 297 boys and 121 girls studying at the undergraduate level of eight affiliated colleges of Gorakhpur University were selected on the basis of the random cluster method.

The following results were obtained from the present study: 1. Students from high socio-economic status were found to have a better social attitude than students coming from lower socio-economic status. 2. Boys with high and low social attitudes were self- confident, and self-reliant. 3. Girls with the same social attitude were tender, dependent, and influential. 4. Boys and girls with a better social attitude had high morality, high sense of duty and high responsibility. 5. Motivation, creativity and morality were found more dominant in students with better social attitude in comparison with those with low social attitude, both boys and girls. 6. Boys and girls with a better social attitude had the characteristics of self – control, alertness and awareness more than those with low social attitude.

Lall (1984) studied the child rearing attitudes, personal problems and personality factors as correlates of Academic Achievement.

The main purpose of the study was (*i*) to investigate the relationship among child-rearing attitudes of parents (termed as parental attitude), youth problems and personality factors such as locus of control, reinforcement, anxiety, extraversion and neuroticism, and (*ii*) to study their relation with academic achievement (termed as academic success). Fourteen hypotheses were examined.

A random sample of 400 class IX and X students (200 boys and 200 girls) was selected from two high schools of Bhagalpur City. Singh's Parental Attitude Scale, Verma's Youth problem Inventory, Levenson's Locus of Control Scale, Sinha's M.A. Self Analysis Form, and Eysenck's Personality Inventory were used. Academic success was determined by marks obtained by students in the annual examination. Correlation analysis, t-test, etc. were employed.

The major findings were 1. Restrictive and protecting attitudes of parents were positively and significantly related to youth problems and anxiety. 2. Restrictive attitudes of parents were negatively and significantly related to internal locus of control and extraversion, whereas they were positively and significantly related with powerful-others, locus of control and neuroticism. Protecting attitudes of parents were positively and significantly related to academic success of boys. 3. Loving attitudes of parents were positively and significantly related to powerful-others, locus of control, extraversion and neuroticism. 4. Academic success was negatively and significantly related to personal problems and sensitivity, anxiety and neuroticism. Internal, powerful-others and locus of control of reinforcement were not significantly related to academic success. 5. Boys were score internally oriented and neurotic than girls, while girls were subjected to more restriction by parents and were more anxious than boys.

The major educational implication of the study is that it is helpful to teachers and others in understanding the problems of adolescent students, their personality and perception of parent child-rearing attitude.

Supts (1983) studied the Personality characteristics of Ninth Grade Over-and Under-achieving Boys and Girls at different levels of Achievement motivation.

The objectives of his were (*i*) to identify the personality factors of ninth grade boys and girls in which there was a significant interaction between over-and under –achievement and achievement motivation, (*ii*) to identify the personality factors of ninth grade boys and girls in which over-achievers differed from under-achievers, (*iii*) to identify the personality factors of ninth class boys and girls in which three levels of achievement motivation showed significant differences, (*iv*) to identify the personality factors of ninth grade boys and girls which showed main effects neither of over-and under-achievement, nor of achievement motivation, nor of the interaction between the two, and (*v*) to identify the personality factors of over-and under-achievers, of high motivated, average motivated and low motivated groups.

A sample of 310 ninth class boys and 312 ninth class girls was chosen randomly from four high schools of Patiala. They were administered the following tools: (*i*) the Tandon Group Test of Intelligence; (*ii*) the adapted version of Catell HSPO (Form B); (*iii*) the Achievement Motivation Inventory. Along with these tools the marks obtained by these students in the eighth class public examination were taken as criterion scores to identify them as high or low achievers. The data were analyzed with the help of un weighted means analysis.

The findings of the study were: 1. The groups of low motivated over-achieving boys was found to be more vigorous and zestful than the group of low motivated under-achieving boys. 2. The high motivated under achieving girls were more submissive and less tense than high motivated over-achieving girls. But low motivated under-achieving girls were less submissive and more tense than the low motivated over-achieving girls. 3. Over achieving boys were les expedient and less shy and had less undisciplined self-conflict than the under-achieving boys. 4. Over-achieving girls were less affected by feelings and more emotionally stable, less shy and more vigorous and zestful and hand less undisciplined self conflict than the under-achieving girls. 5. Among boys, the high motivated group and average motivated group were found to be more sober, less happy-go-lucky, and had less undisciplined self-conflict than the low motivated group. 6. Among girls the high motivated group was more intelligent and less expedient than the low motivated groups, and was less shy and had less undisciplined self-conflict than the low motivated group. The high motivated group did not differ significantly from the average motivated group in shyness and undisciplined self-conflict. 7. The average motivated boys did not differ from low motivated boys in scholastic ability, expediency, shyness and undisciplined self-conflict. 8. Neither the two levels of achievement not the three levels of achievement motivation differed significantly on personality factors- A,B,C,E) and Q3 for boys, and A, D, F, I, O and Q2 for girls. Interactional effect was also not found in these personality factors. 9. Over achievement boys differed from under-achieving girls in G, H and Q3 and over-achieving girls in G, H and Q3 and over-achieving girls differed from underachieving girls in C, H, H and Q3 personality traits. 10. There was significant interaction in academic achievement and achievement motivation both in the case of boys as well as girls in the case of J personality factor.

Khan (1983) studies the personality characteristics of educationally backward pupils of Higher Secondary Schools of Lucknow District.

The objectives of the study were (*i*) to discover the significant variable of personality responsible for low achievement, and (*ii*) to find out the relationship between these variables.

The sample of the study consisted of 600 pupils (150 boys and 150 girls of age range 10 to 12 years and an equal number of boys and girls of age range 13 to 16 years) with an I.Q. ranging from 100-120, studying in classes VII TO x having poor marks in school examinations, and on Schonell's Achievement Test. The sample was selected from 1500 pupils studying in classes VII to X in higher secondary of Lucknow district. The tools used in the study were Jalota's Group Test of Mental ability, Schonell's Test of Achievement, and Cattell's C.P.Q. and H.S.P.Q. Personality Tests prepared in Hindi by Kapoor and Rao and Mehrotra. Examination marks were also used by the investigator. The collected data were tabulated and analyzed using suitable statistical techniques.

Findings of the study were: 1. Educationally backward pupils were more reserved, detached and aloof, less intelligent, more emotionally unstable, more excitable and impatient, more assertive and aggressive, more happy-go-lucky, shy, timed and threat – sensitive, tender- minded and sensitive, more internally reflective, more insecure, worrying and guilt – prone, socially group dependent, uncontrolled and careless of social rules, and tense, over wrought and frustrated. 2. On second order factors the educationally backward pupils were more introverts, tender – mined and subdued, and had more anxiety and poor adjustment. 3. On the whole the girls were found to be a little warmer, more participating, more emotional, having stronger super – ego, more sensitive, tender – minded and guilt- prone than boys who were found more dominating, happy – go – lucky, excitable, tense and ergent. 4. Those who obtained medium sten scores on personality factor were better in achievement than those who obtained high or low sten scores or in other words deviated from the average sten scores to the low or high ends. 5. It was also found that the hampering effects of aloofness, emotional instability, excitability, aggression, dominance, guilt proneness, feeling of insecurity tension and frustration , etc were more prevalent at the adolescent stage (13 to 16 years) than at the preadolescent stage (10 to 12 years ).

Johnson (1983) administered a battery of 15 cognitive tests, the Eysenck Personality Inventory, the 16PF, and the Comrey Personality Scales to members of 105 families (393 subjects) to assess the relationship of scores to educational occupational levels. Results for 4 groups (males and females of Japanese and European ancestry) show that family background, cognitive ability, and personality appear to be associated with educational attainment to much the same degree.

Johnson (1982) studied the Personality characteristics of sports participants in High Schools.

The main objectives were (*i*) to study the Personality characteristics of sports participants, and (*ii*) to compare the personality characteristics of sports participants and non-participants. The hypotheses were: (1) Sports participants are more intelligent, more adjusted and free from abnormal tendencies, and more sociable and less impulsive in terms of temperament than non-participants. (2) Sports participants have greater interest in sports and have a more favorable attitude towards sports than non-participants. (3) Sports participation is related to materialism-spirituality orientation attitude. (4) Socio-economic status, caste membership and perceived degree of encouragement from peers, teachers, and parents are related to sports participation. (5) Sports participation is associated with higher academic achievement.

The sample for the study consisted of two groups-a group of sports participants (n=419) – who had been identified by the Kerala Sports Council, the Government agency for promoting sports, as excelling in sports and who were selected, prepared and tested in academic as well as physical abilities, and a group of non-participants in sports (n=423) who were tested for academic ability alone. The samples were further stratified on the basis of sex. The tools used were Test of Mental Abilities-Verbal (Mathew, 1973), Mathew Maladjustment Inventory (Mathew, 1973), Mathew Temperament Scale (Mathew, 1974) and Mathew Materialism-Spirituality Scale (Mathew, 1980). In addition, an attitude scale to measure attitude towards sports and games, scale to measure attitude towards sports and games and a general data questionnaire were prepared for the purpose of the study. The data were analyzed by applying the two-way analysis of variance technique wherever applicable, of the chi-square test and t-test.

The major findings were: 1. Sports participants differed from non-participants in their personality characteristics. 2. Sports participants were more adjusted, free from abnormal tendencies, more gregarious (sociable) and thoughtful (less impulsive) than non-participants. 3. Sports participants exhibited a more favorable attitude towards sports, and higher interest in sports and games than non-participants. 4. Socio-economic status, caste and religion, and encouragement from parents, peers and teachers were found to be related to sports participation. 5. Sports participation was associated with higher academic achievement.

Pratibha Deo (1980) conducted a study on 50 teachers from Government and private schools belonging to rural and urban areas by using a rating scale for Headmasters and a rating scale for students were used to find out teaching effectiveness. The results show that there is no good agreement amongst the different methods of identifying teaching effectiveness. Secondly, no clear picture has emerged of personality characteristics in relation to teaching effectiveness, though some trends are visible. The high group is ordinarily emotionally more stable, extrovert, dominant and the low group is emotionally more unstable, introverted and submissive, but more sociable.

Kumar (1980), studied some personality correlates of Academic Adjustment.

The main aims of the study were (*i*) to develop a tool for measuring level of academic adjustment of college students and (*ii*) to ascertain the relationships between certain personality dimensions and academic adjustment of college students.

An Academic Adjustment Inventory (AAI) was developed which contained six aspects of academic adjustment, viz., curricular adjustment, level of aspiration, personal efficiency, study skills, personal relations and mental health. The inventory was developed adopting suitable procedures. The reliability and validity of the inventory were found out. Sex difference in academic adjustment of college students was determined. Personality dimensions were ascertained by using the Hindi version of the Eysenck Personality Inventory (EPI). The AAI and EPI were administered to a mixed sample of 500 undergraduate college students of Bihar University.

The major findings were: (1) The AAI was sufficiently reliable and valid for measuring academic adjustment of college students. (2) The AAI was capable of yielding six area scores and one composite score (Inventory Score). (3) The academic adjustment of the female students was significantly much better than that of the male students. (4) No significant difference between the English and Hindi versions of the EPI was observed. (5) The introvert students had better academic adjustment than the extravert students. (6) The normal (or stable) students had better academic adjustment than the neurotic (or unstable) students. (7) The stable-introvert students had the highest academic adjustment, while the unstable extravert students had the lowest adjustment. The significant educational implication is that the AAI can proficiency be used to measure the level of academic adjustment of college students.

Paramesh (1979) administered the Eysenck Personality Inventory to 155 high school boys (mean age 16.14yrs). Scholastic achievement, as measured by scores on a secondary school graduation examination, was also assessed. No significant relationship between personality and scholastic achievement were found.

Singh (1978) investigated the personality factor of successful teachers identified on the basis of public examination results, students' evaluation of their teachers and appraisal of their class room teaching and other activities by the heads of their institutions. He found that high teachers were assertive (factor E), venturesome (factor H). Controlled (factor $Q_3$), emotionally stable (factor C) and trusting (factor L) in comparison to low teachers.

Gupta (1977) studied the personality traits differences of successful and less successful teachers. A group of 400 teachers (200male and 200 female) working in high-higher secondary schools was selected from sixty-seven school of four district in Punjab. A tool was prepared by the investigator to measure teaching success. It was found that success in teaching was significantly related to personality factor A,B,C,F,G,H,I,L,O,$Q_3$ and $Q_4$.

Brar (1976) studied personality traits (extraversion- introversion and neuroticism) and academic achievement in 70 noncommissioned officers (NCOs), 70 junior commissioned officers (JCOs), and 50 commissioned officers (COs) in a training colleges center of the Indian Army. A substantial negative correlation was found between academic achievement and neuroticism. For NCOs and COs there was also a strong negative correlation between academic achievement and extraversion, but for JCOs this correlation was positive. Age was not r elated either to extraversion or neuroticism.

Sharma (1976) investigated into the relationship between personality factors and teaching effectiveness. The sample of the study consists of a purposive sample of 173 cases (103 males and 70 females) of B.Ed. students of students of D.S. College and S.V. College, Aligarh. The criterion scores (i.e. teaching efficiency scores of students teachers) were obtained through a seven point scale prepared by Dr. R.C. Deva, A.M.U., Aligarh. He found only 6 factors out of 16 which are positively correlated with teaching effectiveness. These factors were B (intelligence), L (Trusting, adaptable, free of jealousy), F (happy-go-lucky, impulsive, lively), and M (Practical, careful, regulated by external realities). Intelligence comes out to be a very important factor in teaching effectiveness was .28 which is significant at .01 level.

Gupta (1976) attempted to predict teacher effectiveness through personality test. The sample constituted 300 male trained high school teachers having five to ten years of teaching experience, twenty-five principals and 350 students. Teacher effectiveness measured by using a teacher's rating scale, a teacher attitude inventory and the Jai Prakash's Teaching Aptitude Test. The major findings of the study were as follows//1. In comparison to low effective teachers, the high effective teachers were more warm hearted (A+), intelligent (B+), assertive (E+), emotionally stable (C+), surgent (F+), adventurous (H+), and self-controlled (Q3+), and they were less suspicious (L-), imaginative (M-), apprehensive and guilt prone (O-), experimenting and radical (Q1-), and self sufficient (Q2-).// 2.In comparison to average effective teachers, high effective teachers were significantly more intelligent (B+), emotionally stable (C+), assertive (E+), conscientious (G+), adventurous (H+), tender-minded (I+) and had higher self concept control (Q3+) and they were also less suspicious (L-), less tense and frustrated (Q4-).

Cooper, Boss and Keith (1974) obtained school marks in English, history, mathematics, and science for 582 $10^{th}$ graders. Personality was measured by the

13 non intellective factors of the High School Personality Questionnaire. It was shown that Factors C, G, F, Q2, and Q3 (Ego Strength vs Ego Weakness, Superego Strength vs Superego Weakness, Surgency vs Desurgency, Self-Sufficiency vs Group Dependency, and Strong Self-Sentiment vs Weak Self-Sentiment) were significant discriminators between the subjects who did well in all 4v subjects and those who did poorly in them all. Factors A, E, H, and I (Affectothymia vs Schizothymia, Dominance vs Submissiveness, Parmia vs Threctia, and Premsia vs Harria) were significant discriminators between subjects who performed better in the science than in the humanities.

Bohn (1973) compared biographical, personality, and interest factors of 74 work-study students who completed several personality scales including the California Psychological Inventory (CPI) and the Adjective Check List (ACL), as well as the SVIB. Biographical data and aspiration levels of Persisters and dropouts were very similar. Persisters were found to be more self-assertive, independent, and achievement-oriented than dropouts on the basis of the CPI and ACL scores.

Pandey (1973) administered the 16 Personality Factor Questionnaire to 350 entering freshmen (219 whites, 313 blacks; 193 males, 157 females) at Lincoln University in Missouri in the fall of 1969. 75% of the white students achieved "good" academic standing, 11% became dropouts, and 14% of the blacks students achieved "good" academic standing, 6% dropped out, and 20% were on probation at the end of the fall semester. Analyses of variance indicated ($p<.05$) that the good students were humble and submissive while the dropouts were assertive, stubborn, and independent. Both dropouts and those on probation were assertive, stubborn, and independent. Dropouts, however, were more intelligent and of stronger superego strength than probationers.

Kaul (1973) studied the personality traits of effective teachers identified on the basis of an attitude scale, public examination results and appraisal of teacher's work by the heads of the schools. The study disclosed that effective teachers were more intelligent ($B^+$), emotionally stable ($C^+$), conscientious ($G^+$), tough minded ($I^-$), placid ($O^-$), experimenting ($Q_1^+$), controlled ($Q_3^+$) and relaxed ($Q_4$).

Kaul (1972) conducted a factorial study of certain personality variables of popular teachers in the secondary schools of Haryana. He found that popular teachers distinguished themselves as more outgoing (A+), intelligent (B+), emotionally more stable (C+), sober (F-), conscientious (G+), shrewed (N+), placid (O-), controlled (Q3+) nad relaxed (Q4-).

Berman and Eisenberg (1971) reviewed some previous work on factors in academic achievement and reported a study using 270 final-year high school students. They correlated final-year grades with IQ, family and socio-economic data, and CPI scores in order to define the characteristics of the successful student within a culturally and economically homogenous group. Certain personality traits were found to correlate with achievement, i.e., motivation, sense of well-being, independence, and conformity. Exceptionally high achievement correlated with high IQ, and it is suggested that identification with parents' values and life models may be relevant.

Entwistle and Entwistle (1970) administered the Eysenck Personality Inventory and a questionnaire relating to academic motivation and study methods to 257 undergraduates. A correlation analysis of these scores in relation to academic performance at the end of the 1st year shows superiority of the introverts and subjects with good study methods. Introverts also tended to have better study methods, but this only partially explains their high academic performance. There was no relationship between neuroticism and attainment. A supplementary approach used an item-analysis to identify characteristics of successful students. From this analysis, items which identified good students were also positively related to stability and introversion.

George (1969). Studies the personality patterns of College Students Specializing in Different Fields.

The aim of the study was to find out whether there were significant differences in values, temperament and vocational interests among college students specialization in different fields (science, humanities, engineering, commerce, medicine education, law, agriculture and veterinary sciences).

Nine general education colleges and ten professional colleges were selected to form nine groups of students representing nine subjects, namely science, humanities, engineering, commerce, medicine, education, law, agriculture and veterinary science. Three personality inventories and a vocational interest inventory were developed. Allport-Vernon's Study of Values and the Guliford-Zimmerman Temperament Survey were adapted. The tests were administered to a total of 2407 students. The different samples taken for each test from a college were more or less comparable. The analysis of variance was undertaken for each of the 23 traits to see whether the nine groups of male students differed in the trait concerned. A similar analysis was done for each scale in the case of female students. The important findings of the study: 1. The F-ratio for men was significant of all traits except that of temperament. In the case of women, the F-ratio was significant for twelve scales three of values, two of temperament and all seven vocational interest scales). 2. In values, men were more theoretical, economic and political while women were found social, aesthetic and religious. 3. In temperament, men were found more ascendant, sociable and masculine than women. Women in the humanities group had more restraint than men. They were also emotionally more stable, objective and friendly. Men students in medical colleges were more emotionally stable, and objective, but less thoughtful than the women students. Among student teachers men were more active and emotionally stable. Among science students men were more thoughtful while women were found better in personal relations. 4. In vocational interests men got higher scores in mechanical and persuasive scales, while women were better in outdoor, aesthetic and social work scales. Men in the humanities and medical groups got significantly higher scores on the scientific scale than their women counterparts.

Davis and Satterly (1969) administered 16 P.F. Test to 149 female students of Homarton College at the time of entry and twenty-six months later prior to the final teaching practice. Small groups of students of 'High' and 'low' teaching ability was identified and their personality profiles compared. Poor teachers identified and their personality profiles compared. Poor teachers were less conscientious and persistent (G-) than their successful counterparts, tender-minded and sensitive (I+), prone to feelings of insecurity and timidity (O+), and liable to be tense, excitable and restless (Q4+) on both occasions. On the earlier occasion the low ability group obtained an above average score with regard to factors for unconventional behavior and carelessness in practical matters.

Start (1968) asked the head teacher, along with other things, to select five outstanding and five weakest teachers out of the thirty five members of the staff on the basis of a rating scale comprising nine different criteria, viz., teaching ability, relations with colleagues, class control, relations with parents, administrative ability, relations with children, intelligence, extra-mural contribution and relation with the head teacher. Start concluded that the teacher rated successful in this school was rather like the head teacher but some what more academic (A+ and H+), less sure of himself (G-,Q1- and Q2-), more accommodating (L-) and not as shrewed (N-). The head teacher, therefore, saw the successful teacher as a more intelligent, less confident or less experienced version of himself and one who has to draw from the head teacher's experiences from the field. On the other hand, the teachers rated poorer, appear to be more confidant, tougher, shrewder, tenser, more radical and more unconventional than the head teacher.

Bhatnagar (1966) reported that there is a confusion in the relationship between personality variables and academic achievement due to the (1) use of wide variety of tools, (2) use of invalidated techniques, (3) heterogeneity of samples, (4) inadequate control of correlated variables, (5) imprecise definitions of personality traits, (6) diverse methods of identifying over-and under-achievers, and (7) inherent weakness of the test of significance used in most studies.

Start (1966) studied the relation of teaching ability to measures of personality. He administered the 16 P.F Test to thirty-five members of the staff of a mixed secondary modern school in Lancashire and compared these scores with those of teaching ability as rated by the Headmaster. It appeared that the best teachers differed from the rest on factors A-, B+, E+, L-, M+, Q1- and Q3-. As teaching ability was linked with sex correlations "partialing out" sex indicated that factors

L-, and M+ were significantly (.05) correlated with rated teaching ability and that H+ marginally failed to reach this level of significance.

Tarpey (1965) studied the role of personality factors in teacher-trainee selection. She found the existence of differing patterns of relationship between personality factors and teaching marks among student teachers in different colleges. However, in only one college significant correlations between personality factors and the teaching marks existed. Factor G correlated positively with teaching marks (r=0446) whereas Factor A, (r=-.443), factor H (r=.408) and Factor M (r=-.372) showed negative correlation with teaching marks.

Warbarton, Butcher and Forrest (1963) tested on hundred teachers in the Department of Education, University of Manchester with measures of abilities, personality, interest, Values and general culture. They found the 16 P.F. Test of Cattell to be a fair predictor of teaching mark in that conscientiousness (G+), tender-mindness (I+) and control (Q3+) exhibited relationships significant at the .05 level with teaching ability.

Ryans (1960) identified teachers' effectiveness characteristics by analyzing some other qualities. He conducted that (i) friendly and understanding, and (ii) responsible and systematic and business-like teachers are more effective.

Montross (1954) correlated the scores of 35 high school teachers on Cattell's 16 P.F. with two composite ratings success in teaching. The first was a summation of four ratings given by the principal and two outside raters during the subjects first year of teaching. The second comprised all the ratings included in the first plus an additional one made by the principal made during the subjects second year of teaching. None of the correlation coefficients between scores on the 16 P.F. Test and the first composite rating reached .05 level of significance. Only factor A correlated significantly with the second composite rating (r=.40). Montross (1954, p.96) concluded that "Cattell's 16 P.F. Test seemingly fail (s) to identify aspects of temperamental behavior which are related to success in teaching as measured in this investigation."

Erickson (1954) correlated scores of sixty teachers on parts of the 16 P.F. with nine different measures of teaching effectiveness. Factor 'G' correlated positively with supervisor's ratings ($r$ = +.27) and with pupil evaluation ($r$ = –027). Factor O correlated negatively with teacher's ratings by an outside agency ($r$ = –.27) and with teacher's self-rating ($r$ = –.27). Factor Q3 correlated positively with acceptability to principal (r=.28), with principal's rating during the second year of teaching ($r$ = .28), and with teacher's self evaluation ($r$ = .38).

Lamke (1951) compared the qualities of ten good and eight poor teachers who were identified on the basis of classroom observations combined with head teacher's opinion. While Lamke concluded that Cattell's 16 P.F. test as a whole fails to identify good and poor teachers, he did, however find important differences between good and poor teachers. In such traits as sergency versus desurgency (F), adventurous cyclothymia versus inherent withdrawn schizo thymia (A) and sophistication versus rough simplicity (H). He concluded that good teachers were distinguished by F+, H+, B-, A+ scores while poor teachers tended to have F- and H- scores. Differences in response patterns concerned with these traits appear to indicate that various combinations of personality traits are found in good teachers and in poor teachers. No single ideal type of teacher was identified.

## OTHER STUDIES

In addition to these major studies, several other studies can be mentioned to illustrate the rang of variables that have been related to the perceptions of learning environment. Wisp (1951) and Smith (1954) have shone that psychologically different types of students perceive the same teacher differently. The perception may also be equally dependent upon the sex and grade level of students.

Panda and Samal (1995) presented a comparative study of personality and academic achievement of adolescent daughters of working an non-working mothers. The sample consisted of 120 adolescent girls selected form classes VIII and X in Bhubaneswar, out of which 60 had working mothers and 60 had nonworking mothers. Maudsley personality Inventory and Psychoticism Scale were administered on the sample for data collection. It was found that working mothers' daughters were more extroverted, independent, confident, emotionally stable, aggressive, and less anxious than daughters of nonworking mothers.

Malik (1983) studied the teachers' perception of their classroom learning environments by using LEI. He compared the learning environments of Biology, Physics and Chemistry classes. He found that Biology classes were more diverse and goal directed in comparison to Chemistry classes. No significant difference was observed between the learning environment of physics and Chemistry classes on any dimension of LEI.

Sharan and Yaakob's (1981) use of an adapted version of the LEI with 572students in $10^{th}$ grade Biology classes in Israel revealed that, compared with urban schools, Kibbutz district school had a more positive environment especially in terms of Cohesiveness, Favoritism and Cliqueness.

Pillai (1981) studied affective tone in the primary classroom by using Affective Tone Analysis System (ATAS). This instrument stresses observation of the teachers' positive negative responses to the students, both verbal and non-verbal. What values and attitudes are communicated by the teacher in the classroom is indicated by the ten categories. The ATAS also includes the biographical data of the teachers observed, some items identified as important to teacher effectiveness and the observer is asked to indicate whether the teacher appears clam, confident, cheerful, organized and on task. She found that, in general all the teachers observed in this study exhibit more positive behavior than negative. Positive non-verbal behaviors are greater than positive verbal behavior. There is no significant difference in the affective responses of teachers in terms of sex and years of experience. Urban school teachers have higher affective interaction than the rural teachers and privately-managed teachers exhibit more positive behavior than those managed by local authorities. In general primary teachers are quite well-organized but lack the self-confidence and become nervous when they have visitors observing them. The teachers very rarely praise the children's personal-social behavior, even when the children deserve it.

Sharma and Mahesh (1979) studied the classroom verbal interaction patterns of effective and ineffective teachers. The result shows that effective teachers employ more frequently categories such as "accepts feelings, praises and encourages, asks questions, pupils' response and initiation in their classroom teaching, whereas ineffective teachers use more often "direction", "authority", "lecturing" and "silence/confusion 'categories in their teaching. It seems that effective teachers involve more indirect influence, pupil talk, pupil initiation, teacher question and restrictiveness, restrictive feedback, steady state ratio, negative authority and vicious circle in their classroom teaching. The effective teachers involve creative inquiry model of instruction in their classroom interaction.

Maheswari (1976) studied the classroom verbal interaction patterns of effective and ineffective teachers by using Flanders Interaction Analysis Technique. He founds that effective teachers used the categories of "accept feeling, praise, uses student ideas, questions, student response and initiation, teacher response ratio and pupil steady state ratio, whereas ineffective teachers involved more direct teacher talk, silence or confusion, steady state ratio and non-stimulating situation in classroom behavior. In the effective teachers teaching, student response and initiations were followed by teacher's praise and accepting feelings, whereas ineffective teacher's teaching, student response and initiation were followed by direction and authority. The effective teachers involved more creative teaching models.

Sahgal (1975) studied the environmental learning contact among different types of schools. She found that there were significant differences among different types of schools, in providing the learning environment. Difficulties in learning environment are found in Hindi, English and mixed medium schools. The environment of learning is influenced by the nature of learning group, viz. male group, female group and mixed group.

Brophy (1975) selected those successful teachers for observation whose students achieved well in language arts and also in Mathematics. He found that in high SES schools, the more successful teachers were task-oriented and kept their students on task, had high expectations and were demanding and critical. On the other hand, successful teachers in low SES school had high expectations for students, were more supportive, encouraging and affectively-oriented, were willing to re-teach and to take up personal matters with the students and looked for materials that work. He drew the conclusion that the more successful teachers were those who could teach by keeping in mind the fact how students learn best.

Singh (1973) used his own teat of assessing socio- emotional climate of the classroom instead of using Flanders technique. He developed a pupil rating scale to assess the class room climate consisting of eight dimensions of teachers' behavior. The dimensions are: Warmth, fairness, acceptance, trustfulness, adaptability, status, emotional relationship and communication. Assessment of the climate has been done in terms of pupil perception. The teachers were teaching either General Science or Social Studies to 525 students of class ten. It was concluded that the climate prevailing the classes taught by lady teachers was more conductive to learning. It was further concluded that the climate in rural schools was better than the climate as found in the urban schools.

Randhawa and Michyluk (1973) compared rural and urban classes in Saskatchewan and found the former to be more cohesive and competitive while urban had higher scores on environment.

Walberg and Susan (1972) stated that since students are primary receivers of psychological influence from their teachers, they are more adopt at perceiving, judging and rating multivariate aspects of the teacher's teaching, habits and personality. The perception of the teacher does depend upon the type of student he teaches.

Olson (1971) investigated eleven different variables simultaneously, selecting variables that at one time or another have been thought to be associated with the quality of the educational process in the school classroom. The sample used was 112 largely suburban school district located in eleven metropolitan regions across the United States. In all, 18,528 separated class room observation were conducted (9,961 elementary and 8,567 secondary). He suggested that the teachers sex was found to be insignificant as predictor of the general quality of the educational process in any school classroom at both the elementary and secondary grade levels.

Buch abd Santhanam (1971) conducted a study in which sex as a factor of teachers' classroom behavior had emerged with significance. The study is based on sixteen female teachers of primary and upper primary teachers teaching Science in various schools of Madras city. The researchers in this study sought to answer the questions 'does the sex of the teachers in any way affected the teachers 'classroom behavior = the researchers concluded that male and female teachers differ significantly in respect of their capacity to generate study, Flanders technique was used.

Anderson (1971) used class means on the LEI from a sample of 62 Science, mathematics, humanities (i.e. English literature and History), and French classes in high schools in Montreal. Results indicated that: first, relative to other classes, Mathematics classes Were seen as high on Friction: convergence – divergence contrasted Mathematics with Language arts; substance – syntax contrasted science and Social studies with Language arts and Mathematics; and objectivity- subjectivity contrasted Science with Socio-Favouritism, Difficulty , Disorganization and cliqueness and lover on Formality and Goal direction. Second relative to Humanities classes, science classes were perceived as more formal and fast moving with less friction, Favoritism, cliqueness and disorganization; third, French classes were perceived as higher on Goal Direction and lover on Friction and Disorganization than other classes.

Anderson (1971) investigated the relationship with the teacher sex and course content on fifteen dimensions of classroom learning climate. Sixty two high school classes in s science (physics, biology and chemistry), mathematics (Algebra and geometry), Humanities (English literature and History) and French Comprised the sample. Forty- one male teachers and twenty one female teachers in these sixty two classes were included in his study. The pupils in these sixty-two classes ranged from fifteen to seventeen years in age and were in their tenth or eleventh year of school. The fifteen scales of the learning environment inventory were used as an instrument to describe the class room climate as was unrelated to pupils' perception of learning climate within their classes. Also, he reported that the teachers sex-course content interaction was not statistically significant. Male and female teachers did not have significant different effects on classroom learning climate in four subject areas (Science, Mathematics, Humanities and French).

Zahn (1968) concluded that student teachers undergoing instruction and supervision using interaction analysis had more positive attitude towards teaching. These student teachers tended to modify their teaching attitude and belief system more positively. These changes and modifications ultimately result into bringing about student-teacher effectiveness.

Walberg & Anderson's (1968) study on classroom climate considered the relationship between the individual learning. A series of studies on high school Physics classes throughout the nation had shown that measures of student perception of classroom climate, obtained at midyear, predicted gains in cognitive, affective and behavioral learning criteria during the year.

Small classes were found more cohesive than large classes particularly when the class contain fewer than sixteen pupils (Walberg, 1969 a; Walberg and Ahlgreen, 1970; Anderson and Walberg, 1972), and classes of teachers who are inexperienced with a new course are perceived as more cohesive than those taught by teachers familiar with course (Anderson, Walberg and Welch, 1967). Also classes in history and English were found to be more cohesive than those in other subjects (Shaw and Mackennon, 1973)

Large classes were considered more formal than are small classes and the increase informality is most prominent when the size increases about thirty (Walberg, 1969). Mathematics classes tend to be most informal (Anderson, 1970 b; show and Mackennon, 1973) when compared to classes in science, Humanities and Languages.

Bhatnagar (1966) reported that there is a confusion in the relationship between personality variables and academic achievement due to the (1) use of wide variety of tools, (2) use of invalidated techniques, (3) heterogeneity of samples, (4) inadequate control of correlated variables, (5) imprecise definitions of personality traits, (6) diverse methods of identifying over-and under-achievers, and (7) inherent weakness of the test of significance used in most studies.

Medley and Mitzel (1962) studied teacher behavior as related to its effect on effectiveness of teaching. It was found by them that the teacher needs to know the effects of his behavior in order to make his teaching work effective.

Heil and Washburne (1962) attempted to study teacher effectiveness to determine if the influence of teacher behavior is responsible for change in children and if these pupil changes have any relationship with the types of teachers. He found that work oriented, orderly and self-controlling teachers are liked more by high scorer. These types of teachers were found specially effective with 'opposing' and 'wavering' children. The teachers who were fearful, unsure and anxious proved to be least effective.

Flanders (1962) studied the effects of knowledge of interaction techniques on teacher's classroom effectiveness. By keeping in view this purpose, he observed fifty-five teachers for about six hours before and after their nine-week training in interaction techniques. In a study, the interaction technique provided feed-back to the teachers. Flanders stated that these teachers made significant use of indirect statement and changes in heir classroom behavior. He concluded that knowledge of the technique of interaction analysis is helpful for teaching effectively.

## CONCLUSION

The investigator tried to review this survey of studies to a great extent. It is assumed that the general trend shown by these studies can be considered as a conclusion with regard to the extent of relationship of the variables under this study. Majority of the studies have provide that teaching competencies is influenced by the attitude towards teaching, intelligence an inertest. But almost all studies have been conducted on teachers of general education and not on student teachers of special education. Hence the investigator felt that this study of the relationship between the personality and teaching competency of perspective teachers of special education will be a significant one and that will lead to make some suggestions on the criteria for admission to teacher training courses in special education.

# 4 Methodology

The present study is intended to find out the nature and extend of relationship of personality factors with teaching competency of teacher trainees of special education. The research design, variables selected for the study, tools employed for the collection of data, description of tools, selection of the sample, data collection procedure and statistical techniques used are described in this chapter.

## RESEARCH DESIGN

Descriptive design was used for the study. According to Gay (1990. P,189), "Descriptive research involves collecting data in order to test the hypothesis or to answer the questions concerning the current status of the subject of the study". It is concerned with conditions or relationships that exists, opinions that are held, process that are going on, effects that are evident, or trends that are developing (Best & Kahn, 1992, P. 76). Based on this theoretical aspect descriptive design was employed with all conviction.

## VARIABLES OF THE STUDY

The present study is a descriptive one. It describes recording, analyzing and interpreting conditions that exist. It involves various types of comparisons, contrasts and attempts for finding out relationship between non-manipulated variable. In the present investigation different categories of variables have been used to find out the relationship with teaching competency of teacher trainees of special education. Details of the variables of the study are given below.

### Dependent Variable

In the present study the teaching competency of the teacher trainees of special education.

### Criteria for Selecting the Dependent Variable

The selection of the dependent variable was based on the assumption that teaching competency among the teacher trainees of special education varies in accordance with their personality. This assumption was made in the light of a vast review of related literature. The review of related literature revealed that no attempt to study the teaching competency of the teacher trainees of special education in Kerala have been carried out. So the investigator decided to select teaching competency of the teacher trainees of special education as dependent variable. Also the youths in Kerala are select special education field as a measure of high job opportunity without having interest in the filed of special education.

The investigator assumed that this trend may lead the deficiency of service motive of teachers in the field of special education. As a result, the investigator decided to select teaching competency of the teacher trainees of special education as the dependent variable because of the novelty in the field.

### Independent Variable

The personality factors were taken as the independent variable.

### Criteria Used for Selecting the Independent Variable

The basic consideration for the identification of the independent variable was the review of related literature. The investigator was of the opinion that personality does have some relationship to teaching competency of the teacher trainees of special education. Hence he decided to take personality as independent variable to conduct his study in depth.

### Basal Variables

1. Sex
2. Locality
3. Teaching experience
4. Parental history of teaching
5. Familial background of disability
6. Specialization categories

### Criteria Used for Selecting the Basal Variables

Review of the literature connected with the teaching competency revealed that teaching competency is related to sex, teaching experience. And also the investigator, as a special educator, was of the opinion that certain other variables such as familial background of disability locality of trainees, teacher family background and disability categories such as hearing impaired, visually impaired and mentally retarded do have some relationship to teaching competency of the teacher trainees of special education. Based on these, the investigator decided to select sex, locality, teaching experiences, parental history of teaching, familial background of disability and disability categories as the basal variable of the study.

## TOOLS EMPLOYED FOR COLLECTION OF DATA

Selection of appropriate tools for collecting the data was the main task. Only standardized tools were used in the present study.

The following tools were used for collecting the necessary data for the present study.

1. Sixteen personality factor Questionnaire Form-C

2. General Teaching Competency Scale
3. General Data form

## Description of the Tools

### *Sixteen-personality factor questionnaire form- C (Malayalam Version)*

Due to the great need for a shortened version of 16 PF Questionnaire, Cattell (1965) Standardized 16 PF form C. This is a questionnaire consisting of 105 items, each provided with three alternatives for answers. It is the shortened version of the 16 PF. Completions of form C require 25 to 35 minutes and the reacting level is slightly lower than all other forms.

Cattell's 16 PF Form C was modified by Seetharam (1974) and the language is made simpler than the original form to suit Indian conditions. This modified form of 16 PF form C was translated by Rema and Anitha Ravindran (1989) in to Malayalam language.

## Structure of the Tool (16 PF Questionnaire)

The sixteen PF questionnaire provides measures on 16 personality traits. The 16 PF comes in various forms. Form C consists of 105 items with 6 to 7 items comprising each scale is used in the study.

The traits names assigned to the scales are A) cyclothymia vs Schizothymia B) General intellegence vs mental defect. C) Emotionally stable vs demorating general emotioanality E) Dominance vs submission F) Surgency vs De surgency G) Positive character integration vs Immature dependent character. H) character adventurous vs shy and timed I) Sensitive vs tough L) Suspecting vs trusting M) Unconcerndness vs conventional N) Sophistication vs Rough simplicity O) Free anxiety vs confident adequacy Q1) Redicalism vs Conservation Q2) Self sufficient vs Group dependency Q3) High self sentiment vs poor self sentiment Q4) High ergic, tension,excitable vs low ergic tension composed.

These sixteen dimensions are essential independent that is to say the correlation between one and another is usually quite small. Each of the 16 scale brings an entirely new piece of information about the person Each question carriers 3 possible answers was as A,B and C scores of the items are O, 1 or 2 points except the factor B, which score O, or 1. For each factor, Scores were obtained by summing of scores of all the items belonging to that factor.

## Dimensions Measured by the Questionnaire

Sixteen functionally independent dimensions were measured by this questionnaire.

The Sixteen primary factors covered by the test are as follows:

1. FACTOR A : Cyclothymia Vs Schizothymia
2. FACTOR B : General intelligence Vs Mental defect

| | | |
|---|---|---|
| 3. FACTOR C | : | Emotionally stable Vs Demoralized general emotionality |
| 4. FACTOR E | : | Dominance Vs Submission |
| 5. FACTOR F | : | Surgency Vs De surgency |
| 6. FACTOR G | : | Positive character integration Vs Immature dependent character. |
| 7. FACTOR H | : | Charitable Adventurous Vs Shy and timid. |
| 8. FACTOR I | : | Sensitive Vs Tough |
| 9. FACTOR L | : | Suspecting Vs Trusting |
| 10. FACTOR M | : | Un concernedness Vs Conventional |
| 11. FACTOR N | : | Sophistication Vs Rough Simplicity |
| 12. FACTOR O | : | Free anxiety Vs Confident adequacy |
| 13. FACTOR $Q_1$ | : | Radicalism Vs Conservation |
| 14. FACTOR $Q_2$ | : | Self sufficiency Vs Group dependency |
| 15. FACTOR $Q_3$ | : | High self sentiment Vs Poor self sentiment |
| 16. FACTOR $Q_4$ | : | High ergic, tension, excitable Vs low ergic, tension Composed |

## Administration

Simple and clear instructions were printed on the cover page of the text booklet. To establish a good rapport with the subject, oral instructions were given by the investigator.

After each question three possible answers are given such as A, B and C. Each subject should decided which of the three answers will represent his usual way of acting or feeling and should put a (x) cross mark in the answer sheet, against one of the three alternatives. The investigator gave instruction to avoid middle answers as much as possible. About 25 to 35 minutes was allowed to complete the test. The answer sheets collected were checked to make sure that there are no odd, unscorable responses or omissions.

## Scoring

Each answer scores 0, 1 or 2 points except the factor B (Intelligence) answers which score 0 or 1 for each factor. Scores were obtained by summing of scores of all the items belonging to that factor. Two separate stencile key were used for scoring. One key for scoring the factors A, C, F, H, L, N, Q and $Q_3$ and another for scoring B, E, G, L, M, O, $Q_2$, $Q_4$ factors.

## Reliability

Test-retest reliability of the 16 PF form C established by conducting a test on a population of 200 students by Rema and Anitha Ravindran (1989) are shown in the following table.

**Table 4.1: Test – Retest Reliability of Modified 16 PF Form C**

| No. | Factor | Correlation coefficient |
|---|---|---|
| 1 | A | 0.82 |
| 2 | B | 0.84 |
| 3 | C | 0.81 |
| 4 | E | 0.87 |
| 5 | F | 0.81 |
| 6 | G | 0.77 |
| 7 | H | 0.62 |
| 8 | I | 0.80 |
| 9 | M | 0.73 |
| 10 | L | 0.85 |
| 11 | N | 0.86 |
| 12 | O | 0.82 |
| 13 | $Q_1$ | 0.86 |
| 14 | $Q_2$ | 0.77 |
| 15 | $Q_3$ | 0.89 |
| 16 | $Q_4$ | 0.63 |

For establishing the parallel form reliability of the questionnaire, factor to factor correlations were computed by taking the mean score of each factor of the Malayalam version on each factor of the English version. The coefficient of correlation for the factors ranged from 0-74 to 0-98 as (Rema and Anitha Ravindran 1989) given in the following table.

**Table 4.2: Factor to Factor Correlation Coefficient Between English Version and the Malayalam Version.**

| Factor | R | Factor | R | Factor | R | Factor | R |
|---|---|---|---|---|---|---|---|
| A | 0.98 | F | 0.90 | L | 0.92 | $Q_1$ | 0.89 |
| B | 0.97 | G | 0.90 | M | 0.93 | $Q_2$ | 0.91 |
| C | 0.90 | H | 0.97 | N | 0.91 | $Q_3$ | 0.93 |
| E | 0.74 | I | 0.95 | O | 0.89 | $Q_4$ | 0.78 |

Test-retest reliability of the questionnaire found out by the investigator is given in the following table.

**Table 4.3: Test – Retest Reliability of Malayalam version of 16 PF Form C**

| No. | Factor | R | No. | Factor | R |
|---|---|---|---|---|---|
| 1 | A | 0.79 | 9 | L | 0.72 |
| 2 | B | 0.88 | 10 | M | 0.83 |
| 3 | C | 0.81 | 11 | N | 0.81 |
| 4 | E | 0.82 | 12 | O | 0.80 |
| 5 | F | 0.79 | 13 | $Q_1$ | 0.75 |
| 6 | G | 0.77 | 14 | $Q_2$ | 0.69 |
| 7 | H | 0.75 | 15 | $Q_3$ | 0.78 |
| 8 | I | 0.81 | 16 | $Q_4$ | 0.68 |

## Validity

Validity of the 16 PF Form C was established by finding out the correlation of all items with factors. The mean correlation of all items with factors was 0.37. Also the mean correlation of a factor with the group of six items by which it is represented is about 0.71 which it is decidedly high. (Seetharam, 1974)

Validity of the Malayalam version (Rema and Anitha Ravindran, 1989) of 16 PF Form C was established by calculating the mean of the correlation of the all items with the respective factor scores. It was found that the coefficients of correlation ranged from 0.58 to 0.90 as in the following table.

**Table 4.4: Factor-wise Mean of Correlations**

| Factor | R | Factor | R | Factor | R | Factor | R |
|---|---|---|---|---|---|---|---|
| A | 0.90 | F | 0.65 | L | 0.70 | $Q_1$ | 0.70 |
| B | 0.61 | G | 0.65 | M | 0.64 | $Q_2$ | 0.70 |
| C | 0.58 | H | 0.68 | N | 0.60 | $Q_3$ | 0.59 |
| E | 0.63 | I | 0.71 | O | 0.61 | $Q_4$ | 0.60 |

(Malayalam adaptation of 16 PF Form C Questionnaire, its English version and score sheet are given as Appendix.)

## GENERAL TEACHING COMPETENCY SCALE (GTCS)

The term 'Teaching' has been defined in different ways 'Competency' also has been a debatable term. Thus the lack of clarity and agreement about the concept of teaching competence has made its measurement difficult. Of course, the various teacher institutions have their own tools for assessing teaching competency of student teachers, but there has been no agreement and clarity about such tools. There is no standardized tool in India for measuring teaching competency of teachers/student teachers except the General Teaching Competency scale (GTCS).

GTCS is a Classroom observation schedule prepared by Passi and Lalitha (1979) for ascertaining teaching competency of teachers. Its measurement includes identifying all the teaching skills constituted the entire teaching task and making observation regarding the effectiveness of performance of each of the teaching skill is shown in the following table.

**Table 4.5: Distribution of Items According to the Level of Teaching Competency in the Categories of Teaching skills.**

| Sl. No. | Categories of Teacher skills | No. of Items | Sl. No. of items included in the questionnaire |
|---|---|---|---|
| 1. | Planning | 4 | 1 to 4 |
| 2. | Presentation | 11 | 5 to 15 |
| 3. | Closing | 2 | 16 to 17 |
| 4. | Evaluation | 2 | 18 to 19 |
| 5. | Management | 2 | 20 to 21 |
| | **Total** | **21** | |

## Structure of General Teaching Competency

There are 21 items in the general teaching competency scale related to 21 teaching skills which encompass the entire teaching-learning process in the class-room. They are related to five major aspect of class-room teaching namely, planning, presentation, closing, evaluation and managerial. The items are such that they are centered around teacher class-room behavior in relation to pupil behavior. The various teaching skills included are 1. Related to objectives of the lesson, content, selection, content organization selection of audiovisual materials (planning skills) 2. Introducing the lesson, fluency of questioning, use of probing questions, explaining, illustrating with examples, stimulus variation, use of signs and non-verbal cues, increasing pupil participation, use of blackboard use of verbal and non-verbal cues (presentation skills), 3. Achieving closure, giving assignments (closing) 4. Class room evaluation, diagnosis of pupil difficulties (evaluation) and 5. Recognizing attending behavior and maintaining class-room discipline (managerial skills). The GTCS is a 7 point rating scale measuring the use of the skill by the teacher in the class room corresponding to each item ranging from ' 0' for 'not at all to '6' for 'very much'. The distribution of the various items related to the different classification of teaching skills is given in Table 4.6.

**Table 4.6: Details of Teaching Skills in Each Category of Teaching Aspects**

| Sl. No. | Category | Teaching skills |
|---|---|---|
| 1. | Planning | Objective of the lesson, content selection, content Organization, selection of audio visual materials (4 skills) |
| 2. | Presentation | Introducing the lesson, fluency of questions, use of probing questions explaining, illustrating with examples stimulus variation, use of signs and non-verbal cues, increasing pupil participation, use of black board, use of verbal and non verbal cues (11 skills) |
| 3. | Closing | Achieving closure, giving assignments (2skills) |
| 4. | Evaluation | Classroom evaluation. Diagnosis of pupil difficulties (2 skills) |
| 5. | Managerial | Recognizing attending behavior, maintaining class room discipline (2 skills) |

### Validity of the Scale

The scale has content validity. The factorial validity of the scale was established by Rama (1979) in her doctoral study on factorial structure of teaching competencies among secondary school teachers. Scott's coefficient of inter-observer agreement ranging from 0.78 to 0.82 was obtained while observing teachers on the process variable chosen by passi (1977).

### Reliability of the Scale

Since the scale is an observation test the more appropriate type of reliability is the inter-observer reliability. The reported inter-observer reliability ranges from 0.25 to 0.91 (Passi- 1977 and Joshy, 1977).

Passi's scale was developed in Hindi in the state of Madhyapradesh in the year 1979. There exists cultural differences between the state which the sample was selected and that of Kerala. So it was felt necessary to adopt the test to suit the local condition of Kerala state.

The tool was subjected to scrutiny by a number of experts in the filed of teacher education. The researcher has rich experience in this field as he uses a similar test to rate the classroom observation during the period of practice teaching. Hence the researcher was convinced of the usefulness of the tool and he again tried out for a small sample. Validity and reliability were established (Validity 0.63, Reliability 0.72).

High reliability and validity coefficients of the general teaching competency scale proves to be an efficient-tool for measuring observed teaching competency of the teacher trainees for the present study.

### Procedure

The GTC scale was used for measuring teaching competence of teacher trainees of special education individually by the investigator by means of direct observation of his/her classroom behavior for the entire teaching period. He observed two classes each of a trainee at an interval of 3 months. The observer by sitting at the back of the classroom marked frequencies against each item. Details of the special schools selected for class observation of teacher trainees is presented in the table below:

**Table 4.7: Details of the Special Schools Selected for Class Observation of Teacher Trainees.**

| No. | District | Name of Special School | Category |
|---|---|---|---|
| 1. | Tirvandram | Gvt. School for Deaf | Hearing Impairment |
| 2. | Pathanamthitta | C.S.I. School for partially hearing impaired. | Hearing impairment |
| 3. | Quilon | C.S.I School for Deaf | Hearing impairment |
| 4. | Palakkad | Gvt. School for Deaf | Hearing impairment |
| 5. | Palakkad | H K C M M School for Blind | Visual Impairment |
| 6. | Malappuram | School for Deaf Parappanangadi | Hearing impairment |
| 7. | Malappuram | Karunya Bhavan School for Deaf | Hearing impairment |
| 8. | Malappuram | Good Hope School for Mentally retarded | Mental Retardation |
| 9. | Malappuram | Kerala Schools for Blind | Visual Impairment |
| 10. | Kozhikode | Calicut School for the Handicapped | Hearing Impairments Visual impairment |
| 11. | Kozhikode | Karuna Institute of Speech and hearing | Hearing Impairment |
| 12. | Kozhikode | Rahmaniya Schools for Handicapped | Hearing impairment Mental Retardation and Visual Impairment |
| 13. | Kozhikode | A W H Institute for Mentally Retarded | Mental Retarded |
| 14. | Kozhikode | C.I.C.S Sneha Mahal home for mentally Retarded | Mental Retardation |
| 15. | Kannur | Karunya Nikethan School for Hearing Impaired | Hearing Impairment |

## Scoring

The sum of the ratings against all the 21 items constitutes the score on general teaching competency of the teacher trainees being observed. The maximum possible sore is 126. In the observation of two classes a variation of scores was noticed. Hence the investigator found out the mean difference of the test score and it was found to be insignificant so he took the average score of the observed classes.

## GENERAL DATA FORM

The investigator prepared a data form to collect personal information about the teacher trainees. It includes the name of trainee, sex, local, specializing area of training, qualification, teaching experience, parental history of teaching, familial back ground of disability and motivation behind the selection of the training programme etc. The general data form also included the request of the investigator to the trainees to co operate with his effort to collect the data. It was also ensured that the data collected will be used only for research purpose and will be kept strictly confidential. A copy of the form is appended.

## SAMPLE USED FOR THE STUDY

The population for the present study was teacher trainees of special education of Kerala. Treating this as the reference population, in sample selection the investigator had to take decision on the following aspects:

(*a*) Factors to be considered for selecting the sample.

(*b*) Size of the sample, and.

(*c*) Sample selected for the study.

They are discussed below.

### Factors to be Considered for Selecting the Sample

For selecting the sample the following criteria were taken into consideration. Since it was not possible to include all the teacher trainees in all disability categories of special education, it was considered inevitable to draw a representative sample by adopting stratified random sampling technique.

### Size of the Sample

The investigator considered the following factors in selecting the sample.

(*i*) The size of the sample should be compact enough so as to permit a close study since an observation tool has to be administered in the actual classrooms; the investigator has to limit the sample to a manageable one.

(*ii*) The Size should permit the type of statistical procedures intended to be used in the study.

(*iii*) The investigator has to consider the approximate number of teacher trainees of special education available in each teacher training institutions since all of them have to be observed by the investigator himself the number of schools in which the trainees are deputed for practice teaching to be covered should also be taken in to account.

### Sample Selected for the Study

Considering all the above factors, the investigator arrived at the following decisions about the sample.

1. The sample should be around 150 Teacher trainees of special education
2. The sample should contain male and female teacher trainees in the ratio 1:3 as in almost all the Teacher Education institutions, vast majority are females.
3. Approximately fifty percent each of rural and urban institutions are selected as most of the Teacher Education centers are situated in rural area.

Details of the teacher training institutions from where the teacher trainees were selected for the study are presented in the following table.

**Table 4.8: Type of Teacher Training Institutions from Where the Sample Selected.**

| No. | District | Name of Institution | Area of Specialization |
|---|---|---|---|
| 1. | Trivandrum | National Institute of speech and Hearing (NISH) | Hearing Impairment |
| 2. | Quilon | CSI Institute of Teacher Training in Hearing impaired | Hearing Impairment |
| 3. | Palghad | KFB Teacher training Institute for visual impaired | Visual Impairment |
| 4 | Kozhikode | AWH College of Teacher Education | Hearing Impairment |
| 5. | Kozhikode | Institute of Special Education | Mental Retardation |
| 6. | Kozhikode | Rahmaniya Teacher training institution | Mental Retardation |
| 7. | Bhopal (MP) | Bhoj University (study center Calicut) | Hearing impairment Mental Retardation |

**Table 4.9: Gender Wise Break Up of the Sample.**

| Category specialization | Male | Female | Total |
|---|---|---|---|
| Hearing impaired | 7 | 18 | 25 |
| Visual Impaired | 4 | 19 | 23 |
| Mental Retarded | 11 | 84 | 95 |

## DATA COLLECTION PROCEDURE

The data collection was done in two phases. The first phase was during June-August 2005. During this period the investigator contacted the principles/co-ordinators of the teacher training centers of special education to visit the concerned institutions to collect the general data about the trainees and administer the 16 PF Questionnaire. The time schedule for the administration of 16 PF form C Questionnaire was fixed according to the convenience of the teacher trainees and their Teacher educators.

The Second part of the data collection was completed during the months October 2005 to June 2006 in which the investigator observed the classes of the trainees individually. Details of the data collection are as given below.

The investigator obtained adequate number of copies of all the materials. The trainees in special education who are undergoing D.Ed/B.Ed courses in Visually impaired/Hearing impaired/Mentally retarded were identified and their details were collected using the general data form. All the other data were collected from the trainees by using the selected tools.

## SCORING AND CONSOLIDATION OF DATA

Scoring of the answer sheet was done according to the direction given in the respective tools. The score regarding the General Teaching Competency (GTCS), 16 PF Questionnaire (Factors A, B, C, E, F, G, H, I, L, M, N, O, $Q_1$, $Q_2$, $Q_3$, $Q_4$ and total personality) and other relevant data regarding each teacher trainee were obtained.

The scores of the teachers were tabulated with other relevant data relating to them on consolidated data sheets. Data entered contained scores on various answer sheets and other information such as sex, locality, teaching experience, familial background of disability, parental history of teaching, disability category of training, were converted into suitable codes. The data were entered in such a way that they would be used for computer data processing.

## STATISTICAL TECHNIQUES FOR ANALYSIS

The data for the study has been analyzed using the following techniques. The entire statistical processing was done by the computer.

1. For the preliminary analysis of scores, statistical indices like mean, median, mode, and standards deviation were computed.
2. Correlation analysis to determine the extent of relationship between different variable.
3. Test of significance for difference between means of relevant groups.
4. ANOVA.

# 5 Analysis and Interpretation

## INTRODUCTION

The data analysis using the appropriate quantitative methods will help to understand the influential factors differentiating the General Teaching Competency of the teacher trainees of Special Education. Both Descriptive and Inferential statistical procedures were administered to analyze the data. Frequency Distribution, measures of central tendency and measures of dispersion were used in necessary cases to describe the data. Pearson's coefficient of correlation was used to find out the association between the Personality scores and General teaching competency scores of the respondents. Independent sample t-test was used to find out differences in the General Teaching competency of the respondents with respect to the different variables involved in the study. To know about the existence of significant differences in various basal variable group with the General Teaching Competency (GTC) among the Teacher trainees of Special Education and specialization categories with GTC, One-Way ANOVA was administrated. Appropriate graphical representations showing the association and differences in the variables are also included as part of the analysis. The results of all the above statistical procedures and their interpretation are included in this chapter.

A brief description of statistical techniques used for analysis:

1. Primary analysis of data - descriptive statistics (frequency, percentages, mean, standard deviation).
2. Correlation analysis for personality factors and general teaching competency – Pearson's Coefficient of Correlation.
3. Analysis of general teaching competency and the basal variables of the study (gender, locality, teaching experience , parental history of teaching.) – 't' test.
4. Analysis of general teaching competency on the basis of three categories of specialization in special education – Analysis of variance (ANOVA).
5. Tables, bar diagram and pie diagrams were used for presentation of data.
6. Significance level is fixed as 0.05 $\alpha$ level, but if the value is significant at 0.01 it is also mentioned in the analysis.

## 5.2 ANALYSIS OF PRIMARY DATA OF THE RESPONDENTS

Table 5.1 represents different variables significant to the study relating to the personal profile of the respondents; it covers the variables like gender, locality, teaching experience, parental history of teaching, disability in family, and categories of specialization of the respondents. The gender wise distribution of the respondents indicates that there is a wide difference in the male and female ratio among the respondents. Females cover 84.6% of the total respondents as they form majority in the teaching profession. The table also says that 83.2 percentages of the respondents were from the rural areas. 41.3% of the total respondents were having teaching experience before joining for the teacher training programme in special education. Forty point six percent of the respondents were having a parental history of Teaching; the teacher trainees from the family of disable constitute 14.7% of the total population. Sixty six point four percent of the respondents were from the specialization of Mental Retardation and trainees specializing in hearing impairment and visual impairment are constitute 17.5% and 16.1% respectively of the total population.

**Table 5.1: Primary Data of the Respondents**

| Variable | Attributes | Frequency | |
|---|---|---|---|
| | | Number | Percentage |
| Gender | Male | 22 | 15.4 |
| | Female | 121 | 84.6 |
| | **Total** | **143** | **100** |
| Locality | Urban | 24 | 16.8 |
| | Rural | 119 | 83.2 |
| | **Total** | **143** | **100** |
| Teaching Experience | Yes | 59 | 41.3 |
| | No | 84 | 58.7 |
| | **Total** | **143** | **100** |
| Parental Historyof Teaching | Yes | 58 | 40.6 |
| | No | 85 | 59.4 |
| | **Total** | **143** | **100** |
| Disability in Family | Yes | 21 | 14.7 |
| | No | 122 | 85.3 |
| | **Total** | **143** | **100** |
| Category Ofspecialization | Hearing Impairment | 25 | 17.5 |
| | Visual Impairment | 23 | 16.1 |
| | Mental Retardation | 95 | 66.4 |
| | **Total** | **143** | **100** |

## ASSESSMENT OF THE PERSONALITY OF TEACHER TRAINEES OF SPECIAL EDUCATION

### Personality Factor A

From the above table it is clear that the mean score of personality factor A is 8.224 subject to a standard deviation of 2.177. The minimum Score is 3 and the maximum is 13.000.

**Table 5.2: Description of the Personality Factor A of the respondents**

| | N | Minimum | Maximum | Sten | Mean | S D |
|---|---|---|---|---|---|---|
| **Reserved Vs Out going** | 143 | 3.00 | 13.000 | 8 | 8.224 | 2.177 |

A high score in factor A indicates affectothymic (A+) personality, which is characterized as an out going, warm hearted, easy going and participating nature. Where as a low score (A-) in factor A indicates schizothymeia personality. The data of the above table leads to the conclusion that the teacher trainees of special education possess an out going, warm hearted, easy going and participating nature in their personality.

### Personality Factor B

Table 5.3 reveals that the mean score of personality factor B is 6.762 subject to a standard deviation of 2 the minimum score of factor B is 2 and the maximum is 13.000.

**Table 5.3: Description of the Personality Factor B of the Respondents**

| | N | Minimum | Maximum | Sten | Mean | S D |
|---|---|---|---|---|---|---|
| **Less intelligence Vs More Intelligence** | 143 | 2.000 | 13.000 | 6 | 6.762 | 2 |

A high score in factor B shows higher mental capacity of the respondents (B+). Which is characterized as more intelligent and bright personality. Here as a low score in factor B indicates lower mental capacity (B-) the mean value in the table shows that the teacher trainees of special education possess an average mental capacity.

### Personality Factor C

As per the table 5.4 the mean score of personality factor C is 7.378 with a standard deviation 2.122. The minimum personality score for factor C is 2 and the maximum score is 12.000.

**Table 5.4: Description of the Personality Factor C of the Respondents**

| | N | Minimum | Maximum | Sten | Mean | S D |
|---|---|---|---|---|---|---|
| **Affected by feeling Vs Emotionally stable** | 143 | 2.000 | 12.000 | 7 | 7.378 | 2.122 |

A high score in factor c indicates higher ego strength (C+) personality. Which is characterized as an emotionally stable & calm personality. Where as low score in factor C indicates lower ego strength (C-) the mean value shows that the ego strength of teacher trainees of special education is above average.

## Personality Factor E

Table 5.5 says that the mean score for personality factor E is 2.175 subject to a standard deviation of 2.005. The minimum score is '0' and 8 is the maximum score.

**Table 5.5: Description of the Personality Factor E of the Respondents**

| Humble VsAssertive | N | Minimum | Maximum | Sten | Mean | S D |
|---|---|---|---|---|---|---|
| | 143 | "000" | 8.000 | 7 | 2.175 | 2.005 |

A high score in factor indicates trite of personality (E+) where as assertive humble is the characteristic of the low scorers (E-) in factor E the table shows that the mean value is very low. Hence it can be concluded that the teacher trainees of special education are humble and less assertive in their personality.

## Personality Factor F

From the above table it is clear that the personality factor F records a minimum score of 2 and maximum 12. The mean score is 7.301 and standard deviation is 2.201.

**Table 5.6: Description of the Personality Factor F of the Respondents**

| Sober VsHappy- go- lucky | N | Minimum | Maximum | Sten | Mean | S D |
|---|---|---|---|---|---|---|
| | 143 | 2.000 | 12.000 | 7 | 7.301 | 2.201 |

A high score in factor F/ indicates surgency (F+) which is characterized as a happy go lucky, impulsively lively & enthusiastic personality. Where as low score in factor F/indicates desurgency (F-) which is the opposite pole of the same personality trait.

## Personality Factor G

According to the table 5.7 it is recorded a mean score of 8.112 subject to a standard deviation 1.947 for personality factor G. the minimum score is to and the maximum score is 12.00.

**Table 5.7: Description of the Personality Factor G of the Respondents**

| Expedient Vsconscen- tious | N | Minimum | Maximum | Sten | Mean | S D |
|---|---|---|---|---|---|---|
| | 143 | 2.000 | 12.000 | 7 | 8.112 | 1.947 |

A high score in factor G (G+) indicates positive character integration whereas a low score in factor G/ (G-) means immature dependent character. The table shows that the teacher trainees of special education generally possess positive character integration.

## Personality Factor H

It is clear from the table 5.8 that the mean score for the personality factor H is 8.524 with a standard deviation 2.136.The minimum and maximum score of factor H is 4 and 12 respectively 2.038.

**Table 5.8: Description of the Personality Factor H of the Respondents**

| Shy Vs Venturesome | N | Minimum | Maximum | Sten | Mean | S D |
|---|---|---|---|---|---|---|
| | 143 | 4.000 | 12.000 | 8 | 8.524 | 2.136 |

A high score in factor H (H+) is characterized as venturesome likes meetings people, active, responsive, friendly and has emotional as well as artistic interests whereas the lower score (H-) indicates the shyness personality, as far as the teacher trainees of special education concerned they are coming in the venturesome character group.

## Personality Factor I

The Table 5.9 shows that the minimum score of personality factor is 2 and the maximum is 12. The mean score is 12 subject to standard deviatio 2.038

**Table 5.9: Description of the Personality Factor I of the Respondents**

| Tough minded Vs Tender minded | N | Minimum | Maximum | Sten | Mean | S D |
|---|---|---|---|---|---|---|
| | 143 | 2.000 | 12.000 | 7 | 7.958 | 2.038 |

High score in factor I ($I^+$) characterized as tender minded, dependent over protected and sensitive. Where as a low score in factor I ($I^-$) characterized as tough-minded; here according to the table, the teacher trainees of special education possess an average reflection of the trait.

## Personality Factor L

From the above table it is clear that the mean score of personality factor L is 7.084 with a standard deviation 2.105. The minimum score of '0' and the maximum is 12.00.

**Table 5.10: Description of the Personality Factor L of the Respondents**

| Trusting Vs suspicious | N | Minimum | Maximum | Sten | Mean | S D |
|---|---|---|---|---|---|---|
| | 143 | "000" | 12.000 | 6 | 7.084 | 2.105 |

A high score in factor L (L+) characterized as suspicious where as low score in factor L (L–) indicates trusting trait of personality the table revels that the teacher trainees of special education in between the two extremes of their characteristic features.

## Personality Factor M

As per table no. 5.11 the mean score of personality factor M is 6.056 subject to a standard deviation of 1.868. The minimum and maximum score are 2.00 and 11.000 respectively.

**Table 5.11: Description of the Personality Factor M of the Respondents**

| Practical Vs Imaginative | N | Minimum | Maximum | Sten | Mean | S D |
|---|---|---|---|---|---|---|
| | 143 | 2.000 | 11.000 | 6 | 6.056 | 1.868 |

A high score in factor M of the personality factor characterized as imaginative (M+) whereas the low score indicates practical or conventional. Here is also the teacher trainees of special education come in the average group.

## Personality Factor N

Table 5.12 reveals that the maximum score is 9 and the minimum score is 0. The mean score is 4.280 with a standard deviation of 2.050.

**Table 5.12: Description of the Personality Factor N of the Respondents**

| Forth- right VsShrewed | N | Minimum | Maximum | Sten | Mean | S D |
|---|---|---|---|---|---|---|
| | 143 | "000" | 9 | 5 | 4.280 | 2.050 |

A high score in factor N of the personality factor characterized s sophistication (N+) and low score indicates (N-) rough simplicity. The shows a low mean value which table is evident of the rough simplicity with regard to the personality of teacher trainees of special education.

## Personality Factor O

According to the Table 5.13 the mean score of personality factor O is 5.189 subject to a standard deviation of 1.906.The minimum score id'0' and 11 is the maximum score.

**Table 5.13: Description of the Personality Factor O of the Respondents**

| Self assured Vs Apprehensive | N | Minimum | Maximum | Sten | Mean | S D |
|---|---|---|---|---|---|---|
| | 143 | "000" | 11 | 6 | 5.189 | 1.906 |

A high score factor O indicates a guilt prone (O+) personality which is characterized as apprehensive worrying, depressive and trouble nature where as a low score in factor O indicates untroubled adequacy (O-) which is characterized as placid, self assured and confident with regard to the above trait the teacher trainees of special education comes as an average group.

## Personality Factor Q1

From the above information is the 5.14 it is clear the personality factor Q1 has a mean score 5.234 subject to a standard deviation1.914.The minimum score is '0' and the maximum is 10.000.

**Table 5.14: Description of the Personality Factor Q1 of the Respondents**

| Conservative Vs Experimenting | N | Minimum | Maximum | Sten | Mean | S D |
|---|---|---|---|---|---|---|
| | 143 | "000" | 10.000 | 5 | 5.234 | 1.974 |

A high score in factor Q1 (Q1+) of the personality factor characterized as experimenting personality where as a low score indicates (Q1-) conservation personality. Here in the case of teacher trainees of special education they possess a middle position of the two extremes of the character.

## Personality Factor Q2

Table 5.15 says that the mean score of personality factor Q2 is 6.888 with a standard deviation 2.032.The minimum score is 2 and the maximum score is 12.00.

**Table 5.15: Description of the Personality Factor Q2 of the Respondents**

| Group independant Vs Self sufficent | N | Minimum | Maximum | Sten | Mean | S D |
|---|---|---|---|---|---|---|
| | 143 | 2.000 | 12.00 | 7 | 6.888 | 2.032 |

A high score on this factor (Q2+) indicates self sufficiency, resourcefulness and preferences of own decisions, whereas low scores on this factor that is Q2- indicates group dependency and tendency to join and follow the group. Table reveals that the teacher trainees of special education neither posses a complete self sufficiency nor a complete group dependency in their personality.

## Personality Factor Q3

As per the table, the personality factor Q3 records a minimum score 2 and a maximum of 8.00. The mean score is 6.839 and the standard deviation is 2.661.

**Table 5.16: Description of the Personality Factor Q3 of the Respondents**

| Un desciplined Vs Controlled | N | Minimum | Maximum | Sten | Mean | S D |
|---|---|---|---|---|---|---|
| | 143 | 2.000 | 8.000 | 7 | 6.839 | 2.661 |

A high score in factor Q3 indicates high self concept (Q3+) which is characterized as controlled and self disciplined personality. Whereas a low score in factor Q3 characterized as undisciplined (Q3-) has self-conflicts, follows own urges and is careless of the protocol. It is impossible to make a judgment that all the teachers trainees of special education posses self disciplined personality or undisciplined personality on the basis of the above table they posses a position in between in these two extremes.

## Personality Factor Q4

Table 5.17 reveals that mean score of personality factor Q4 is 4.956 subject to a standard deviation of 2.404.The minimum score ia '0' and the maximum score is 12.000.

**Table 5.17: Description of the Personality Factor Q4 of the Respondents**

| Relaxed Vs Tence | N | Minimum | Maximum | Sten | Mean | S D |
|---|---|---|---|---|---|---|
| | 143 | "000" | 12.000 | 5 | 4.956 | 2.404 |

A high score in factor Q4 indicates high ergic tension (Q4) which is characterized as tensed frustrated and over worried nature, whereas low score in factor Q4 (Q4–) indicates low ergic tension, which is characterized as relaxed, tranquil and un frustrated. In the case of teacher trainees of special education the table shows that they possess a relaxed and unfrustrated personality.

## Personality – Total Score

It is clear from the table 5.18 that the mean personality score for the respondents is 102.4825 subject to a standard deviation of 8.9039. The Minimum score is 73.00 and the maximum score is 127.00.

**Table 5.18: Description of the Total Personality of the Respondents**

| Personality Scores (Total) | N | Minimum | Maximum | Mean | S.D |
|---|---|---|---|---|---|
| | 143 | 73.00 | 127.00 | 102.4825 | 8.9039 |

## A Brief Description of the Assessment of 16 Personality Factors

The teacher trainees of special education possess a high score in factor A. It indicates affectothymic personality, which is characterized as an outgoing, warm hearted, easy going and participating nature. The score in factor B. shows higher mental capacity which is characterized as more intelligent and bright personality. The score in factor c indicates higher ego strength personality which if characterized as an emotionally stable & calm personality. In factor E (assertive vs humble) the data shows that the mean value is very low hence it can be concluded that the teacher trainees of special education are humble and less assertive in their personality.

The high score obtained by the trainees in factor F indicates surgency which is characterized as a happy go lucky, impulsively lively & enthusiastic personality. As per the analysis of factor G, it is understood that the teacher trainees of special education generally possess positive character integration. The trainees possess high score in factor H. It is characterized as venturesome. Likes meetings people, active, responsive, friendly and has emotional as well as artistic interests. In the case of factor I, the teacher trainees possess an average reflection of the trait. Since the sten score in the factor L is 6 it reveals that the respondents falls in between the two extremes of their characteristic features trusts vs. suspicious.

With regard to the analysis of factor M (practical vs. imaginative) the position of the teacher trainees of special education stands as average. The personality factor N characterized sophistication rough simplicity, the data shows a low mean value which is evident of the rough simplicity with regard to the personality. The analysis of the factor O shows an average position of the trainees, with regard to guilt proneness vs. untroubled adequacy. In the case of factor Q1 the respondents possess a middle position of the two extremes of the character conservative vs. experimenting.

With regard to the personality factor Q2, it is clear that the teacher trainees of special education neither possess a complete self sufficiency nor a complete group dependency in their personality. In the case of personality factor Q3, it is impossible to make a judgment that all the trainees possess self discipline personality or undisciplined personality. On the basis of score obtained in this regard, it can be concluded that they possess a position in between in these two extremes.

The personality factor Q4 characterized as relaxed tranquil, and un frustrated. The data shows that trainees possess a relaxed and un frustrated personality.

## Profile of the Respondents

The scores obtained by the respondent in each personality factor were converted in to Standard Ten Score Scale (STEN) for the preparation of profile. The sten ranges from 1 to 10 ie, low score to high score. The scores of the respondents in standard ten score (Sten) is presented in Table 5.19(a) and these profile in Fig. 5. 2.

**Table 5.19 (a): Description of the Standard Scores (STEN) of the Respondents for 16 Personality Factors**

| Sl. No. | Personality Factor | STEN | Sl. No. | Personality Factor | STEN |
|---|---|---|---|---|---|
| 1 | A | 8 | 9 | L | 6 |
| 2 | B | 6 | 10 | M | 6 |
| 3 | C | 7 | 11 | N | 5 |
| 4 | E | 7 | 12 | O | 6 |
| 5 | F | 7 | 13 | Q1 | 5 |
| 6 | G | 7 | 14 | Q2 | 7 |
| 7 | H | 8 | 15 | Q3 | 7 |
| 8 | I | 7 | 16 | Q4 | 5 |

Since the mean sten of factor A is 8, naturally shows affectolgming. It is also evident that they are ready to corporate, attentive to people, soft hearted, kindly and adaptable. They likes occupations dealing with people and socially impressive situations in the case scholastic mental capacity the profile shows a sten score of 6 which is average factor C ie, related to ego strength proves the ego strength of the trainees which is above average. It is evident in their performance that they are realistic about life, possessing ego strength and better able to maintain solid group morale.

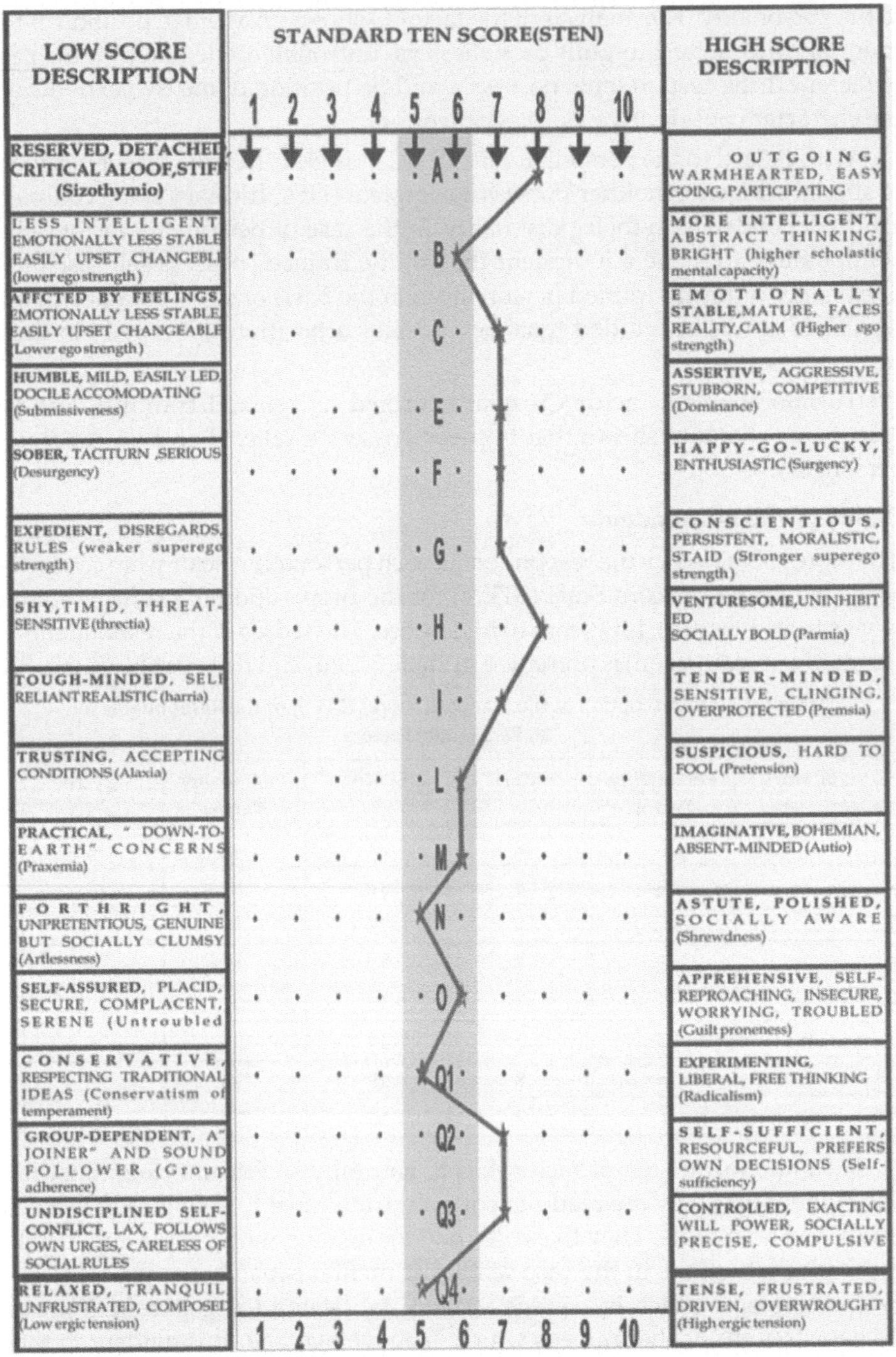


**Fig. 5.1: 16 PF test profile respondents according to the personality score.**

In the case of dominance ie factor E of 16 PF sten score is 7 ie they are self assured and independent minded. The sten score 7 marked in the profile for factor F shows the cheerful, active, talkative expressive traits of the trainees. The nature of happy go lucky reflects in their behaviors. Who scores high on factor G tends to be exacting in character. Hence in the profile the sten score is 7. Hence it is concluded that the teacher trainees are dominated by sense of duty, perspective, responsible and plan full. They are conscientious. High scores in factor H indicates venturesome socially bold and spontaneous. As far as teacher trainees are concerned it is found that they are sociable, bold and ready to try new things. The profile made clear that the mean sten score for factor I is 7, which is above average. It means the teacher trainees are tender minded. They some time demands the attention and help. The sten scores of factor L and M are 6 each. Which are average records it reveals the traits of suspicious and imaginative respectively. From the profile it can be concluded that the teacher trainees are average in suspicious. The personality factor N is 5, O is 6 and QI is 5. The personality traits shrewd, apprehensive and experimenting, representing the factors N, O and Q1 respectively scored an average in the Rest profile. The sten score of the 16 PR test profile indicates that the teacher trainees of special education are emotionally expressive easy going and tends to be good natured. Hence it can conclude that the teacher trainees of special education possess an average shrewdness, appreheveness and experimenting behaviors in their personality.

According to the profile the teacher trainees scored a sten score of 7 on factor Q2. A high score on factor Q2 is shows temperamentally independent, accustomed to going his own way. But is not necessarily dominant in his relations with others. Does not dislike people but simply doe's mot need their agreement or support. The teacher trainees score reflect that they are above average in the traits of self sufficiency and taking their own decisions in the case of factor Q3 trainees obtained a mean sten score 7. here the trainees have an above average position to have strong control of emotions and general behavior on factor Q4 the mean sten score obtained is 5.hence it can conclude that the teacher trainees shows an average tense and frustration in their behavior.

## ASSESSMENT OF THE GENERAL TEACHING COMPETENCY OF TEACHER TRAINEES OF SPECIAL EDUCATION

Table 5.20 reveals that the mean score of respondents in the General Teaching Competency assessment is 83.4895 subject to a standard deviation of 13.4247. 60 is the minimum Score and maximum score is 110.

**Table 5.20: Description of the General Teaching Competency of Respondents**

| | N | Minimum | Maximum | Mean | Std. Deviation |
|---|---|---|---|---|---|
| General Teaching Competency | 143 | 60.00 | 110.00 | 83.4895 | 13.4247 |

## Classification of the Respondents on the Basis of GTC score.

The respondents are again classified in to three groups on the basis of the mean and standard deviation of the scores of General Teaching Competency Assessment, and it presented in the table 5.21 below.

High Group > 96.9142 (83.4895 + 13.4247)

Average Group = between 96.9142 and 70.0648

Law Group < 70.0648 (83.4895 –13.4247)

**Table 5.21: Categorization of Respondents on the Basis of General Teaching Competency**

| Category | Frequency | Percent |
|---|---|---|
| High Group | 40 | 28.0 |
| Average Group | 79 | 55.2 |
| Low Group | 24 | 16.8 |
| Total | 143 | 100.0 |

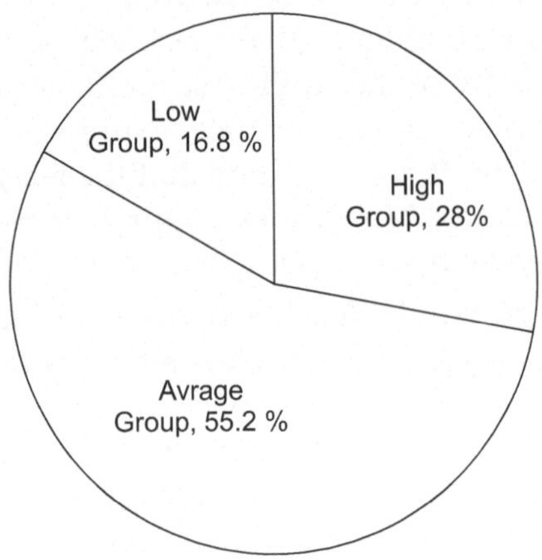


**Fig. 5.2: Pie diagram of categorization of respondents on the basis of General Teaching Competency**

It is clear from the table 5.21 and Fig. 4.3 that 55.2% of the respondents are belonging to the "average group" in the classification of respondents according to the General Teaching competency. 28.0 % belong to the high group and 16.8% belong to the low group category.

## CORRELATION ANALYSIS OF EACH OF THE 16 PERSONALITY FACTORS OF THE RESPONDENTS WITH THE GENERAL TEACHING COMPETENCY.

In order to assess the personality of the respondents, 16 personality factors are considered. A correlation analysis of each of these factors with the General Teaching Competency of the respondents will help to measure the depth of the relationship between the Personality and General Teaching competency of the respondents. The factors which are highly associated and least associated with the General Teaching Competency of the respondents can also be detected. In order to find the association, Pearson's coefficient of correlation method is administrated.

### Correlation of First Personality Factor (Factor A. Affectothymia V/S Schizothimia) with the General Teaching Competency

Table 5.22 shows that the Pearson's coefficient of correlation obtained in .008. This is not significant that is the personality factor A. (Reserved v/s out going traits) of the respondents has not significant correlation with their teaching competency.

**Table 5.22: Correlation of Factor A with GTC**

| Description | GTC | PA |
|---|---|---|
| PA Pearson Correlation Sig (2-tailed) 0.05 level N | 1.000<br><br>143 | .008<br>.922<br>143 |
| GTC Pearson Correlation Sig (2-tailed) 0.05 level N | .008<br>.922<br>143 | 1.000<br><br>143 |

### Correlation of Second Personality factor B- (More Intelligence V/s Less Intelligence) with the General Teaching Competency

From the above table it is very clear that there is significant correlation between personality factor B (more intelligent V/S less intelligent) and General Teaching Competency of the respondents. The obtained coefficient of correlation is .233 which is significant at 0.01 levels.

**Table 5.23: Correlation of Factor B with GTC**

| | GTC | PB |
|---|---|---|
| P.B Pearson Correlation Sig (2-tailed) 0.05 level N | 1.000<br><br>143 | .233**<br>.005<br>143 |
| GTC Pearson Correlation Sig (2-tailed) 0.05 level N | .233**<br>.005<br>143 | 1.000<br><br>143 |

** Correlation is significant at the 0.01 level

### Correlation of Third Personality factor C (Emotionally stable Vs Demoralized general emotionality) with the General Teaching Competency

According to the table 5.24 there is no significant correlation between personality factor C and General Teaching Competency. Hence it is shows that emotional stability of the respondents is not related with teaching competency.

**Table 5.24: Correlation of Factor C with GTC**

| | GTC | PC |
|---|---|---|
| PC Pearson Correlation Sig (2-tailed) 0.05 level N | 1.000<br><br>143 | .032<br>.704<br>143 |
| GTC Pearson Correlation Sig (2-tailed) 0.05 level N | .032<br>.704<br>143 | 1.000<br><br>143 |

## Correlation of Fourth Personality factor E (Dominance Vs Submissiveness) with the General Teaching Competency

Table 5.25 reveals that significance correlation is there in between personality factor E and General Teaching Competency of the teacher trainees of special education.

**Table 5.25: Correlation of Factor E with GTC**

| | GTC | PE |
|---|---|---|
| GTC Pearson Correlation Sig (2-tailed) 0.05 level N | 1.000<br><br>143 | .284**<br>.001<br>143 |
| PE Pearson Correlation Sig (2-tailed) 0.05 level N | .284**<br>.001<br>143 | 1.000<br><br>143 |

**Correlation is significant at the 0.01 level

## Correlation of Fifth Personality factor F (Factor F Surgency Vs Desergency) with the General Teaching Competency

As per the information shows in table No. 4.26 the personality factor F has no significant correlation with General Teaching Competency

**Table 5.26: Correlation of Factor F with GTC**

| | GTC | PF |
|---|---|---|
| GTC Pearson Correlation Sig (2-tailed) 0.05 level N | 1.000<br><br>143 | .080<br>.342<br>143 |
| PF Pearson Correlation Sig (2-tailed) 0.05 level N | .080<br>.342<br>143 | 1.000<br><br>143 |

**Correlation of Sixth Personality Factor (Factor G. Positive Character integration V/S immature Dependent Character) with the General Teaching Competency**

From the above table 5.27 it is clear that there is no significant correlation in between Personality factor G and General Teaching Competency

**Table 5.27: Correlation of Factor G with GTC**

| | GTC | PG |
|---|---|---|
| GTC Pearson Correlation Sig (2-tailed) 0.05 level N | 1.000<br><br>143 | .008<br>.924<br>143 |
| PG Pearson Correlation Sig (2-tailed) 0.05 level N | .008<br>.924<br>143 | 1.000<br><br>143 |

**Correlation of Seventh Personality factor (Factor H. Venturous V/S Shy and Timid) with the General Teaching Competency.**

As per the details contains in table 5.28 shows that personality factor H has no significant correlation with teaching competency.

**Table 5.28: Correlation of Factor H with GTC**

| | GTC | PH |
|---|---|---|
| GTC Pearson Correlation Sig (2-tailed) 0.05 level N | 1.000<br><br>143 | .085<br>.311<br>143 |
| PH Pearson Correlation Sig (2-tailed) 0.05 level N | .085<br>.311<br>143 | 1.000<br><br>143 |

**Correlation of Eighth Personality factor (Factor I .sensitive/S tough) with the General Teaching Competency.**

Table No. 5.29 reveals that the personality factor I have no significant correlation with the General Teaching Competency of teacher trainees of special education

**Table 5.29: Correlation of Factor I with GTC**

| | GTC | PI |
|---|---|---|
| GTC Pearson Correlation Sig (2-tailed) 0.05 level N | 1.000<br><br>143 | .085<br>.313<br>143 |
| PI Pearson Correlation Sig (2-tailed) 0.05 level N | .085<br>.313<br>143 | 1.000<br><br>143 |

**Correlation of Ninth Personality factor (Factor L. Suspecting V/S Trusting) with the General Teaching Competency.**

The above table reveals that there is no significant correlation in between Personality factor L and General Teaching Competency of teacher trainees of special education.

**Table 5.30: Correlation of Factor L with GTC**

| | GTC | PL |
|---|---|---|
| GTC Pearson Correlation Sig (2-tailed) 0.05 level N | 1.000<br><br>143 | .096<br>.254<br>143 |
| PL Pearson Correlation Sig (2-tailed) 0.05 level N | .096<br>.254<br>143 | 1.000<br><br>143 |

**Correlation of Tenth Personality factor (Factor M. Unconcerndness V/S Conventional) with the General Teaching Competency.**

According to the table 5.31, the personality factor M has significant correlation with General Teaching Competency of teacher trainees of special education. The obtained coefficient in .268 which is significant at 0.01 level.

**Table 5.31: Correlation of Factor M with GTC**

| | GTC | PM |
|---|---|---|
| GTC Pearson Correlation Sig (2-tailed) N | 1.000<br><br>143 | .268**<br>.001<br>143 |
| PM Pearson Correlation Sig (2-tailed) N | .268**<br>.001<br>143 | 1.000<br><br>143 |

**Correlation is significant at the 0.01 level

**Correlation of Eleventh Personality Factor (Factor N Sophistication V/S Rough simplicity) with the General Teaching Competency**

Table 5.32 reveals that personality factor N has no significant correlation with General Teaching Competency of teacher trainees of special education.

**Table 5.32: Correlation of Factor N with GTC**

| | GTC | PN |
|---|---|---|
| GTC Pearson Correlation Sig (2-tailed) 0.05 level N | 1.000<br><br>143 | .125<br>.135<br>143 |
| PN Pearson Correlation Sig (2-tailed) 0.05 level N | .125<br>.135<br>143 | 1.000<br><br>143 |

## Correlation of 12th Personality factor (factor O.Guilt Proneness V/S Confident Adequacy) with the General Teaching Competency

According to the information from the table 5.33, personality factor O has not any significant correlation with General Teaching Competency of teacher trainees of special education.

**Table 5.33: Correlation of Factor O with GTC**

| | GTC | PO |
|---|---|---|
| GTC Pearson Correlation Sig (2-tailed) 0.05 level N | 1.000<br><br>143 | .064<br>.444<br>143 |
| PO Pearson Correlation Sig (2-tailed) 0.05 level N | .064<br>.444<br>143 | 1.000<br><br>143 |

## Correlation of 13th Personality Factor (Factor Q1 Radicalism V/S Conservation) with the General Teaching Competency.

Table 5.34 reveals that there is no significant correlation in between Personality factor Q1 and General Teaching Competency of teacher trainees of special education.

**Table 5.34: Correlation of Factor Q1 with GTC**

| | GTC | PQ1 |
|---|---|---|
| GTC Pearson Correlation Sig (2-tailed) 0.05 level N | 1.000<br><br>143 | .070<br>.403<br>143 |
| PQ1Pearson Correlation Sig (2-tailed) 0.05 level N | .070<br>.403<br>143 | 1.000<br><br>143 |

## Correlation of 14th Personality Factor (Factor Q2.Self Sufficiency V/S Group Dependency) with the General Teaching Competency

As per the correlation shows in the table 5.35 it is very clear that it is significant in the case of personality factor Q2 and General Teaching Competency of the teacher trainees of special education.

**Table 5.35: Correlation of Factor Q2 with GTC**

| | GTC | PQ2 |
|---|---|---|
| GTC Pearson Correlation Sig (2-tailed) 0.05 level N | 1.000<br><br>143 | .130<br>.123<br>143 |
| P Q2Pearson Correlation Sig (2-tailed) 0.05 level N | .130<br>.123<br>143 | 1.000<br><br>143 |

**Correlation of 15th Personality factor (Factor Q3. High Self Concept V/S Low Integration) with the General Teaching Competency**

Table 5.36 shows that there is significant correlation in between personality factor Q3 and General Teaching Competency of the teacher trainees of special education.

**Table 5.36: Correlation of Factor Q3 with GTC**

| | GTC | P Q3 |
|---|---|---|
| GTC Pearson Correlation Sig (2-tailed) 0.05 level N | 1.000<br><br>143 | .164<br>.050<br>143 |
| P Q3 Pearson Correlation Sig (2-tailed) 0.05 level N | .164<br>.050<br>143 | 1.000<br><br>143 |

**Correlation of 16th Personality Factor (Factor Q4. High Ergic Tension V/S Low Ergic Tension) with the General Teaching Competency.**

As per the table 5.38 the Pearson's coefficient of correlation obtained is .399 and is significant at 0.01 levels. So there exist a positive correlation between the Personality Scores and General Teaching Competency Scores of the teacher trainees of special education. To be more clear, those who acquired higher personality scores acquired higher General Teaching Competency scores also. But the positive relation ship is only on a moderate level since the value of coefficient of correlation is .339.

**Table 5.37: Correlation of Factor Q4 with GTC**

| | GTC | PQ4 |
|---|---|---|
| GTC Pearson Correlation Sig (2-tailed) 0.05 level N | 1.000<br><br>143 | .147<br>.080<br>143 |
| PQ4 Pearson Correlation Sig (2-tailed) 0.05 level N | .147<br>.080<br>143 | 1.000<br><br>143 |

**Table 5.38: Pearson's Coefficient of Correlation of the Relationship Between General Teaching Competency and Total Personality Score.**

| Description | | GeneralTeaching competency | Personality Scores |
|---|---|---|---|
| General Teaching Competency | Pearson CorrelationSig. (2-tailed ) N | 1,000<br><br>143 | .399**<br><br>143 |
| Personality Scores | Person CorrelationSig- (2-tailed)N | .399**<br>.000<br>143 | 1,000<br><br>143 |

**Correlation is significant at the 0.01 level (2-tailed)

The factor wise correlation analysis presented in the Table 5.22 to 5.37, the personality factors B, E, Q, Q3 and Q4 (intelligence, emotional stability, assertiveness, self sufficiency discipline and ergic tension) of teacher trainees of special education shows, a positive correlation with General Teaching Competency whereas all other factors do not have any significant relationship with General Teaching Competency

## ANALYSIS OF RESPONDENTS GENERAL TEACHING COMPETENCY AND THE BASAL VARIABLES OF THE STUDY

Respondents on the basis of the difference in the teaching competency of the based variables such as sex, locality, teaching experience, parental history of teaching, disability background and disability categories of visual impairment, hearing impairment and mental retardation are analyzed by using 't' test and ANOVA.

### 't' test for Gender Difference in General Teaching Competency of the Teacher Trainees of Special Education

Table 5.39 shows that the mean score obtained by the male in General Teaching Competency test is 84.4091 subject to a standard deviation of 11.6155 and the mean score obtained by the females is 83.3223. The 't' value obtained is .348. The 'p' value is .728 (P >.05) which is grater than .05. The conclusion is that there is no significant difference in the mean scores obtained by the male and female respondents. So it is concluded that there is no significant gender difference in the General Teaching Competency of Teacher Trainees of Special Education.

**Table 5.39: Gender Difference and General Teaching Competency**

| Variables | Gender of the Respondents | N | Mean | Std. deviation | 't'value | P value (0.05 level) |
|---|---|---|---|---|---|---|
| General Teaching Competency | Male | 22 | 84.4091 | 11.6155 | 0.348 | 0.728 |
| | Female | 121 | 83.3223 | 13.7648 | | |

### Gender Wise Categorization of Respondents on the Basis of General Teaching Competency

The respondents are classified into three groups on the basis of the mean and standard deviation presented in table 4.40 as High group > 96.9142 (83.3223 + 13.7648), Average group between 96.9142 and 70.0648, and Low group < 70.0648 (83.4895 – 13.4247).

**Table 5.40: Categorization of Respondents on the Basis of General Teaching Competency**

| Categorizing respondents on the basis of General Teaching Competency | Gender of the Respondents | | | | Total No | Percent |
|---|---|---|---|---|---|---|
| | Male | % | Female | % | | |
| High Group | 6 | 27.27 | 34 | 28.09 | 40 | 28 |
| Average Group | 14 | 63.63 | 65 | 53.73 | 79 | 55.2 |
| Low Group | 2 | 9.09 | 22 | 18.18 | 24 | 16.8 |
| Total | 22 | 100 | 121 | 100 | 143 | 100 |

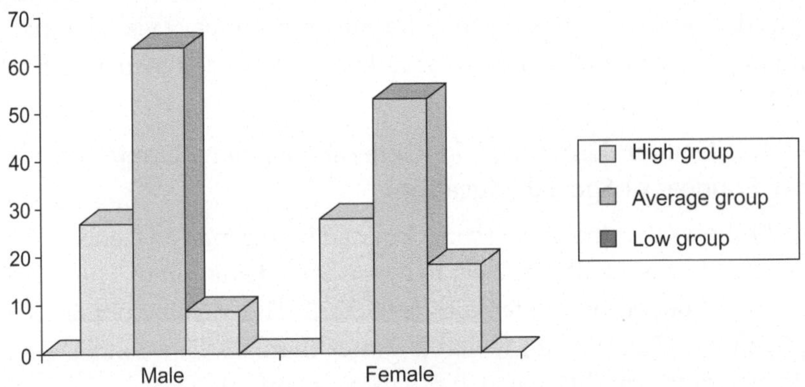


**Fig. 5.3: Bardiagram of categorisation of respondents on the basis of gender and their General Teaching Competency.**

Table 5.40 and Fig. 5.3 is indicating that both male and female respondents are more in the average group category in the classification based on General Teaching Competency constituting 55.2 percent. Twenty eight percent, respondents are grouped as high in teaching competency and 16.8 percent teacher trainers were in low group.

Twenty seven point two seven percent male respondents performed high competency in teaching whereas it is 28.09 % in the case of female. Sixty three point six three percent male trainees are included in the average group and 53.73% female trainees are included in this group. While 18.18% females were grouped as low in teaching competency and only 9.09% trainees are included from male group.

## 't' test for Difference Among Locality Categories in General Teaching Competency of Respondents

According to table No.5.41 the 't' value obtained in 0.427 and the 'p' value is 0.746. The 'p' value in higher than the 't' value. Hence it can be concluded that there is no significant difference in teaching competency among locality categories. The respondents are classified as three groups on the basis of mean and standard deviation and presented in table 5.42. High group > 96.3635 (82.6271 + 13.7364), Average group between 96.3635 and 68.8907, and low group < 68.8907 (82.6271-13.7364).

**Table 5.41: Difference Among Locality Categories in General Teaching Competency**

| Variables | Locality category | N | Mean | Standard deviation | 't' value | P(0.05 level) |
|---|---|---|---|---|---|---|
| General Teaching Competency | Urban | 24 | 82.6271 | 13.7364 | 0.427 | .746 |
| | Rural | 119 | 83.0486 | 12.1576 | | |

## Categorization of Respondents on the Basis of Locality and General Teaching Competency of Respondents

As per the above table 5.42 and Fig. 5.4, among the urban respondents 50.1% belongs to average group category and 56.30% of the rural respondents were also belongs to the same category. Thirty three percent trainees of both urban and rural respondents perform high competency in teaching. It is very clear from this information presented in table 5.41 and 5.42 that there is no significant difference among locality categories in teaching competency.

**Table 5.42: Categorizing of Respondents on the Basis of Locality and General Teaching Competency**

| Locality of the Respondents | Categorizing of respondents on the basis of locality and General Teaching Competency | | | | | | Total | |
|---|---|---|---|---|---|---|---|---|
| | High Group | | Average Group | | Low Group | | | |
| Urban | 7 | 33% | 12 | 50.1% | 5 | 16.9% | 24 | 16.78% |
| Rural | 33 | 33% | 67 | 56.3% | 19 | 10.7% | 119 | 83.22% |
| Total | 40 | | 79 | | 24 | | 143 | |

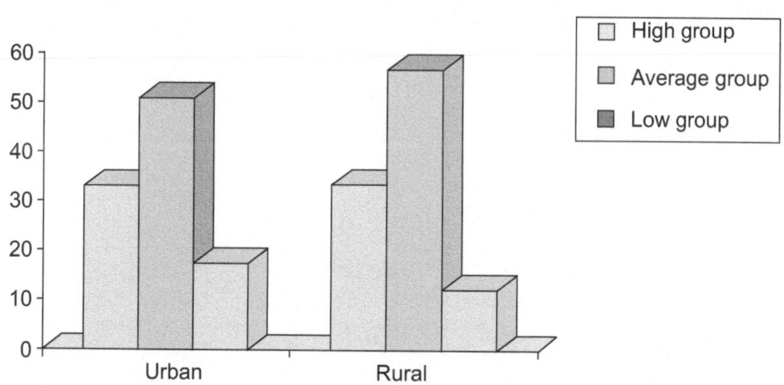


**Fig. 5.4: Bardiagram – categorization of respondents on the basis of locality and their General Teaching Competency**

### t' test for Difference in General Teaching Competency Among Respondents having Teaching Experience and not Having Teaching Experience

Table 5.43 shows that the mean score obtained by the respondents with teaching experience is 86.5424 subject to a standard deviation of 13.1730 and the mean score obtained by the respondents without teaching experience is 81.3452 subject to a standard deviation of 13.2588. It reveals that the 't' value is 2.314 and the 'p' value is .022. The 'p' value is less than .05 (P<.05), Hence there exists a significant difference in the teaching competency of Teacher trainees of special education with teaching experience and without teaching experience.

**Table 5.43: Difference Among Respondents on the Basis of Having Teaching Experience and not Having Teaching Experience**

| Variables | Teaching Experience of the Respondents | N | Mean | Std. Deviation | 't' value | P value (0.05 level) |
|---|---|---|---|---|---|---|
| General Teaching Competency | Yes | 59 | 86.5424 | 13.1730 | 2.314 | 0.022 |
| | No | 84 | 81.3452 | 13.2588 | | |

### Categorization of Respondents as High, Average and Low Group in Teaching Competency on the Basis of having Teaching Experience and not Having Teaching Experience

(High group > 94.6040 (81.3452+13.2588) Average in between 94.6040 and 68.0864 low <68.0864.)

**Table 5.44: Categorizing of Respondents on the Basis of General Teaching Competency**

| Teaching Experience of the Respondents | Categorizing of respondents on the basis of General Teaching Competency | | | Total |
|---|---|---|---|---|
| | High Group | Average Group | Low Group | |
| Yes | 21(35.59%) | 30 (50.84%) | 8(13.55%) | 59 |
| No | 19(22.61%) | 49(58.33%) | 16 (19.04%) | 84 |
| Total | 40 | 79 | 24 | 143 |

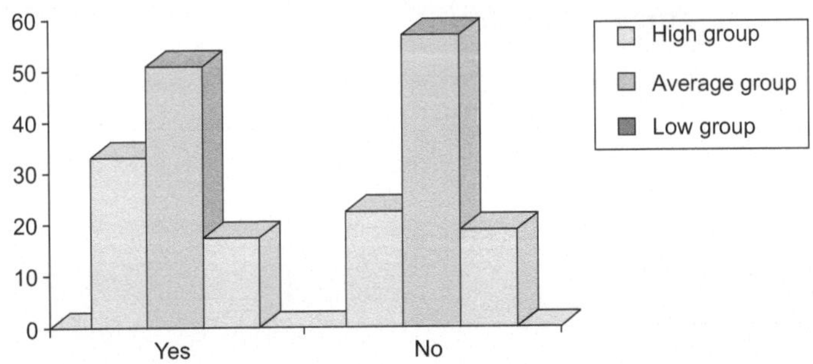


**Fig. 5.5: Bar diagram – Categorization of respondents on the basis of teaching experience and their teaching competency**

Among the respondents who are having teaching experience, 50.84% were belonging to the average group category in the classification based on teaching competency and the 35.59 % comes in high group and another 13.55% trainees are grouped in low category. In the respondents without teaching experience, 58.33 % were coming in the average group category in the classification based on General Teaching Competency and 22.61% trainees coming in high group and 19.04% are included in low group category.

### 't' Test for Difference in General Teaching Competency Among the Respondents Having Parental History of Teaching and not Having Parental History of Teaching

The mean score obtained by the respondents with parental history of teaching as per table No 4.45 is 84.0000 subject to a standard deviation of 12.7733 and that without a parental history of teaching is 83.1412 subject to a standard deviation of 13.9157. The 't' value is .374; the 'p' value is .709 which is greater than .05. ( P >.05) So the research hypothesis is rejected. We can conclude that there exists no significant difference between the General Teaching Competency of respondents with a parental history of teaching and without parental history of teaching.

**Table 5.45: General Teaching Competency of Respondents Having Parental History of Teaching and not Having Parental History of Teaching**

| Variables | Parental Historyof Teaching | N | Mean | Std. Deviation | 't' value | P value (0.05 level) |
|---|---|---|---|---|---|---|
| General Teaching Competency | Yes | 58 | 84.0000 | 12.7733 | 0.374 | 0.709 |
| | No | 85 | 83.1412 | 13.9157 | | |

### Categorization of Respondents having Parental History of Teaching on the Basis of and not having High Group > 97.0569, Average – between 97.0569 and Low < 69.2245 69.2245.

Among the respondents with parental history of Teaching, 58.62% were in the average group category, 27.58% trainees are in high group whereas 13.79% comes

**Table 5.46: Categorizing of Respondents Having Parental History of Teaching and not Having Parental History of Teaching on the Basis of General Teaching Competency**

| Parental History of Teaching | Categorizing of respondents on the basis of General Teaching Competency | | | Total |
|---|---|---|---|---|
| | High Group | Average Group | Low Group | |
| Yes | 16 (27.58%) | 34 (58.62%) | 8(13.79%) | 58 |
| No | 24(28.23%) | 45(52.94%) | 16(18.82%) | 85 |
| Total | 40 | 79 | 24 | 143 |

in low groups in the grouping based on General Teaching Competency. Among the respondents with out parental history of teaching, 52.94 were, 28.23% comes in high groups and 18.82% trainees are coming in low group in the grouping based on General Teaching Competency.

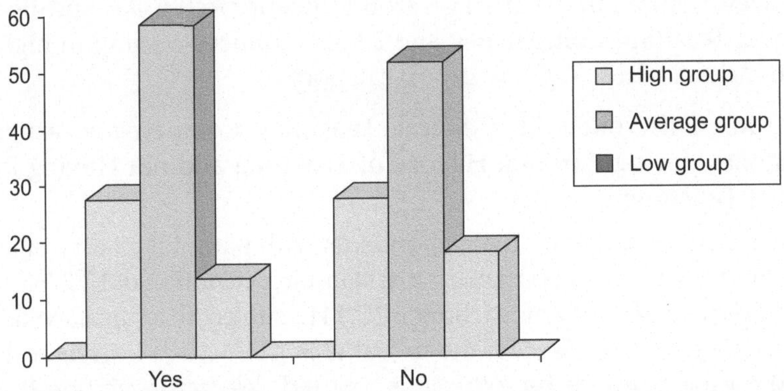


**Fig. 5.6: Bar diagram categorization of respondents on the basis of parental history of teaching and their teaching competency**

## 't' Test for Difference in General Teaching Competency of the Respondents Having Familial Background of Disability and not Having Familial Background of Disability

According to the table No.5.47 the mean score obtained by the respondents, who are belonging to the family of disabled, in the General Teaching Competency assessment is 92.2381 subject to a standard deviation of 3.3173 and the same by the respondents who are not belonging to the family of a disabled is 81.9836 subject to a standard deviation of 1.1371. The 't'- value obtained is 3.347 and the 'p' value is .001. The 'p' value is less than the .05. Hence it can be conclude that there exists a significant difference in the General Teaching Competency of respondents belonging to the family of disabled and not belonging to the family of disabled.

**Table 5.47: Familial Background of Disability and General Teaching Competency**

| Variables | Disability in Family | N | Mean | Std. Deviation | 't' value | P value (0.05 level) |
|---|---|---|---|---|---|---|
| General teaching Competency | Yes | 21 | 92.2381 | 15.2017 | 3.347 | 0.001 |
| | No | 122 | 81.9836 | 12.5593 | | |

## Categorization of Respondents of Having Familial Background of Disability and not Having Familial Background of Disability on the Basis of Teaching Competency.

(High > 94.5429, Average – between 94.5429 and low <69.4243. 69.4243)

Among the respondents coming from the family of disabled, 66% are in the high group category in the grouping based on General Teaching Competency. Out of the remaining, 14.28% comes in average group and 19.04% comes in low group. In the case of not having familial background of disability 21.31% trainees are grouped as high and 62.29% are in the average group category. Remaining 16.39% trainees comes in low group.

**Table 5.48: Categorizing of Respondents Having Familial Background of Disability and not Having Familial Background of Disability on the Basis of General Teaching Competency**

| Disability In Family | Categorizing of respondents on the basis of General Teaching Competency | | | Total |
|---|---|---|---|---|
| | High Group | Average Group | Low Group | |
| Yes | 14(66%) | 3 (14.28%) | 4(19.04%) | 21 |
| No | 26(21.31%) | 76(62.29% | 20(16.39%) | 122 |
| Total | 40 | 79 | 24 | 143 |

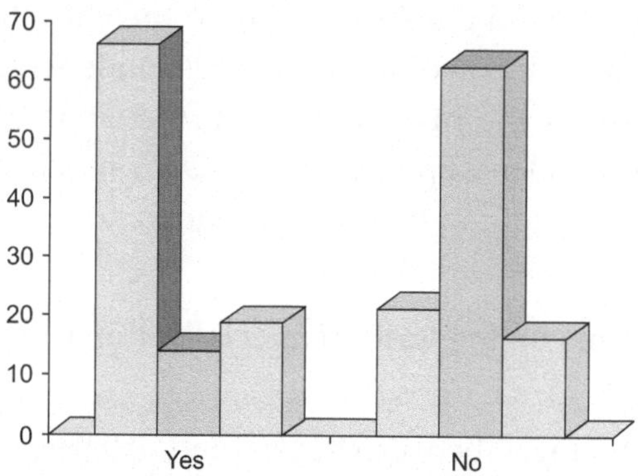


**Fig. 5.7: Bar diagram categorisation of respondents on the basis of familial background of disability and their teaching competency.**

## Analysis of Variance (ANOVA) of the General Teaching Competency of the Respondents and their Areas of Specialization

Table No 5.49 shows that the F value obtained is 5.237 and the 'p' value is .006 which is less than .05 (P< .05). Hence it is concluded that there exists a significant difference in the General Teaching Competency of Teacher Trainees Specializing in Hearing Impairment, Visual Impairment and Mental Retardation.

**Table 5.49: ANOVA Summary Table General Teaching Competency and Areas of Specialization of the Respondents**

| Group variance | Sum of Squares | Df | Mean square | F | Sig (0.05 level) |
|---|---|---|---|---|---|
| Between Groups | 1781.344 | 2 | 890.672 | 5.237 | .006 |
| Within Groups | 23810.391 | 140 | 170.074 | | |
| Total | 25591.734 | 142 | | | |

**Table 5.50: Description of Respondents Specialization Categories and GTC**

| Variables | N | Mean | SD. | Std. Error | 95% Confidence Intvl | | Mnm | Mxm |
|---|---|---|---|---|---|---|---|---|
| | | | | | Lower Bound | Upper Bound | | |
| HI | 25 | 90.6400 | 2.4993 | 85.4818 | 85.4818 | 95.7982 | 68.00 | 108.00 |
| VI | 23 | 84.8261 | 2.6804 | 79.2673 | 79.2673 | 90.3848 | 67.00 | 104.00 |
| MR | 95 | 81.2842 | 1.3563 | 78.5912 | 78.5912 | 83.9772 | 60.00 | 110.00 |
| Total | 143 | 83.4895 | 1.1226 | 81.2703 | 81.2703 | 85.7087 | 60.00 | 110.00 |

As per the table no 5.50 the mean score obtained by the respondents who are specializing in hearing impairment is 90.6400 subject to a standard deviation of 12.4963. The mean score obtained by the respondents who are specializing in visual impairment is 84.8261 subject to a standard deviation of 12.8546. The mean Score obtained by those who are specializing in mental retardation is 81.2842, subject to a standard deviation of 13.296. The respondents specializing in hearing impairment possess the highest score in the General Teaching Competency assessment, Respondents Specializing in visual impairment scored the next and those who specializing in mental retardation acquired the third position in the assessment.

## Categorization of Respondents on the Basis of Specialization Categories and their Teaching Competency

(High group > 82.6405, Average – between 82.6405 and 79.9279 low <79.9279)

(HI – Hearing impairment specialization category

VI – Visual impairment specialization category

MR – Mentally retarded Category)

**Table 5.51: Categorizing of Respondents on the Basis of Specialization Categories and General Teaching Competency**

| Area of Specializations | Categorizing of respondents on the basis of General Teaching Competency | | | Total |
|---|---|---|---|---|
| | High Group | Average Group | Low Group | |
| HI | 12 (48%) | 11(44%) | 2(8%) | 25 |
| VI | 7(30.43%) | 12(52.17%) | 4(17.39%) | 23 |
| MR | 21(22.10%) | 56(58.94%) | 18(18.94%) | 95 |
| Total | 40(27.97%) | 79(55.24%) | 24(16.78%) | 143 |

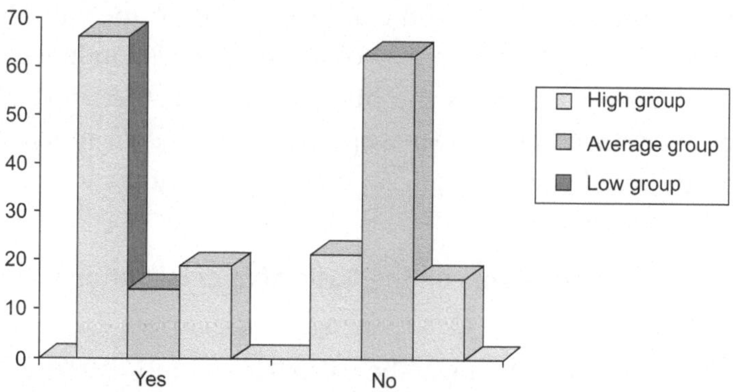

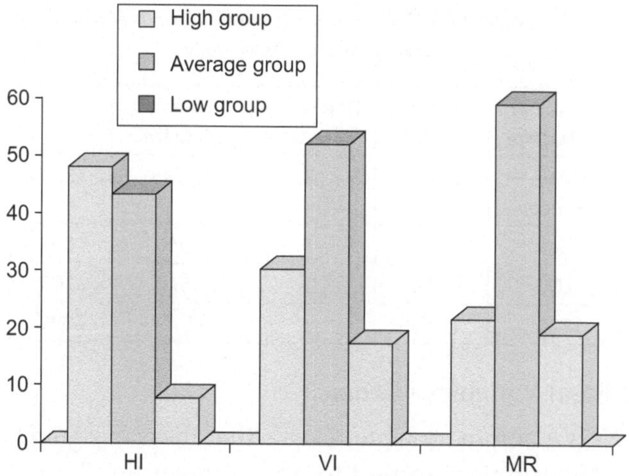


**Fig. 5.8: Bar diagram-categorization of respondents on the basis of specialization in training and their teaching competency**

As per table 5.51 and figure 5.8, out of 143 respondents 40 respondents constitute the 27.97 percent comes high group with respect to teaching competency and 55.24% comes under average group where as 16.78 % of total respondents are in low group. The table also shows that in the specialization category of hearing impairment 48% trainees are comes in high group,44% and 8% trainees are come under average and low group respectively 30.43 % trainees of visual impairment specialization grouped as high and 52.17% trainees are comes in average group. Another 17.39% grouped as low with respect to the General Teaching Competency. Among the category of mental retardation 18.94% comes in low group. 58.94 % trainees are included in average group where as 22.10% trainees shows high competency in teaching.

## SUMMARY OF ANOVA OF BASAL VARIABLES WITH REGARD TO RESPONDENTS GROUPED ON THE BASIS OF SEX–LOCALITY – PARENTAL HISTORY OF TEACHING (GROUP 1 ) AND TEACHING EXPERIENCE – FAMILIAL BACKGROUND OF DISABILITY - PARENTAL HISTORY OF TEACHING (GROUP 2)

### Significance of the Effect of the Sex, Locality and Parental History of Teaching (group 1) on 16 Personality Factors

#### *Factor A and basal variables Group 1*

The teacher trainees of special education coming from teacher family have high significant difference in the personality factor A whereas it is not statistically significant in the case of basal variables sex and locality.

**Table 5.52: The Summary of ANOVA of the Personality Factor A with Respect to Sex, Locality and Teacher Family**

| | Source of variation | Sum of squares | Degrees of freedom | Mean Square | F | P value (0.05 level) |
|---|---|---|---|---|---|---|
| A Reserved Vs Out going | Main Effects | 11.844 | 3 | 3.948 | .819 | .485 |
| | Sex | .040 | 1 | .040 | .008 | .928 |
| | LOC | .510 | 1 | .510 | .106 | .746 |
| | TFAMI | 11.495 | 1 | 11.495 | 2.385 | .125 |

## Factor B and Basal Variables - Group 1

The above ANOVA summary table reveals that there is significant difference in personality factor B with respect to sex but regarding locality and teacher family there is no significant difference.

**Table 5.53: The Summary of ANOVA of personality factor B with Respect to Gender, Locality and Parental History of Teaching**

| | Source of variation | Sum of squares | Degrees of freedom | Mean Square | F | P value (0.05 level) |
|---|---|---|---|---|---|---|
| BLess intelligence Vs more intelligence | Main Effects | 8.990 | 3 | 2.997 | .744 | .528 |
| | Sex | 7.840 | 1 | 7.840 | 1.947 | .165 |
| | LOC | .248 | 1 | .248 | .062 | .804 |
| | TFAMI | .626 | 1 | .626 | .156 | .694 |

## Factor C and Basal Variables - Group 1

Table 5.54 shows that there is significant difference in personality factor C with respect to sex and teacher family but there is no significant difference in personality factor with regards to locality.

**Table 5.54: The summary of ANOVA of the Personality Factor C with Respect to Gender, Locality and Parental History of Teaching**

| | Source of variation | Sum of squares | Degrees of freedom | Mean Square | F | P value (0.05 level) |
|---|---|---|---|---|---|---|
| C Emotionally less stable Vs Emotionaly stable | Main Effects | 32.001 | 3 | 10.667 | 2.454 | .066 |
| | Sex | 2.966 | 1 | 2.966 | .682 | .410 |
| | LOC | 0..2 | 1 | .002 | .000 | .985 |
| | TFAMI | 30.207 | 1 | 30.207 | 6.949 | .009 |

## Factor E and Basal Variables - Group 1

From the above table it is clear that the variable sex and parental history of teaching have significantly difference with respect personality factors. But there is no significant difference in the case of locality of respondents.

**Table 5.55: The Summary of ANOVA of the Personality Factor E with Respect to Gender, Locality and Parental History of Teaching**

| | Source of variation | Sum of squares | Degrees of freedom | Mean Square | F | P value (0.05) |
|---|---|---|---|---|---|---|
| EHumble Vs Assertive | Main Effects | 22.806 | 3 | 7.602 | 1.973 | .121 |
| | Sex | 18.417 | 1 | 18.417 | 4.780 | .031 |
| | LOC | .014 | 1 | .014 | .004 | .953 |
| | TFAMI | 3.134 | 1 | 3.134 | .814 | .369 |

## Factor F and Basal Variables - Group 1

The above summary shows that with respect to sex and locality there is significant difference in personality factor F of the teacher trainees of special education, whereas there is no significant difference in the case of teacher family.

**Table 5.56: The Summary of ANOVA of the Personality Factor F with Respect to Gender, Locality and Parental History of Teaching Experience.**

| | Source of variation | Sum of squares | Degrees of freedom | Mean Square | F | P value (0.05) |
|---|---|---|---|---|---|---|
| FSober Vs Happy-go-lucky | Main Effects | 16.613 | 3 | 5.538 | 1.167 | .325 |
| | Sex | 12.124 | 1 | 12.124 | 2.554 | .112 |
| | LOC | 4.739 | 1 | 4.739 | .998 | .319 |
| | TFAMI | 1.097 | 1 | 1.097 | .231 | .631 |

## Factor G and Basal Variables Group 1

Since the Pvalues of F with regard to sex and locality are higher than the F value it is clear that there is no significance difference in the personality factor G with regard to these variable, but there is significant difference with respect to teacher family.

**Table 5.57: The Summary of ANOVA of the Personality Factor G with Respect to Gender, Locality and Parental History of Teaching Experience.**

| | Source of variation | Sum of squares | Degrees of freedom | Mean Square | F | P value (0.05) |
|---|---|---|---|---|---|---|
| G Expedient Vs conscentious | Main Effects | 3.879 | 3 | 1.293 | .329 | .804 |
| | Sex | .000 | 1 | .000 | .000 | .998 |
| | LOC | .130 | 1 | .130 | .033 | .856 |
| | TFAMI | 3.773 | 1 | 3.773 | .960 | .329 |

## Factor H and Basal Variables - Group 1

There is significant difference in personality factor H with regard to sex and teachers family. But there is no significant difference with regard to locality. The main effect of these three variable are also significant.

**Table 5.58: The Summary of ANOVA of the Personality Factor H with Respect to Gender, Locality and Parental History of Teaching Experience.**

| | Source of variation | Sum of squares | DF | Mean Square | F | Signi (0.05) |
|---|---|---|---|---|---|---|
| HShy Vs Venturesome | Main Effects | 20.260 | 3 | 6.753 | 1.491 | .220 |
| | Sex | 9.358 | 1 | 9.358 | 2.066 | .153 |
| | LOC | .666 | 1 | .666 | .147 | .702 |
| | TFAMI | 12.078 | 1 | 12.078 | 2.667 | .105 |
| | | | | | | |

## Factor I and Basal Variables - Group 1

From table 5.59 it is very clear that all the three variables F values are high than the P value. Hence there is significant difference in personality factor I with regard to sex, locality and teacher family.

**Table 5.59: The Summary of ANOVA of the Personality Factor I with Respect to Gender, Locality and Parental History of Teaching Experience.**

| | Source of variation | Sum of squares | Degrees of freedom | Mean Square | F | P value (0.05) |
|---|---|---|---|---|---|---|
| ITough minded Vs Tender minded | Main Effects | 26.610 | 3 | 8.870 | 2.225 | .088 |
| | Sex | 7.597 | 1 | 7.597 | 1.906 | .170 |
| | LOC | 5.074 | 1 | 5.074 | 1.273 | .261 |
| | TFAMI | 12.450 | 1 | 12.450 | 3.123 | .079 |

## Factor L and Basal Variables - Group 1

As per the above table there is significant difference in personality factor L with respect sex and locality and there is no significant difference in respect to teachers family.

**Table 5.60: The Summary of ANOVA of the Personality Factor L with Respect to Gender, Locality and Parental History of Teaching Experience.**

| | Source of variation | Sum of squares | Degrees of freedom | Mean Square | F | P value (0.05) |
|---|---|---|---|---|---|---|
| L Trusting Vs suspicious | Main Effects | 8.650 | 3 | 2.883 | .653 | .583 |
| | Sex | 2.212 | 1 | 2.212 | .501 | .480 |
| | LOC | 5.562 | 1 | 5.562 | 1.259 | .264 |
| | TFAMI | .507 | 1 | .507 | .115 | .735 |

## Factor M and Basal Variables - Group 1

The table shows that there is significance difference in personality factor M with respect to sex, locality and teacher family.

**Table 5.61: The Summary of ANOVA of the Personality Factor M with Respect to Gender, Locality and Parental History of Teaching Experience.**

| | Source of variation | Sum of squares | Degrees of freedom | Mean Square | F | P value (0.05) |
|---|---|---|---|---|---|---|
| MPractical Vs Imaginative | Main Effects | 14.877 | 3 | 4.959 | 1.464 | .227 |
| | Sex | 3.674 | 1 | 3.674 | 1.085 | .300 |
| | LOC | 9.828 | 1 | 9.828 | 2.902 | .091 |
| | TFAMI | 2.727 | 1 | 2.727 | .805 | .371 |

## Factor N and Basal Variables Group 1

From the above table the personality factor N shows significance difference in respect to sex and locality. There is no significance difference in personality factor N with respect to teachers family.

**Table 5.62: The Summary of ANOVA of the Personality Factor N with Respect to Gender, Locality and Parental History of Teaching Experience.**

| | Source of variation | Sum of squares | Degrees of freedom | Mean Square | F | P value (0.05) |
|---|---|---|---|---|---|---|
| NForth- right Vs Shrewed | Main Effects | 7.071 | 3 | 2.357 | .548 | .650 |
| | Sex | 4.411 | 1 | 4.411 | 1.027 | .313 |
| | LOC | 2.288 | 1 | 2.288 | .532 | .467 |
| | TFAMI | .034 | 1 | .034 | .008 | .929 |

## Factor O and basal variables - Group 1

As per the above table the personality factor O has significant difference with respect to all the three variables sex, locality and teachers family.

**Table 5.63: The Summary of ANOVA of the Personality Factor O with Respect to Gender, Locality and Parental History of Teaching Experience.**

| | Source of variation | Sum of squares | Degrees of freedom | Mean Square | F | P value (0.05) |
|---|---|---|---|---|---|---|
| OPlacid Vs Apprehensive | Main Effects | 41.528 | 3 | 13.843 | 3.972 | .009 |
| | Sex | 17.306 | 1 | 17.302 | 4.965 | .028 |
| | LOC | 8.665 | 1 | 8.665 | 2.486 | .117 |
| | TFAMI | 20.147 | 1 | 20.147 | 5.781 | .018 |

## Factor Q1 and Basal Variables-Group 1

From the above data it is very clear that Personality Factor Q has significance difference in regard to sex. But with regard to locality and teacher family there is no significant difference.

**Table 5.64: The Summary of ANOVA of the Personality Factor Q with Respect to Gender, Locality and Parental History of Teaching Experience.**

| | Source of variation | Sum of squares | Degrees of freedom | Mean Square | F | P value (0.05) |
|---|---|---|---|---|---|---|
| Q1 Conservative Vs Experimenting | Main Effects | 6.089 | 3 | 2.030 | .527 | .665 |
| | Sex | 3.325 | 1 | 3.325 | .863 | .355 |
| | LOC | 1.841 | 1 | 1.841 | .478 | .491 |
| | TFAMI | 1.586 | 1 | 1.586 | .412 | .522 |

## Factor Q2 and Basal Variables - Group 1

Table 5.65 shows that there is significance difference in personality factor Q2 with regard to sex and teachers family. But in the case of locality there is no significant difference.

**Table 5.65: The Summary of ANOVA of the Personality Factor Q2 with Respect to Gender, Locality and Parental History of Teaching Experience.**

| | Source of variation | Sum of squares | Degrees of freedom | Mean Square | F | P value (0.05) |
|---|---|---|---|---|---|---|
| Q2 Self sufficient Vs Group dependent | Main Effects | 16.183 | 3 | 5.394 | 1.294 | .279 |
| | Sex | 3.934 | 1 | 3.934 | .943 | .333 |
| | LOC | .025 | 1 | .025 | .006 | .939 |
| | TFAMI | 13.225 | 1 | 13.225 | 3.172 | .077 |

## Factor Q3 and basal variables - Group 1

According to the information of Table 4.75 there is significant difference in personality factor Q3with regard to teachers family. But there is no effect on personality factor Q3 by sex and locality.

**Table 5.66: The Summary of ANOVA of the Personality Factor Q3 with Respect to Gender, Locality and Parental History of Teaching Experience.**

| | Source of variation | Sum of squares | Degrees of freedom | Mean Square | F | P value (0.05) |
|---|---|---|---|---|---|---|
| Q3 Un desciplined Self conflit Vs Controlled | Main Effects | 13.205 | 3 | 4.402 | .608 | .611 |
| | Sex | .027 | 1 | .027 | .004 | .951 |
| | LOC | 1.042 | 1 | 1.042 | .144 | .705 |
| | TFAMI | 11.874 | 1 | 11.874 | 1.642 | .202 |

## Factor Q4 and Basal Variables - Group 1

There is significant effect of sex and teachers family on personality factor Q4. But there is no significant difference with respect to locality.

**Table 5.67: The Summary of ANOVA of the Personality Factor Q4 with Respect to Gender, Locality and Parental History of Teaching Experience.**

| | Source of variation | Sum of squares | Degrees of freedom | Mean Square | F | P value (0.05) |
|---|---|---|---|---|---|---|
| Q4 Relaxed Vs Tence | Main Effects | 111.586 | 3 | 37.195 | 7.316 | .000 |
| | Sex | 77.413 | 1 | 77.413 | 15.226 | .000 |
| | LOC | .090 | 1 | .090 | .018 | .894 |
| | TFAMI | 41.866 | 1 | 41.866 | 8.234 | .005 |

## Significance of the Effect of Teaching Experience, Disability Background and Parental History of Teaching

The above summary table reveals that there is significant difference in personality factor total with respect to teachers family. Since the 'p' values of sex and locality are greater than F value it is concluded that the effect of sex and locality of the respondents on personality is not significant.

**Table 5.68: The Summary of ANOVA of the Personality Factor Total with Respect to Gender, Locality and Parental History of Teaching Experience.**

| | Source of variation | Sum of squares | Degrees of freedom | Mean Square | F | P value (0.05) |
|---|---|---|---|---|---|---|
| Personality factor total | Main Effects | 181.056 | 3 | 60.352 | .674 | .570 |
| | Sex | 1.659 | 1 | 1.659 | .019 | .892 |
| | LOC | 18.160 | 1 | 18.160 | .203 | .653 |
| | TFAMI | 158.182 | 1 | 158.182 | 1.766 | .186 |

## Significance of the Effect of Teaching Experience, Disability Background and Parental History of Teaching (Group 2) on /16 Personality Factors

### Factor A and Basal Variables - Group 2

Table shows that the effect of teaching experience, disability background and teachers family are there on the personality factor A of teacher trainees of special education. There is significant difference in the personality factor A with respect to these variables.

**Table 5.69: The Summary of ANOVA the Personality Factor A with Respect to Teaching Experience, Disability Background and Teacher Family**

| | Source of variation | Sum of squares | Degrees of freedom | Mean Square | F | P value (0.05) |
|---|---|---|---|---|---|---|
| A Reserved Vs out going | Main Effects | 39.442 | 3 | 13.147 | 3.151 | .027 |
| | TEXP | 5.085 | 1 | 5.085 | 1.219 | .272 |
| | DISA | 20.868 | 1 | 20.868 | 5.001 | .027 |
| | TFAMI | 11.486 | 1 | 11.486 | 2.752 | .099 |

## Factor B and Basal Variables - Group 2

From Table 5.70 it is very clear that the personality factor B has no any significant difference with regard to teacher family teaching experience and familial background of disability.

**Table 5.70: The Summary of ANOVA of the Personality Factor B with Respect to Teaching Experience, Disability Background and Parental History of Teaching**

| | Source of variation | Sum of squares | Degrees of freedom | Mean Square | F | P value (0.05) |
|---|---|---|---|---|---|---|
| BLess intelligence Vs More intelligence | Main Effects | 1.558 | 3 | .519 | .132 | .941 |
| | TEXP | .268 | 1 | .268 | .068 | .794 |
| | DISA | .211 | 1 | .211 | .054 | .817 |
| | TFAMI | 1.047 | 1 | 1.047 | .266 | .607 |

## Factor C and Basal Variables - Group 2

As per the above information the personality factor C has significant difference with regard to teaching experience, disability background and teacher family.

**Table 5.71: The Summary of ANOVA of the Personality Factor C with Respect to Teaching Experience, Disability Background and Parental History of Teaching**

| | Source of variation | Sum of squares | Degrees of freedom | Mean Square | F | P value (0.05) |
|---|---|---|---|---|---|---|
| C Emotionally less stable Vs Emotionaly stable | Main Effects | 44.729 | 3 | 14.910 | 3.519 | .017 |
| | TEXP | 3.017 | 1 | 3.017 | .712 | .400 |
| | DISA | 13.751 | 1 | 13.751 | 3.245 | .074 |
| | TFAMI | 26.846 | 1 | 26.846 | 6.335 | .013 |

## Factor E and Basal Variables Group 2

Table 5.72 reveals that there is significant difference in personality factor E with respect to teaching experience and teachers family, whereas there is no effect of disability background on personality factor E.

**Table 5.72: The Summary of ANOVA the Personality Factor E with Respect to Teaching Experience, Disability Background and Parental History of Teaching**

| | Source of variation | Sum of squares | Degrees of freedom | Mean Square | F | P value (0.05) |
|---|---|---|---|---|---|---|
| **E Humble Vs Assertive** | Main Effects | 11.309 | 3 | 3.770 | .934 | .426 |
| | TEXP | 6.899 | 1 | 6.899 | 1.710 | .193 |
| | DISA | .186 | 1 | .186 | .046 | .830 |
| | TFAMI | 4.962 | 1 | 4.962 | 1.230 | .269 |

## Factor F and Basal Variables - Group 2

From the above table it is clear that only disability back ground of the teacher trainees special factor F. there is no significant difference in factor F in respect to teaching experience and teacher family.

**Table 5.73: The Summary of ANOVA of the Personality Factor F with Respect to Teaching Experience, Disability Background and Parental History of Teaching**

| | Source of variation | Sum of squares | Degrees of freedom | Mean Square | F | P value (0.05) |
|---|---|---|---|---|---|---|
| **F Sober Vs Happy-go-lucky** | Main Effects | 4.223 | 3 | 1.408 | .294 | .830 |
| | TEXP | .762 | 1 | .762 | .159 | .691 |
| | DISA | 2.639 | 1 | 2.639 | .551 | .459 |
| | TFAMI | .533 | 1 | .533 | .111 | .739 |

## Factor G and Basal Variables - Group 2

The personality factor G has influenced by disability background and teachers family background of the teacher trainees of special education whereas the table says that the teaching experience has shown no significant difference in factor G.

**Table 5.74: The Summary of ANOVA the Personality Factor G with Respect to Teaching Experience, Disability Background and Parental History of Teaching**

| | Source of variation | Sum of squares | Degrees of freedom | Mean Square | F | P value (0.05) |
|---|---|---|---|---|---|---|
| **G Expedient Vs conscentious** | Main Effects | 6.878 | 3 | 2.293 | .658 | .580 |
| | TEXP | 1.380 | 1 | 1.380 | .396 | .530 |
| | DISA | 2.037 | 1 | 2.037 | 1.185 | .278 |
| | TFAMI | 4.133 | 1 | 4.133 | 1.185 | .278 |

## Factor H and Basal Variables - Group 2

Table 5.75 shows that the teacher trainees with teaching experience, disability background and teacher family background have significant difference on personality factor H by comparing with to their not having counter parts.

**Table 5.75: The Summary of ANOVA of the Personality Factor H with Respect to Teaching Experience, Disability Background and Parental History of Teaching**

| | Source of variation | Sum of squares | Degrees of freedom | Mean Square | F | P value (0.05) |
|---|---|---|---|---|---|---|
| H Shy Vs Venturesome | Main Effects | 47.048 | 3 | 15.683 | 3.574 | .016 |
| | TEXP | 8.662 | 1 | 8.662 | 1.974 | .162 |
| | DISA | 24.834 | 1 | 24.834 | 5.660 | .019 |
| | TFAMI | 10.518 | 1 | 10.518 | 2.397 | .124 |

## Factor I and Basal Variables Group 2

Table 5.76 reveals that the personality factor I has significant difference with respect to variables disability background and teachers family. Whereas teaching experience has no effect on personality factor I.

**Table 5.76: The Summary of ANOVA of the Personality Factor I with Respect to Teaching Experience, Disability Background and Parental History of Teaching**

| | Source of variation | Sum of squares | Degrees of freedom | Mean Square | F | P value (0.05) |
|---|---|---|---|---|---|---|
| I Tough minded Vs Tender minded | Main Effects | 44.750 | 3 | 14.917 | 3.716 | .013 |
| | TEXP | .335 | 1 | .335 | .083 | .773 |
| | DISA | 28.990 | 1 | 28.990 | 7.222 | .008 |
| | TFAMI | 15.593 | 1 | 15.593 | 3.885 | .051 |

## Factor L and Basal Variables - Group 2

From the above table it is clear that the scores in personality factor l of the teacher trainees of special education having disability background is significantly different. The variables teaching experience, teacher family has shown no effect on factor L.

**Table 5.77: The Summary of ANOVA the Personality Factor L with Respect to Teaching Experience, Disability Background and Parental History of Teaching**

| | Source of variation | Sum of squares | Degrees of freedom | Mean Square | F | P value (0.05) |
|---|---|---|---|---|---|---|
| L Trusting Vs suspicious | Main Effects | 11.618 | 3 | 3.873 | .858 | .465 |
| | TEXP | .119 | 1 | .119 | .026 | .871 |
| | DISA | 10.715 | 1 | 10.715 | 2.373 | .126 |
| | TFAMI | .594 | 1 | .594 | .131 | .717 |

## Factor M and Basal Variables-Group 2

As per table 5.78 personality factor M is significantly different with respect to teacher family background of trainees of special education. Teaching experience and disability background has no significant effect on factor M.

**Table 5.78: The Summary of ANOVA of the Personality Factor M with Respect to Teaching Experience, Disability Background and Parental History of Teaching**

| M Practical Vs Imaginative | Source of variation | Sum of squares | Degrees of freedom | Mean Square | F | P value (0.05) |
|---|---|---|---|---|---|---|
| | Main Effects | 3.333 | 3 | 1.111 | .314 | .815 |
| | TEXP | .386 | 1 | .386 | .109 | .742 |
| | DISA | 1.068 | 1 | 1.068 | .302 | .584 |
| | TFAMI | 2.138 | 1 | 2.158 | .610 | .436 |

## Factor N and Basal Variables - Group 2

Table 5.79 shows that personality factor N has significantly difference in respect to disability background of the teacher trainees of special education. But in the case of teaching experience and parental history of teaching there is no significant difference in the personality factor N.

**Table 5.79: The Summary of ANOVA of the Personality Factor N with Respect to Teaching Experience, Disability Background and Parental History of Teaching**

| | Source of variation | Sum of squares | Degrees of freedom | Mean Square | F | P value (0.05) |
|---|---|---|---|---|---|---|
| NF orth-right Vs Shrewed | Main Effects | 13.239 | 3 | 4.413 | 1.039 | .378 |
| | TEXP | .857 | 1 | .857 | .202 | .654 |
| | DISA | 12.882 | 1 | 12.882 | 3.032 | .084 |
| | TFAMI | .005 | 1 | .005 | .001 | .973 |

## Factor O and Basal Variables - Group 2

Table 5.80 reveals that there is significant difference in the personality factor O with respect to teachers' family. but teaching experience and disability background has no influence on personality factor O of the teacher trainees of special education.

**Table 5.80: The Summary of ANOVA of the Personality Factor O with Respect to Teaching Experience, Disability Background and Parental History of Teaching**

| O Placid Vs Apprehancive | Source of variation | Sum of squares | Degrees of freedom | Mean Square | F | P value (0.05) |
|---|---|---|---|---|---|---|
| | Main Effects | 18.010 | 3 | 6.003 | 1.738 | .162 |
| | TEXP | 1.104 | 1 | 1.104 | .320 | .573 |
| | DISA | .160 | 1 | .160 | .046 | .830 |
| | TFAMI | 16.245 | 1 | 16.245 | 4.704 | .032 |

## Factor Q1 and Basal Variables - Group 2

It is very clear from the above table that there is no significant difference in personality factor Q1 with respect to teaching experience, disability background and teacher family of the teacher trainees of special education.

**Table 5.81: The Summary of ANOVA of the Personality Factor Q1 with Respect to Teaching Experience, Disability Background and Parental History of Teaching**

| | Source of variation | Sum of squares | Degrees of freedom | Mean Square | F | P value (0.05) |
|---|---|---|---|---|---|---|
| 1 Conservative Vs Experimenting | Main Effects | 2.433 | 3 | .811 | .208 | .890 |
| | TEXP | .816 | 1 | .816 | .210 | .648 |
| | DISA | .556 | 1 | .556 | .143 | .706 |
| | TFAMI | 1.320 | 1 | 1.320 | .339 | .561 |

## Factor Q2 and Basal Variables - Group 2

Table 5.82 shows that teaching experience and teacher family have influence on personality factor Q2 with regard to these variables whereas there is no significant difference in personality factor Q2 with respect to disability background of teacher trainees of special education.

**Table 5.82: The Summary of ANOVA of the Personality Factor Q2 with Respect to Teaching Experience, Disability Background and Parental History of Teaching**

| Q2 Group dependent Vs Self sufficient | Source of variation | Sum of squares | Degrees of freedom | Mean Square | F | P value (0.05) |
|---|---|---|---|---|---|---|
| | Main Effects | 34.635 | 3 | 11.545 | 2.960 | .035 |
| | TEXP | 21.359 | 1 | 21.359 | 5.476 | .021 |
| | DISA | .333 | 1 | .333 | .085 | .771 |
| | TFAMI | 10.818 | 1 | 10.818 | 2.773 | .098 |

## Factor Q3 and basal variables - Group 2

As per table No.5.83, the personality factor Q3 has significant difference with regard to teaching experience, disability background and teachers family of the teacher trainees of special education.

**Table 5.83: The Summary of ANOVA of the Personality Factor Q3 with Respect to Teaching Experience, Disability Background and Parental History of Teaching**

| Q3Un desciplined Self conflit Vs Controlled | Source of variation | Sum of squares | Degrees of freedom | Mean Square | F | P value (0.05) |
|---|---|---|---|---|---|---|
| | Main Effects | 24.674 | 3 | 8.225 | 1.158 | .328 |
| | TEXP | 9.890 | 1 | 9.890 | 1.392 | .240 |
| | DISA | 3.694 | 1 | 3.694 | .520 | .472 |
| | TFAMI | 10.655 | 1 | 10.655 | 1.500 | .223 |

## Factor Q4 and Basal Variables - Group 2

From the table 5.84 is clear that all the three based variable have significant influence on personality factor Q4 there is significant difference with respect to teaching experience, disability background and teachers family of the respondents.

**Table 5.84: The Summary of ANOVA of the Personality Factor Q4 with Respect to Teaching Experience, Disability Background and Parental History of Teaching**

| | Source of variation | Sum of squares | Degrees of freedom | Mean Square | F | P value (0.05) |
|---|---|---|---|---|---|---|
| Q4 Relaxed Vs Tense | Main Effects | 51.950 | 3 | 17.317 | 3.520 | .024 |
| | TEXP | 4.750 | 1 | 4.750 | .892 | .347 |
| | DISA | 11.513 | 1 | 11.513 | 2.161 | .144 |
| | TFAMI | 34.018 | 1 | 34.018 | 6.385 | .013 |

## Personality Factor Total and Basal Variables - Group 2

Table 5.85 shows that the F values of teaching experience disability back ground and teachers family are greater than their corresponding P value hence the effect of these variables on personality factor total is significant. Those teacher trainees of special education having teaching experience, having disability back ground and coming from the family of teachers have secured high score in the personality factors than those trainees without having teaching experience, disability background and familial background of teaching.

**Table 5.85: The Summary of ANOVA of the Personality Factor Total with Respect to Teaching Experience, Disability Background and Parental History of Teaching**

| Personality factor Total | Source of variation | Sum of squares | Degrees of freedom | Mean Square | F | P value (0.05) |
|---|---|---|---|---|---|---|
| | Main Effects | 679.253 | 3 | 226.418 | 2.663 | .051 |
| | TEXP | 196.832 | 1 | 196.832 | 2.315 | .131 |
| | DISA | 273.711 | 1 | 273.711 | 3.219 | .075 |
| | TFAMI | 155.872 | 1 | 155.872 | 1.833 | .178 |

# 6 Summary, Findings and Suggestions

Education is a life long process involving many planned and unplanned experiences that enable children and adults alike to develop and learn through interaction with the society and culture in which they live. It involves experiences at all stages of life, from infancy through to old age. Education also involves adaptations to society and culture. With all the combinations of life event, adaptation will mean that each person is subject to a unique set of learning and problem solving experiences that constitute an understanding of the world and the events that take place in it.

There are many children who, for some reason, are unable to take full advantage of the school curriculum as it is normally offered. For these children special arrangements must be made to ensure that they receive the opportunities and experiences, which will help them to learn and develop to the extent of their capabilities. There are several hearing impaired and visual impaired children in the classrooms who achieve low in spite of their average or above average intelligence. And also there are educable children with mental retardation in the class room but unidentified. Hence parents become highly disappoints when children fall behind in performance. The reasons for the above scenario are numerous. Poor family background, emotional conflicts at home and lack of motivation are some of them. Inefficiency of the teacher is however, considered as the most critical reason for the backwardness of the children with special needs.

Playing a significant role in the all round development of the children with disabilities, the teachers should be trained effectively to meet the challenge. Hence in order to equip the trainees to meet the challenges and to manage the children with special needs the following objectives should be followed strictly in the teacher training programme in special education.

(1) To develop an awareness that all school teachers, whatever the age group of their pupils or level of their work, are likely to be concerned with helping some children who have special educational needs. (2) To enable teachers to recognize early signs of variable special educational needs. (3) To give the knowledge of the part which they can play in the amount of child's educational needs and in the execution of any special measures prescribed. (4) To give teachers what special education is like together with the knowledge or range of various forms of special educational provision and of specialist advisory services. (5) To provide some acquaintance with the school classes and units, to give teachers understanding of how to communicate effectively with parent's

anxieties and encouraging their continued involvement in their child's progress. (6) To give teachers in service training of when and where to refer for special help and knowledge in general terms of teaching to handicapped. (7) To develop Practical skills in observation of children both individually and in groups and to help teachers sharpen their perception of variations in children's learning and behavior and develop their awareness of variation in children's circumstances (home-school difficulties). (8) Appreciation of the educational needs of children with developed difficulties-physical, sensory, emotional behavioral or learning the needs of their parents, and the value of the contribution which parents can make to their children's development. (9) Understanding of the practical steps necessary for meeting a child's special needs and an ability to adopt the attitude must suit to dealing with particular difficulties and to appreciate the need for modification of the school or classroom organization the curriculum or teaching techniques. (10) Appreciation of the special services available to children with epical needs of their familiar and of the advisory services available to teachers. This might be developed by inviting professionals for the various services to visit the college so that through discussion, the students can contributions which different specialist can make, the services to expect from them, and the kind of question to put to time and (11) Awareness of the range of career and professional opportunities in special education and the availability of further qualification in special education and the fact that special education offer the teachers engaged in it ,an intellectual challenge.

Various studies have been taken up by different researchers regarding scholastic backwardness of the children with special needs in general. However a comprehensive yet concise research work focusing on the personality and Teaching competency of teacher trainees of special education could not be located. Hence much work needs to be done with reference to the above mentioned areas in India especially in Kerala Culture. Thus, this study aim at a new perspective with an earnest attempt to satisfy the need of presenting the picture of teacher training in special education and the factors related to it. The findings of the study would equip the authorities with information about the required strategies in alleviating the condition of inefficiency of the special educators and low performance of the children with special needs.

## THE STUDY IN RETROSPECT

The study as stated earlier was an attempt to find out the nature and extent of relationship of personality with teaching competency of prospective teachers of special education. The problem was stated as personality as correlates teaching competency among teacher trainees of special education

### Research Problem Re-stated

"PERSONALITY AS CORRELATES OF TEACHING COMPETENCY AMONG TEACHER TRAINEES OF SPECIAL EDUCATION"

## Objectives of the Study

The present study was under taken with the following objectives.

1. To asses the personality of the teacher trainees of special education.
2. To evaluate general teaching competency and to categorize the teacher trainees in regard to their general teaching competency.
3. To find out whether the personality of the teacher trainees of special education has significant relationship with teaching competency.
4. To understand the gender differences in the teaching competency of teacher trainees of special education
5. To examine whether there is any significant difference in the General Teaching Competency of Teacher Trainees of Special education, who belongs to the family of disabled and who do not belongs to the family disabled.
6. To examine whether there is any significant difference in the general teaching competency of teacher trainees of special education on the basis of locality (i.e. Urban and Rural).
7. To find out whether there is any significant difference in the general teaching competency of teacher trainees of special education, who have teaching experience and those who have not teaching experience.
8. To find out whether there is any significant difference in the general teaching competency of teacher trainees of special education with the parental history of teaching and without the parental history of teaching.
9. To find out whether there is any significant difference in the teaching competency of teacher trainees of special education specializing in visual impairment, hearing impairment and mental retardation.

## Hypotheses

The following hypotheses were formulated for testing in the study.

1. There exist significant correlation between the personality and General teaching competency of teacher trainees of special education.
2. There exists significant Gender difference in the personality of teacher trainees of special education.
3. There exists significant Gender difference in the teaching competency of teacher trainees of special education.
4. There exists significant difference in the General Teaching Competency of Teacher Trainees of special education, who belong to the family of disabled and those who do not belong to the family of disabled.
5. There exists significant difference in the General Teaching Competency of Teacher Trainees of Special education, who have teaching experience and those who have not teaching experience.

6. There exists significant difference in the General teaching competency of teacher trainees with parental history of teaching and without parental history of teaching.
7. There exists significant difference in the teaching competency of Teacher Trainees of special education on the basis of specialization in visual impairment, Hearing impairment and Mental retardation.

## Methodology in Brief

The present study is intended to find out the nature and extend of relationship of personality with teaching competency of teacher trainees of special education. Hence descriptive method was used for the study. Personality factors considered as independent variable and teaching competency is considered as dependent variables. Sex, locality, teaching experience, Parental history of teaching, Familial background of disability and area of specialization are considered as basal variables.

## Sample

143 Teacher trainees of special education of seven teacher training institution form Trivandram, Quilon, Palakkad, and Kozhikkode District were selected.

Disability area of specialization, Male- female, urban-rural, Trainees having teaching experience and not having teaching experience, family background of disability and parental history of teaching were considered for sub samples.

## Tools Employed

The following tools were employed in the study.

1. 16P.F Questionnaires (C-Form)- R.B cattle.
2. General Teaching Competency Scale (GTCS) developed by Passi (1979)
3. General data form

## Procedure of Data Collection

The data collection was done in two phases. The first phase was during 2005 June – 2006 August – during the period General data were collected and 16PF Questionnaire administered. The second part of the data collection was conducted during the month of October 2005 to April 2006 in which the investigator observed the classes of the trainees individually.

## Statistical Techniques Used

The data for the study has been analyzed using the following techniques. The entire statistical processing was done by the computer.

1. For the preliminary analysis of scores, statistical techniques like mean, median, mode, and standards deviation and skew ness and kurtosis were computed.

2. Correlation analysis to determine the extent of relationship between different variable.
3. Test of significance for difference between means of relevant groups (t, test).
4. ANOVA.

## SUMMARY

1. 143 Teacher Trainees of special education were included in the study. Their teaching competency was measured by using General Teaching Competency Scale. The trainees were grouped on the basis of mean score and standard deviation. 55.2% of the trainees have average teaching competency. But 16.8% trainees did not have the required level of teaching competency, while 28 percent of the total sample is seen highly competent in teaching. The categorization is presented below.

**Table 6.1: Categorization of Respondents on the Basis of General Teaching Competency**

| Category | Frequency | Percent |
|---|---|---|
| High Group > 96.9142 (83.4895+ 13.4247) | 40 | 28.0 |
| Average Group = between 96.9142 and 70.0648 | 79 | 55.2 |
| Low Group < 70.0648 (83.4895 -13.4247) | 24 | 16.8 |
| Total | 143 | 100.0 |

2. The assessment of the personality scores of 143 Teacher trainees of special education reveals that, Majority of the trainees are comes under the category of average scoring group. 103 trainees consist of 72 percentages of the total sample fall in the average scoring group. 17 teacher trainees that is 11.9 percentage secured high personality scores where as 16.1 percentage consisting of 23 teacher trainees comes under the personality category of low group. The categorization of the teacher trainees of special education is presented in the table below.

**Table 6.2: Categories of Respondent's According to the Personality Scores**

| Category | Frequency | Percent |
|---|---|---|
| High Group > Mean + Standard Deviation | 17 | 11.9 |
| Average Group = Mean +/- Standard Deviation | 103 | 72.0 |
| Low Group < Mean – Standard Deviation | 23 | 16.1 |
| Total | 143 | 100.0 |

3. Relationship of all the personality factors with teaching competency was found out for the whole sample. The result reveals that there exist positive correlation between the personality and general teaching competency among teacher trainees of special education. The obtained 'r' and their significance is presented below.

**Table 6.3: Relationship of the Personality Factor Total with teaching competency**

| Independent Variable | Relationship variable | 'r' | Level of significance |
|---|---|---|---|
| Personality factor total | GTC | 0.399 | Significant at 0.01 level |

4. Out of 143 teacher trainees there are 22 male trainees and 121 female trainees. 27.27% trainees come under high group where as 63.6% trainees were grouped as average and another 9.09% trainees were included in low group with respect to general teaching competency. In the case of female trainees it is 28.09%, 53.73% and 18.18% trainees grouped as high, average and low group respectively. Since the 't' value obtained is 348 and the 'p' value is 728 (p>05). It is found that there is no significant difference in the mean scores of general teaching competency scored by the male and female respondents. Hence it is concluded that there is no significant relationship between sex and teaching competency of the teacher trainees of special education.

5. There are 24 trainees belongs to urban and 119 trainees are coming from rural. Both urban respondents and rural respondents are more in the average group with respect to teaching competency. Among the urban respondents 501 percent were belongs to average group category and 56.30 percent of the rural respondents were also belongs to the same category 33 percent trainees of both urban and rural perform high competency in teaching. On the basis of the above it is very clear that there is no significant difference in the teaching competency on the basis of locality.

6. Out of the whole sample, 59 respondents have previous teaching experience and the rest 84 trainees comes under the group of with out having teaching experience. 35 percent of the trainees having teaching experience found to have high competency in teaching while only 22 percent comes under high competent group from not having teaching experience category with regard to teaching competency. It shows that the previous teaching experience positively influenced on the performance of teacher trainees in their teaching. The mean score obtained by the respondents with teaching experience in 86.5424 and with out teaching experiences 81.3452 subject to a standard deviation of 13.1730 and 13.2558 respectively. The p value is (.022) less than .05 (p<.05) hence it is concluded that there exists a significant difference in the teaching competency of teacher trainees of special education with teaching experience and without teaching experience.

7. Fifty eight out of 143 teacher trainees of special education have parental history of teaching. In this group 60% were in the average group category and 27% belongs to low group in respect of general teaching competency. Where as it is 28%, 53% and 19% for high, average and low respectively in the group of trainees without having parental history of teaching. So it is found that the parental history of teaching has no influence on the performance of the teacher trainees in their teaching. It is also seen that the t value obtained in the

independent sample test is 374 the p value is 709 which is greater than .05 (p>.05). Hence it is concluded that there exist no significant difference between general teaching competency of teacher trainees with parental history of teaching and without parental history of teaching.

8. Among the 143 trainees 21 teacher trainees are belongs to the family of disabled and 122 trainees have not any familial background of disability, 66% teacher trainees having familial background of disability come under high group and 14.28% trainees were grouped as average and another 19.04% teachers come under low group with respect to general teaching competency. Out of 122 teacher trainees without having familial background of disability 21.31% teacher trainees performed high level competency in teaching where as 62.29% teacher trainees comes in average and 16.39% trainees comes under low group respectively with respect of teaching competency. Hence it is concluded that the teacher trainees coming from the families of person with disabilities perform high competency in teaching than other teachers with out having any familial background of disabilities.

**Table 6.4: Relationship Between Basal Variables (Sex, Locality, Teaching Experience, Familial Background of Disability, Parental History of Teaching) and General Teaching Competency**

| Sl No. | Basal variables | GTC | 't' | 'P' | Level of significance at 05 level |
|---|---|---|---|---|---|
| 1. | Sex | GTC | 3.48 | 7.28 | Not significance |
| 2. | Locality | GTC | 0.427 | 0.746 | Not significant |
| 2. | Teaching experience | GTC | 2.134 | 0.22 | Significant |
| 4. | Familial background of disability | GTC | 3.347 | .001 | Significant |
| 5. | Parental history of teaching | GTC | .374 | .709 | Not Significant |

9. According to the area of specialization 25 teacher trainees were categorized as hearing impairment group 23 included in visual impairment group and 95 trainees were there in the category of mental retardation. In hearing impairment category 48% trainees were high competent in teaching where as it is 30.43% and 22% in visual impairment and mental retardation respectively. 59% teacher trainees of mental retardation grouped as average in general teaching competency whereas it is 52 and 44 percentages in visual impairment and hearing impairment respectively. Only 8% teacher's shows poor performance in teaching among the hearing impaired category. But 17% trainees of visual impairment and 19%of trainees from the area of mental retardation (MR) come under low group category with regard to general teaching competency. The 'F' value obtained in the statistical analysis (ANOVA) of the three categories HI, VI and MR is 5.237 and the p value is .006 which is less than.05 (p<.05). Hence

there exists a significant difference in the general teaching competency of teacher trainees specializing in HI, VI and MR. The trainees specializing in hearing impairment possess the highest score in the general teaching competency assessment. The trainees of VI scored the next and those who specializing in MR acquired at the third Preston in the assessment.

**Table 6.5: Categorizing of Respondents on the Basis of Specialization Categories and General Teaching Competency**

| Area of Specializations | Categorizing of respondents on the basis of general teaching competency | | | Total |
|---|---|---|---|---|
| | High group > 82.6405 | Average – between 82.6405 and 79.9279 | low <79.9279 | |
| HI | 12 (48%) | 11(44%) | 2(8%) | 25 |
| VI | 7(30.43%) | 12(52.17%) | 4(17.39%) | 23 |
| MR | 21(22.10%) | 56(58.94%) | 18(18.94%) | 95 |
| Total | 40(27.97%) | 79(55.24%) | 24(16.78%) | 143 |

10. The effect of parental history of teaching, sex and locality on the personality of teacher training of special education was found by using ANOVA technique. The F value is greater than the P value in the case of parental history of teaching. But sex and locality have no effect on the personality of teacher trainees of special education. The F value of sex is 0.019 and its P value is 0.892 and in the case of locality it is 0.203 and 0.653 respectively. Both these values clearly give evidence that there is no sign cant difference in the personality of teacher trainees with regard to sex and locality.

**Table 6.6: The Personality Factor Total and Gender, Locality and Parental History of Teaching Experience.**

| | Source of variation | F | P value (0.05) |
|---|---|---|---|
| **Personality factor total** | Main Effects | .674 | .570 |
| | Sex | .019 | .892 |
| | Locality | .203 | .653 |
| | Parental history of teaching | 1.766 | .186 |

11. The effect of teaching experience, disability background, and parental history of teaching on personality of teacher training is significant. The F values of these variables (teaching experience F value 2.315, P value 0.131, disability background F value 3.219, P value 0.075 and teachers family F value 1.833, P value 0.178) are greater than their corresponding P value. Hence the effect of these variables on personality (total) is significant. Those teacher trainees of special education having teaching experience, having disability back ground and coming from the family of teachers have secured high score in the personality

factors than those trainees without having teaching experience, disability background and familial background of teaching.

**Table 6.7: The Personality Factor Total and Teaching Experience, Disability Background and Parental History of Teaching**

| | Source of variation | F | P value (0.05) |
|---|---|---|---|
| Personality factor Total | Main Effects | 2.663 | .051 |
| | Teaching Experience | 2.315 | .131 |
| | Disability background | 3.219 | .075 |
| | Parental History of Teaching | 1.833 | .178 |

## TENABILITY OF THE HYPOTHESES

### There Exists Significant Correlation Between the Personality and General Teaching Competency of Teacher Trainees of Special Education

It is clear from the Table 6.6 and Fig. 6.3 that there exists a significant correlation between the personality and General Teaching Competency of Special Education Teacher trainees of special education. The coefficient of correlation obtained is .399 showing a moderate positive relationship between the variables. The p value obtained is .000 and is less than 0.01 levels, P<.01 and so the research hypothesis is accepted. All the above mentioned things are leading to the conclusion that there exist a significant positive relationship between the personality and General Teaching Competency of the respondents.

### There Exists Significant Gender Difference in the Personality of Teacher Trainees of Special Education

To test this hypothesis the total respondents are classified in to the groups of males and females and the Independent sample t-test is administered.

The Group statistics is revealing the mean score obtained by the male respondents in the personality test is 102.7727 subject to a standard deviation of 8.4003 and that of females is 102.4298 subject to a standard deviation of 9.0248. The t- value is .166 and the p value is .869 which is greater than 0.05. So the research hypothesis is rejected leading to the conclusion that, there is no gender difference in the personality of Teacher trainees of special education.

### There Exists Significant Gender Difference in the General Teaching Competency of Teacher Trainees of Special Education

To test the hypothesis the total respondents are classified in to the groups of male and female and administrated the independent sample t-test.

The group statistics shows that the mean score obtained by the male in General Teaching Competency test is 84.4091 subject to a standard deviation of 11.6155 and the mean score obtained by the females is 83.3223. The t value obtained is .348. The p value is .728 (P >.05) which is grater than .05. The conclusion is that there is no significant difference in the mean scores obtained by the male and female respondents. So the research hypothesis is rejected. So there is no significant gender difference in the General Teaching Competency of Special Education Teacher trainees.

### There Exists Significant Differences in the General Teaching Competency of Teacher Trainees of Special Education, Who Belongs to the Family of Disabled and Who not Belongs to the Family of Disabled

Independent sample t-test is used to test the hypothesis after classifying the respondents in two groups on the basis of their belongingness to the family of a disabled.

The Group Statistics shows that the mean score obtained by the respondents, who are belonging to the family of disabled, in the General Teaching Competency assessment is 92.2381 subject to a standard deviation of 3.3173 and the same by the respondents who are not belonging to the family of a disabled is 81.9836 subject to a standard deviation of 1.1371. The t- value obtained is 3.347 and the p value is .001. The p value is less than the .05 and so the research hypothesis is accepted. Hence it can be conclude that there exists a significant difference in the General Teaching Competency of respondents belonging to the family of disabled and not belonging to the family of disabled. The Respondents who are belonging to the family of disabled gained more score in the General Teaching Competency assessment than the respondents not belonging to the family of disabled.

### There Exists Significant Difference in the General Teaching Competency of Teacher Trainees with Teaching Experience and Without Teaching Experience

Independent sample t-test is used to test this hypothesis after dividing the total respondents in to two groups on the basis of their teaching experience. The first Group consists of the respondents with teaching experience and the second group consists of the respondents without teaching experience.

The mean score obtained by the respondents with teaching experience is 86.5424 subject to a standard deviation of 13.1730 and the mean score obtained by the respondents without teaching experience is 81.3452 subject to a standard deviation of 13.2588. The t-value is 2.314 and the p value is .022. The p value is less than .05 (P<.05), so the research hypothesis is accepted. Hence there exists a significant difference in the teaching competency of Teacher trainees of special education with teaching experience and without teaching experience. Those who have teaching experience acquired high score in the General Teaching Competency Assessment.

### There Exists Significant Difference in the General Teaching Competency of Teacher Trainees with Parental History of Teaching and Without Parental History of Teaching

In order to test the hypothesis the respondents were grouped as respondents with parental history of teaching and respondents without parental history of teaching and the independent sample t-test is administered to find the difference in the mean scores obtained by the respondents in the General Teaching Competency assessment .

The mean Score obtained by the respondents with parental history of teaching is 84.0000 subject to a standard deviation of 12.7733 and that without a parental history of teaching is 83.1412 subject to a standard deviation of 13.9157. The t value is .374; the p value is .709 which is greater than .05. (P >.05) So the research hypothesis is rejected. We can conclude that there exists no significant difference between the General Teaching Competency of respondents with a parental history of teaching and without parental history of teaching.

### There Exists Significant Difference in the Teaching Competency of Teacher Trainees of Special Education Specializing in Visual Impairment, Hearing Impairment and Mental Retardation

Three groups of respondents are involved in this analysis, ie the respondents specializing in Visual Impairment, the respondents specializing in Hearing Impairment and the respondents specializing in Mental Retardation. So Analysis of Variance (ANOVA) method is used to find out the difference in the General Teaching Competency of Teacher Trainees of Special Education Specializing in the above mentioned areas of Special Education.

The mean score obtained by the respondents who are specializing in hearing impairment is 90.6400 subject to a standard deviation of 12.4963. The mean Score obtained by the respondents who are specializing in Visual Impairment is 84.8261 subject to a standard deviation of 12.8546. The mean Score obtained by those who are specializing in Mental Retardation is 81.2842, subject to a standard deviation of 13.296. The F value obtained is 5.237 and the p value is .006 which is less than .05 (P< .05) and so the research hypothesis is accepted. There exists a significant difference in the General Teaching Competency of Teacher Trainees Specializing in Hearing Impairment, Visual Impairment and Mental Retardation. The respondents Specializing in Hearing impairment possess the highest Score in the General Teaching Competency assessment, Respondents Specializing in Visual Impairment Scored the next and those who specializing in Mental Retardation Acquired the third position in the assessment.

## FINDINGS

1. The teacher trainees of special education possess an outgoing behavior and they are socially bold. They possess the traits of assertiveness and

conscientious. They are tender minded and self sufficient. They are above average in the trait of intelligence.

2. Whereas 28% of teacher trainees of special education possess high competency in teaching, 55.2% shows and average competency and 16.8% comes in the low group.
3. The teaching competency of the teacher trainees of special education is influenced by their personality.
4. The locality of teacher trainees of special education has not any role in their teaching competency.
5. Gender differences of the teacher trainees of special education is not a factor in determining their competency in teaching.
6. The teacher trainees of special education having familial background of disability are more competent in teaching than those trainees with out having familial background of disability.
7. The teacher trainees of special education having teaching experience shows high competency in teaching than those who have not teaching experience.
8. Parental history of teaching is not a determining factor of teaching competency of teacher trainees of special education.
9. The teacher trainees of special education who are specializing in teaching of hearing impaired category are more competent than the trainees who are specializing in the visual impaired and mental retarded categories.

The first outcome of the study reveals that the candidates having assertiveness and conscientious selected the teacher training programmes in special education. Tender mindedness and self sufficiency are other qualities of the trainees. It also reveals that the trainees posses outgoing behavior and social boldness. These findings are clear proof that they are eligible to deal children with special needs.

In the case of teaching competency it is almost normally distributed among the samples. Average consisting 55.2% and a high competency shown by 28%. This reveals that competency among trainees in teaching is normally distributed.

With regard to the influence of the personality factors in teaching the findings show that those who posses high scores in certain factors such as intelligence emotional control self sufficiency posses high teaching competency. Hence it can be concluded that it is good to conduct a personality test or including testing of personality as one of the criteria for admission to the training programmes.

The study shows that locality, gender and parental history of teaching are not determining factors of the teaching competency of teacher trainees. It shows that there is no need to make any kind of discrimination or reservation in this regard to ensure the candidate on the basis of the above categories in admission.

According to the outcome of the study familial background of disability and teaching experience are influential factors in determining the teaching competency. Hence the authorities can think about to set apart certain percentages of seats for the candidates having teaching experience and having familial background of disability for admission.

As per the findings of the study trainees from hearing impaired category shows more competency in teaching than other two categories. The reason behind this fact should be examined by the authorities and should ensure that the teachers are competent to deal with students having visual impairment and mental retardation. Curriculum of the academic programme should also be reviewed and admission procedure is revised accordingly.

## EDUCATIONAL IMPLICATIONS

From this study it is possible to conclude that the teaching competency is influenced by personality of the teacher trainees of special education. And it is also influenced by the disability background of the family of teacher trainees of special education, their teaching experience and their parental history of teaching. These factors are also to be taken into account be fore admitting the students for teacher training courses in special education. As such an entrance test to measure the candidates' personality is highly required. It is also required to reserve a certain percentage of seats to the candidates belonging to the family of disabled and also for those candidates having teaching experience. It is to ascertain that no candidate who is not having genuine interest in the profession enters in this noble profession i.e. , teaching the differently able children. At present anybody who acquires minimum marks in the qualifying examination and ready to pay the capitation fee is admitted to the course. This practice should be stayed.

## SUGGESTIONS FOR THE FURTHER RESEARCH

The findings of the study have helped to identify the areas of research in personality and teaching competency that need more attention from researchers. On the basis of present study the investigator would like to suggest the following areas for further research:

1. Replication of the present study with other adjustment variables and on the other categories of disabilities such as students with learning disability and students with multiple disabilities
2. Correlation between the variables such as job stress, job satisfaction, role conflict and role ambiguity and teaching competency.
3. A study can be conducted to critically evaluate the curriculum of teacher training courses in special education.
4. A study can be conducted on the organization and functioning of teacher training institutes of special education.

# Bibliography


Aaron, P.G. (1996). "Attitude and Motives of Teachers and Pupils-A Study Conformity", *Journal of the College of Education*, Kurukshetra University, Kurukshetra.

Abirami P.C. Perr, R.P. and Leventhal, L. (1987). The Relationship Between Students Personality Characteristics, Teacher Ratings and Students Achievement, *Journal of Educational Psychology*. Feb-Vol. 74(1) III-125.

Aggarwal, S.S. (1996).*The Study of Attitude of Training College Teachers of Agra Univ. Towards their Profession*, Unpublished M.Ed. Dissertation, Central Institution of Education, Delhi.

Allport, G.W. (1961). *Pattern and Growth in Personality*, New York : Holt, Rinehart and Winston.

Anderson, C.C. and Hunka S.M. (1963). "Teacher Education: Some Problems and a Proposal". *Harvard Educational Research*. 33, 74-95.

Anderson, H.M. (1954). Study of Certain Criteria of Teaching Effectiveness". *Journal of Educational Research*, 22, 41-71.

Anderson, G.J.(1971). "Effects of Course Content and Teacher Sex on the Social Climate of Learning". *American Educational Research Journal*, 8, 649-663.

Azad, Y. (1996). Integration of Disabled in Common Schools. A Survey Study of IEDC in the Country. New Delhi: Department of Education NCERT.

Barkley and Denyse, Olivia (1995). "Role Perception, Personality Type and Academic Achievement in a Practical Nursing School", *Dissertation Abstract International*, Vol. 57/08, p. 116.

Barr, A.S. (1929). *Characteristic Difference in the Teaching Performance of Good and Poor Teachers of Social Studies*. Bloomington Illinois: Public School Publishing Co..

Barr, A.S. and Associates (1961). *Wisconsisn Studies of the Measurement and Prediction of Teacher Effectiveness: A Summary of Investigations*. Madison: Wis. Dember Publication.

Beck, W.R.(1967). "Pulips" Perceptions of Teacher Merit: A Factor Analysis of Five Postulated Dimensions". *Journal of Educational Research*, 61,3, 127-128.

Berman, G. and Eisenberg, M. (1971). Psycho Social Aspects of Academic Achievement. *American Journal of Ortho Psychiatry*. Apr. Vol. 41 (3), 406-415.

Best, John S. (2003). *Research in Education*, New York: Prentice Hall.

Bohn, M.J. (1973). Personality Variables in Successful Work-Study Performance. *Journal of College Students Personal*. Mar. Vol. 14(2). 135-140.

Bose, E.V.C. (1993) *Correlation of Teacher Effectiveness of Student Teacher of Biology* M.Phil Thesis, University of Kerala.

Brar, J.S.(1976). Relationship Between Extrovert Introvert Neurotism and Academic Achievement Experience of Army Educational Corps. *Indian Educational Review Journal*. Vol. 11 (3). 105-110.

Brophy, J.E. (1976). "Reflections on Research in Elementary Schools". *Journal of Teacher Education*, XXVII, 1, 31-34.

Buch, M.B. (1975). *Studies in Teaching and Teacher Behaviors*, Centre of Advance Studies in Education (CASE) Baroda.

Buch, M.B. (1979). *Second Survey of Research in Education*, Society for Educational Research and Development, Baroda.

Buch, M.B. (1991). *Fourth Survey of Research in Education*, NCERT, Vol. 1, p. 366.

Busato, V.V. Prins, F.J., Elshout, J.J, and Aumaker, C.T. (1989). The Relationship Between Learning Styles, the Big Five Personality Traits and Achievement Motivation in Higher Education. Personality and Individual differences. Jan. Vol. 20 (1), 129-140.

Catell, R.B. (1931). "The Assessment of Teaching Ability". *British Journal of Educational Psychology*, 1, 48-71.

Catell, R.B.(1965). *The Scientific Analysis of Personality*. Baltimore: Penguin.

Cattell, R.B. and Eber, H.W. (1970). *Handbook for the Sixteen Personality Factor Questionnaire.* Champaign Illinois: Institute for Personality and Ability Testing.

Chhaya (1979). *An Investigation into the Certain Psychological Characteristics of an Effective School Teacher*. Ph.D Thesis, In .B. Buch(Ed.), *Second Survey of Research in Education* Baroda : CASE, 1979.

Chitra, J.U., Thyagarajan, A.P. and Krishnan, S.S. (1994). Psycho Socio Educational Factors of Schedule Caste Students in Higher Secondary Schools. Indian Journal of Psychometry and Education. Vol. 25 (12). 91-94.

Clarke, S.C.T.(1970). "General Teaching Theory", *Journal of Teacher Education*, 21, 403.

Cornolius (200). *Teacher Competence Associated with Intelligence, Attitude Towards Teaching Professions and Academic Achievements of Teacher Trainers*, M-Phil Thesis, University of Kerala.

Cornolius (2000). *Teacher Competence Associated with Intelligence, Attitude Towards Teaching Professions and Academic Achievements of Teacher Trainees*, M-Phil thesis, University of Kerala.

Cooper, M. Boss, M. and Keith, V. (1974). Personality Factors as Predictors of General and Differential Performance in High School. *Multivariate Experimental Clinic Research*. Vol. 1 (2). 46-57.

Dash, S. (2006). Quality Improvement in Teacher Education - An Analysis of Present and Future, *Edutrackes* - 5 (10), 12-14.

Davis, T.N. and Satterly, D.J. (1969). "Personality Profiles of Student Teacher". *British Journal of Educational Psychology*, 39,183-187.

Debnath, H.N. (1971). *Teaching Efficiency : Its Measurement and Some Determinants*, Unpublished Ph.D. Thesis, Lucknow University, 1971.

Deva, R.C. (1966). *Prediction of Student Teaching Success*. Ph.D Thesis, Aligarh Muslim University.

Edwards, A.L. (1975). *Techniques of Attitude Scale Construction*, New York : Appleton Century–Crafts.

Entwistle, N.S., Entwistle, D. (1970). The Relationship Between Personality, Study Methods and Academic Performance. *British Journal of Educational Psychology*. Vo. 40(2), 132-143

Erickson , H.E. (1954). A Factorial Study of Teaching ability". *Journal of Experimental Education*, 23,1-39.

Evan, K.M. (1952). "Study of Teacher Towards Teaching as a Career", *British Journal of Educational Psychology*, 22, 63.

Evans, P., and Verma, V. (eds), (1990). *Special Education Past, Present and Future*, London: The Falmer Press.

Flanders, N. A. (1969). "Teacher Effectiveness" In R.Ebel (Ed), *Encyclopaedia of Educational Research*. New York: The Macmillan Co. 1423- 143.

Gage, N.L. (1968). "An Analytical Approach to Research on Instructional Methods", *Phi Delta Kappa*, 49, 601.

Gage, N.L. (1972). *Teacher Effectiveness and Teacher Education : The Search for a Scientific Basis*, Palto Alto, California: Pacific Book Publishers.

Giancarlo and Carol, Ann Facione (1996). "Critical Thinking, Culture and Personality: Predicting Lationos Academic Success", *Dissertation Abstracts International*, Vol. 57/09, p. 289.

Green, Peters & Webster (1991). "Personality and Academic Success", In G. Lindzey (Ed.) *Handbook of Social Psychology*, Addison – Wesley Publishing Company, Inc, Reading Mass.

Guilford , J.P. (1959). *Personality*, New York : Mc Graw Hill.

Gupta, R.C. (1979). *Prediction of Teacher Effectiveness through Personality Test*. Ph.D Thesis, In M.B. Buch (Ed.) *Second Survey of Research in Education*, Baroda: CASE.

Gupta, V.P. (1979). "Personality Characteristics, Adjustment Level, Academic *Achievement and Professional Attitude of Successful Teachers"*. Ph.D. Thesis, In M.B. Buch (Ed.) *Second Survey of Research in Education*, Baroda: CASE, M.B. University, 1979.

Hallahan. D.P. & Kauffman. J.M.(1991). *Exceptional Children; Introduction to Special Education*, Allyes.

Harris, C.W. (Ed.) (1960). *Encyclopedia of Educational Research*, New York, The Mac Millian Company.

Hart, W.F. (1934). *Teachers and Teaching*. New York : Macmillan.

Heil, L.M. and Washburne, C (1962). "Brooklyn College Research in Teacher Effectiveness."*Journal of Educational Research*, 55, 347-351.

Heward, W, L. and Orlanksky, M.D. (1992) Exceptional Children ($4^{th}$ ed) New York, Macmillan.

Hewett, F.M. and Forness, S.R. (1984), Education of Exceptional Children, London, Allyn and Bacon.

Jangira, N.K. (1986). *Special education, Scenario in Britain and India: issues, practice and perspective*. Hanging: The Academic Press.

Jayamma, M.S. (1974). *Construction and Standardisation of an Inventory for Predicting Teacher Efficiency*. In M.B. Buch (Ed.), *A Survey of Educational Research in Education*. Baroda: CASE, 428-429.

Johnson, (Jr), G.B. (1997). "An Evaluation Instrument for the Analysis of Teacher Effectiveness". *Journal of Experimental Education*, 23, 331-344.

Johnson and Carol Bradley (1996). "Personality Traits and Learning Styles: Factors Affecting the Academic Achievement of Underachieving Gifted Students", *Dissertation Abstracts International*, Vol. 57/11, p. 132.

Jones K (1972) A History of the Mental Health Services, Roultedge & Kegan Paul, London.

Kauffaman. M.J., Gottlieb. J., Agar. J.A., and Kukic. M., (1975). " Mainstreaming: Toward an Explication of the Constuct'. In E.L. Meyen, G. A. Vergason, and R.J. Whelan (Eds), *Alternatives of Teaching Exceptional Children*, (pp. 34-54). Denver: Love.

Kaul, L. (1972). *Factorial Study of Certain Personality Variables of Popular Teachers*. Unpublished Ph.D. Thesis, Kurushethra University.

Kaul, L. (1973). "Personality Traits of Effective Teachers". *Educational Psychological Journal*, 1,1, 29-36.

Khan, S.B. and J. Weiss (1973). "The Teaching of Affective Responses", In Roberst M.W. Travers (Ed.), *Second Handbook of Research on Teaching* , Chicago: Rand McMally Publishing Co., p. 766.

Khan, A.H. (1990). *Personality Structure of Blind Children and Its Relationship with their Mental Ability and Educability*, Ph.D, Dissertation, Utakal University.

Khan, S.B. (1970). "Affective Correlates of Academic Achievement: A Longitudinal Study", *Measurement and Evaluation in Guidance*, 3.

Kirk, S. (1962), Educating Exceptional Children, Boston, Haughton Mifflin.

Kirk, S. & Chackfant J. (1984). *Academic and Development Learning Disabilities.* New York: Denver love.

Knight, E.W. (1940). "Twenty Centuries of Education", Boston: Cinn and Co., p. 62.

Krishna Bhattachrya (1994) Attitude of Student Teachers Towards Teaching Profession. University Press P.

Kunda, C.L. (Ed) (2000). *Status of Disability in India 2000.* New Delhi: Rehabilitation Council of India.

Lamke, T.A. (1951). "Personality and Teaching Success". *Journal of Experimental Education,* 20, 217-260.

Leonoff and Deborah, (1993). "Parental, Peer and Personality Factors in Adolescent Academic Underachievement (Underachievers)", *Dissertation Abstracts International,* Vol. 54/08, p. 277.

Lins, L.J. (1946). "The Prediction of Teaching Efficiency". *Journal of Experimental Education,* 15, 2-60.

Loeb, R., and Sarigini, P. (1986). " The Impact of Hearing Impairment on Self Perception of Children", *Volta Review,* 88, 89-91.

Loree, M.R. "Shaping Teacher's Attitude", (1971). In B.O. Smith (Ed.) *Research in Teacher Education: Asymposium,* New Jersey: Prentice Hall Inc. Englewood Cliffs.

Maheshwari, V.A. (1976). *Study into the Classroom Verbal Interaction Pattern of Effective and Ineffective Teachers.* Ph.D. Thesis, In M.B. Buch (Ed.), *Second Survey of Research in Education.* Baroda: CASE.

Malik, J.S. (1983). "Teacher's Perception of Their classroom Learning Climate". *The Progress of Education,* LVII, 8, 173-176.

Mani, M.N.G., (1993). *Report of PIED, SRK College of Education,* Coimbatore, NCERT.

Mani, M.N.G. (1997). *Techniques of Teaching Blind Children,* Sterling Publishers, New Delhi.

Medley, D.M. and H.E. Mitzel (1962). "A tentative Frame Work for the Study of Effective Teacher Behavior", *Journal of Experimental Education,* 30. 317.

Mehrota, R.N. (1973). *Effect of Teacher Education Programme on the Attitude of Teachers Towards the Teaching Profession,* Delhi: Central Institute of Education.

Ministry of Human Resource Development (1986) National Policy on Education Governement of India, New Delhi.

Mitzel, H.E. (1989). "Teacher Effectiveness?", *Encyclopedia of Educational Research* 3rd ed. New York: The McMillian Co.

Mohan, R. (1998). Teaching Effectiveness. A Factorial Approach. *Experiments in Education,* Vol. XXVI, No.6 January, 97-103.

Montross , H.W. (1954). "Temperament and Teaching Success". *Journal of Experimental Education,* 23,73-97.

Mutha (150) Intelligence as Correlate of Teaching Competency of Perspective Teacher Prentice Hall New Delhi.

Nair, P.K. (2003). *A Study of the Problems Experienced by Student Teachers at Primary Level.* Unpublished Masters Thesis, Mahatma Gandhi University, Kottayam

Narayan, J. (1992). *Comparison of the Effectiveness of Adult and Peer Model on the Learning and Retention of Performance Skills Among Mentally Retarded Children,* Ph. D Dissertation, Utkal University.

Narsimhan, M.C., and Mukherjee, A.K., (1986), *Disability:* A *Continued Challenge,* New Delhi: Wiley Eastern.

NCTE Bulletin (1991), Volume III, No : 2/4, NCTE, New Delhi. National Policy of Education (1986/1992), MHRD, Government of India, New Delhi.

NCERT (1969). "Survey of Secondary School Teachers in India – Reaction of Teachers Towards Teaching Profession", A study NCERT, New Delhi.

Ngati and Jerry, (1996). "The Relationship between Personality Characteristics and Academic and Demongraphic Variables Adult Learners", *Dissertation Abstract International,* Vol. 58/02, p. 114

Olson, M.N. (1971)."Ways to Achieve Quality in School Classroom: Some Definitive Answers". Phi Delta Kappan, 53,63-65.

Panda, K.C., (1994). "Psycho Educational Assessment in Special Education: Issues and Concerns". *Indian Journal of Psychological Issues,* 2, 1, 1-20.

Pandey, G.S. (1973). *A Study of Teachers Adjustment in Relation to Professional Efficiency,* Ph.D Thesis, Gorakhpur University.

Pandey, R.S. and Advani, Lal, (1995). *Perspectives in Disability and Rehabilitation,* New Delhi: Vikas.

Parashar, O.D. (1963). *A Study of Attitude of Teachers of Secondary School in Delhi Towards Teaching Profession,* Unpublished M.Ed. Dissertation, Central Institution of Education, Delhi, 1963.

Pareek, U. and T.V. Rao. (1974). " Handbook of Psychological and Social Instruments", Ahmedabad: Samasti.

Passi, B.K. (1976). *Becoming Better Teacher: Microteaching Approach,* Ahmedabad: Sahitya Mudranalya.

Passi, B.K. and M.S. Lalitha (1976). "*Microteaching, Skill – Based Approach,* in B.K. Passi (Ed.), *Becoming Better Teacher Microteaching Approach,* Sahitya Mudranalya, Ahammadabad,

Passi, B.K. and S.K. Sharma (1981). *A Study of Teaching Competencies Among Secondary Teachers,* Department of Education, University of Indore.

Paunen, S.V. and Ashton, M.C. (2001). Big Five Predictors of Academic Achievement. *Journal of Research in Personality.* Mar. Vol. 35-(11), 78-90.

Peronto, A.L. (1996). Ability and Patterns of Behavior of Good and Poor Teachers". *Journal of Experimental Education,* 30,1,88-106.

Peterson (1976). *Penelope Loraine.* "Interactive Effects of Student Anxiety, Achievement Orientation and Teacher Behavior on Student Achievement and Attitude", Ph.D. Stanfcar University, 37.

Pillai, J.K.(1981). "Affective Tone in the Primary Classroom" *Indian Educational Review,* XVI, 3, 35-42.

Polleys.M.T (2001). A Study of Relationship Between Self Regulated Learning, Personality and Achievement. *Dissertation Abstract International.* Apr. Vol. 61(9a), 34-67

Prasad, M. (1970). *Evaluation of Professional Efficiency of Primary School Teachers In Service.* Ph.D. Thesis, Sagar University.

Pratibha, Deo (1980). "Some Personality and Adjustment Correlates of Teaching Effectiveness". *Journal of the Institute of Educational Research*, IV, 2.

Radhawa, B.S. and Michayluk, J.O. (1973). *Perceptions of Learning Environment in Rural and Urban Classroom*. Saskatchewan School Trustee Association.

Rajagopalan, S. (1976). "Measurement of Teaching Success". *Experiments in Education*, 4,1,1-19.

Rajagopalan, S. and Sundararajan, S. (1977). "The Pupils Concept of a Good Teacher: Its Implication for Teacher Education Programmes". *Experiments in Education*, 1-3-10.

Randhawa, B.S. and Fu, L.L.W,(1973). " Assessment and Effect of Some Classroom Environment Variables". *Review of Educational Research*, 43,3,303-322.

Ranganathan, V. (2008). Self Esteem and Teaching Aptitude of D.T.Ed Students. *Journals of Psychological Researchers. An International Journal*, Vol. No. 52, No.1, P. 49-49.

Rinderman, H., and Neubauer, A.C, (2001). The Influence of Personality on Three Aspects of Cognitive Performance: Processing, Speed, Intelligence and School Performance. *Personality and Individual Difference*. Apr. Vol.30 (5) 829-842.

Roy, S.G.K. (1971). *A Study of Teacher Attitude and its Relationship with Teaching Efficiency*. Ph.D Thesis, Sambalpur University,

Ryans, D.G. (1951). "A study of the Extent of Association of Certain Professional and Personal Data with Judged Effectiveness on Teacher Behaviors". *Journal of Experimental Education*, 20,77.

Sayles and Juliet Pamela, (1995). "The Relationship among Selected Personality, Identity, Status and Academic Achievement Factors among Black Adolescents", *Dissertation Abstracts International*, Vol. 86/05, p. 171.

Schwartz, A.N. (1950)." A Study of the Discrimining Efficiency of Certain Tests of the Primary Source of Personality Traits of the Primary Source of personality Traits of Teachers". *Journal of Experimental Education*, 19, 1, 63-94.

Seagoe, M.V.(1945). "Prognostic Tests and Teaching Success. " *Journal of Educational Research*, 39, 685-690.

Sehal, M. (1975). *A comparative Study of Environment Learning contacts Among Different Types of Schools*. M.Ed. Dissertation, Bhopal University, Bhopal.

Sharma, G.R. (1976). "An Investigation into the Relationship between Personality Factors and Teaching Effectiveness". *Journal of Education and Psychology*. 33, 4, 258.

Sharma, R.A. and Mahesh, V.(1979). "The Classroom Verbal Interaction Pattern of Effective and Ineffective Teachers". *Journal of Education and Psychology*. 90-95.

Sharma, R.A. (1974). *A Study into the Relationship of Predictors of Teachers Effectiveness at Elementary Level and Follow – Up After One Year of Training*. D. Phil. Education, In M.B. Buch (Ed.), A *Survey of Research in Education*, Baroda: CASE.

Sharma, R.C. (1984). *Teaching Aptitude, Intelligential Level and Morality of Prospective Teachers*, Doctoral Dissertations: Ed.M.S University .

Sharma, Rajeev. (1975). *Madhyamik Vodyalayon Men Sevarat Andhypakon Ke Monabal Ka Ek Adhyayan*, M.Ed. Dissertation, Rajasthan University. Jaipur.

Sharn, S. and Yaakobi D. (1981). "Classroom Learning Environmental of City and Kibbutz Biology Classrooms in Israel". *European Journal of Science Education*, 3, 321-328.

Sherry, G.P. (1974). *A Battery of Psychological Tests for Prediction of Success in Teaching*. Ph. D. Thesis, In M.B. Buch (Ed.), *A survey of Research in Education*, Baroda: CASE.

Simon, D.L. (1936). "Personal Reasons for the Dismissal of Teachers in Small School". *Journal of Educational Research*, 29,585-588.

Singh, I.M. (1987). *A Comparative Study of Creative B.Ed Pupil Teachers in Relations to Teaching Effectiveness, Self Concept and Some Personal Values* in MS Doctoral thesis Education Bhopal University .

Singh, R.P.(1973). "Achievement and Behaviors Outcomes as Functions of Pupil Perception of Classroom Climate". *Journal of Board of Secondary Education*, Rajasthan, IX, 2,6-10.

Singh, L.P. (1981). "Research Classroom Climate." *Indian Educational Review*, XVI, 3, 27-33.

Singh, S.(1978). *Relationship between Teacher's Personality Teaching Success and Behavioral Changes in Students*. Unpublished Ph.D Thesis, University of Udaipur,

Singh, S.K. (1974). *A Study of the Relationship Between Verbai Interaction of Teaching (with Special Reference to B.Ed, Students)* Ph.D. Education, Meerut Univ.

Sinha, S.P.(1980). "A Study of Interest and Personality Patterns of Successful Men in Different Occupations." XV, 4, 68-70.

Sivarajan, K. (2002). *Trends and Developments in Modern Educational Practice.* Calicut University Central Co-operative Store, University of Calicut.

Sivaarajan, K. (2002). *Psychology of Learning and Instruction.* Calicut University Central Co-operative Store, University of Calicut.

Smith, K.R. (1972). *A Comparative Study of the Morale of Teachers in a Sample of Catholic Primary and Secondary Schools with Emphasis on One School Distinguished by Exceptionally High Morale*, Unpublished Dip. In Education Admini. Univ. of New Eugland.

Start, K.B. (1966). "The Relations of Teaching Ability to Measures of Personality". *British Journal of Educational Psychology*, 36,159-169.

Start, K.B. (1968). "Rater – Ratee Personality in the Assessment of Teaching Ability." *British Journal of Educational Psychology*, 38,1,14-20.

Super (1949) the Filed of Personality British Journel of Educational Psychology, 1, 48 – 71.

Sumarntarory, G.K. (1971). *A Study of Teacher's Attitude and Its Relationship with Teaching Efficiency*, Unpublished Ph.D. Thesis, Utkal University.

Tarpey, M.S.(1965). "Personality Factors in Teacher – Trainee Selection." *British Journal of Educational Psychology*, 35,140-149.

Taylor, P.H. (1962). "Children Evaluation of the Characteristics of a Good Teacher". *British Journal of Educational Psychology*, 32,258,266.

Van, Heyningen and Julie, (1997). "Academic Achievement in College Students: What Factors Predict Success?", *Dissertation Abstracts International*, Vol. 55/06, p. 135.

Vijayakumariamma (2002). Doctorial Dissertation. University of Kerala, Trivandrum.

Vincente, A.Q. (1970). "Socio Economic Factors Related to Morale of Adults in Economically Disadvantaged Rural". *Dissertation Abstract International.* Vol. 32/7, p. 78.

Wangoo (1982) Teaching Skill and Intelligent of Students Teachers a Brief Study Bhopal University Bhopal.

Wills, and Cora Deanne, (1996)." An Investigation of Personality Variables that Discriminate Between Succeeding and Non-succeeding Disadvantaged College Students", *Dissertation Abstracts International*, Vol. 57/09, p. 103.

Wright, W.W. (997). "The Development and Use of a Composite Achievement Test", Indian Univ. Bulletin of School of Education.

Yeh, Yu-chu (2001). Aptitude Treatment Instructions in Preserves Teacher's Behavior Change During Computer Stimulated Teaching . (EJ 747149) ERIC.

Yeung, K.W. Watkins, D. (2000). Hong Kong Student Teacher's Personal Constructions of Teaching Efficacy, Educational Psychology, Vol. 20, No. 2.

# Index

**U**



**V**